W9-BKN-393

Everything
YOU NEED TO KNOW
to Talk
YOUR WAY TO
Success

BURTON KAPLAN

PRENTICE HALL
Englewood Cliffs, New Jersey 07632

Prentice-Hall International (UK) Limited, *London*
Prentice-Hall of Australia Pty., Limited, *Sydney*
Prentice-Hall Canada, Inc., *Toronto*
Prentice-Hall Hispanoamericana, S.A., *Mexico*
Prentice-Hall of India Private Limited, *New Delhi*
Prentice-Hall of Japan, Inc., *Tokyo*
Simon & Schuster Asia Pte. Ltd., *Singapore*
Editora Prentice-Hall do Brasil, Ltda., *Rio de Janerio*

©1995 by
Burton Kaplan

All rights reserved. No part of this
book may be reproduced in any form or
by any means, without permission in
writing from the publisher.

10 9 8 7 6 5 4

Library of Congress Cataloging-in-Publication Data

Kaplan, Burton
Everything you need to know to talk your way to success /
Burton Kaplan.
    p.   cm.
Includes index.
ISBN 0-13-289067-4, — ISBN 0-13-289059-3
   1. Persuasion (Psychology).   2. Interpersonal communication.
3. Influence (Psychology) 4. Success—Psychological aspects. I.
Title.
BF637.P4K26 1995
158′.2—dc20   94–28916
                                      CIP

ISBN 0-13-289059-3

ISBN 0-13-289067-4 (pbk)

PRENTICE HALL
Career & Personal Development
Englewood Cliffs, NJ 07632

A Simon & Schuster Company

Printed in the United States of America

Other Books by the Author

"THE MANAGER'S COMPLETE GUIDE TO SPEECH WRITING"
(MACMILLAN)

"STRATEGIC COMMUNICATION: HOW TO MAKE YOUR IDEAS THEIR IDEAS"
(HARPERCOLLINS)

Dedication

For Edward

This Book Is Guaranteed to Turn Your Life Around

Do You Need This Book?

True or False?

1. Do you sometimes have the unhappy feeling your career is shrinking to the confines of a narrow job description?

2. Do you come out on the short end of the stick more often than you like when it comes to winning an argument, persuading somebody else, or sharing . . . at home, in the community, or at work?

3. Are your kids or loved ones flirting with alcohol, drugs, or cults . . . are your family relationships headed for the rocks . . . are you tired of not having enough friends?

4. Do you hate new social situations, especially with the opposite sex, because you are afraid you'll be ignored?

5. Is it uncomfortable to speak in public . . . or write down your thoughts?

6. Have you ever gotten turned down for a promotion or a raise you deserved?

Is your life and the lives of those around you all that you want them to be? All that they can and should be?

If even one of your answers is yes, chances are you—or someone close—are feeling the effects of a breakdown in communication that blocks the full measure of happiness and fulfillment you want and deserve at home and on the job.

But no matter why you hold this book in your hands now, please do us both a big favor: Read on.

What I am about to show you will turn things around—not in a year, not in a month, but starting right here and now when I explain the proven, practical way to start reprogramming your life in the time it takes to read the next few pages.

Why Your Worst Enemy Isn't Your Worst Enemy

I figure you've been around the block once or twice. Whether you are twenty-something or approaching the silver years, woman or man, parent or child, straight or gay, these breakdowns—you're not imagining them.

They're real, and if you don't start getting rid of them soon, or help others start wiping the slate clean, you'll find that the rest of your life will turn out to be less than you want and wish for.

You see, my friend, what we're looking at here—failures of communication—are at the root of every human problem that ever was or will be.

And when that's the case, it turns out that your worst enemy really isn't your worst enemy after all. No, you are up against an even more formidable adversary. Yourself.

This case of bad communications—it's not something you or your kids or your boss or your main squeeze caught. It is something you or they—and perhaps you *and* they—create.

And the driving idea behind this book is that *if, alone or together, we create bad communication, we can un-create it.* I say this not because I am a wishful thinker but because, like you, I've gone through the school of communication hard knocks.

The Reason My Problems Are Your Answers

Today I am a communication consultant for some of the biggest companies in the country. For the past 25 years I've been teaching thousands of rising managers how to win instant support for their views and ideas—practical, well-tested, proved ways to inform, inspire, and persuade others at home, on the job, and in the community. Several of the people I worked with over the years are now leading chief executives in their own right.

But effective communications never came easily to me. Like you in this moment, I had to find ways to get rid of the things that were shooting me in the foot. Perhaps if I had been born a natural communicator I would not have had to solve the problems of getting my views across. I would not have had to grope my way through impasse after impasse in search of easy-to-follow programs to make my ideas their ideas.

I would not have had to study so hard or read so much to discover how successful people—everyone from billionaire Ross Perot to world-renowned sex researcher Dr. Alfred Kinsey, from America's favorite author, Mark Twain, to America's top TV preachers—got the results you seek now, *results that got them what they wanted from others.*

Here Comes Better News

But on the other hand, if communication was not a problem for me, I wouldn't feel so qualified to help you overcome the deficits you now face.

And neither I nor my publisher, one of the world's largest and most respected, would be able to offer you this ironclad, money back guarantee:

No matter what your education or position in life, if you've got a hot enough fire burning in your belly, if you've got a will strong enough to take what is and change it into all that it can be, over the next 30 days this book—this comprehensive source of personal power and magnetism—will revolutionize your thinking and turn your life around.

Here's even better news: You don't have to read it from cover-to-cover to get the *immediate relief* you want and need.

If you're pressed to solve a specific problem immediately, by all means turn now to *Chapter 14*, look up the source of trouble, and instant relief is just pages away. Whether it is a matter of winning the *attention* of your boss to the fact that you deserve a raise, or *zeroing* in on the causes of defiance in children—or anything in between—you'll find specific, concrete, and practical help—step-by-step guides, honest-to-life examples you can follow and be guided by—to turn your problems into opportunities.

A Matter of Leverage

Now let me tell you how the rest of the book works.

In the hope that you will treat this as your lifelong personal user's manual, it is organized into 13 subject chapters. Each chapter is oriented to a specific communication skill with broad application at home, in the community, and on the job.

While each chapter stands on its own, they are arranged to build on the ones that come before and to lay down the foundations of the ones to follow. Each makes a uniform presentation: a brief introduction to the skill, the practical benefits of learning it, a specific, concrete program complete with self-analysis and realistic and pin-pointed suggestions for perfecting it quickly, and a summary.

This approach means you can practice skills selectively if you wish, in any order you choose. It frees you to spend more time mastering areas where you feel the need for help and less on the ones you feel confident about.

Using the book's individual chapters in response to specific issues is a sensible idea. But if you really want to get ahead of the curve, give some thought to reading a chapter a week. The choice is yours: either way, this book is a problem solver . . . an answer book . . . *an ideas book that adds value to your life by dealing specifically with what to say and how to say it to talk your way to success in the least time possible.*

On the belief that you don't leave your humanity at home on the doorstep when you head out to work, each chapter covers family, social, and business situations. As you will see, tested concepts of human interaction are both universal and portable—the real McCoy. They work as well in business settings as in social ones.

In *Chapter 1*, I give you 14 workable ways to stop shooting yourself in the foot and start getting what you want. Basically, this chapter shows you two very big things.

First, it exposes the self-defeating myth that miscommunications are always—or, even, usually—the other person's fault.

You see, my friend, we are the enemy within. We are the ones sabotaging our own conversations. And our weapons are the words we choose. Don't make the mistake of blindly believing that people are too sensitive, that words don't matter, that "Sticks and stones may break my bones but words will never harm me." Words are the most powerful tools we have. They are the magic we use to create pleasure, the weapons we apply to cause pain. They endow our lives and work with meaning, warn us, propel us.

The impressions they create put love in our souls, money in our pockets, and if we do not consider the impact of our words on others, chill the hearts of the people we most wish to affect.

I want you to see for yourself how we use words to dig ourselves into conversational traps that appear so logical and well-intentioned they escape question.

Only when you recognize and understand that the impact of your words causes people to respond to you in the ways they do can you hope to find a way past your mistakes and their defenses.

But, helping you understand yourself better is only half of what this chapter will do for you. Doing something about it is the rest.

Once you know what causes you to unwittingly work against your own interests, this chapter gives you 14 workable ways to stop shooting yourself in the foot and start getting what you want.

By getting rid of the problems you unconsciously put in the way, you will automatically create the conditions that encourage others to respect your wishes and defer to your needs.

Family, friends, co-workers, customers—here you get the conversational skills to come out of every encounter feeling like a winner—even if there's mistrust between you, or you had a falling out.

Chapter 2 reveals the magic formula guaranteed to get people to do it your way every time—the proven way to appeal to anybody and everybody from the guy in your shipping department to your child. Here, you will quickly see that while it seems easier to talk about your thoughts and plans in the ways you yourself think about them, that is like leaving the landing lights on for Amelia Earhart. Using the secret method of every great communicator, you will happily discover that it is just as easy, and far more rewarding, to slant those same thoughts and plans to appeal to the self interests of others. Step-by-step, you will learn to think more about what they want to hear than what you want to say—see things from their angle as well as your own. The outcome is certain to be a solid foundation for relationships stronger than any you may have known before.

The subject of *Chapter 3*, with its 16 workable ways to listen with your eyes, is the vitally important skill of nonverbal communication. When you learn to listen with your eyes and act on what you see, you hold the key to controlling one of life's most complex events—a face-to-face encounter with another human being.

Here, I give you the unspoken signs to watch for in conversation, signals that are invariably better indicators of what is really going on than words alone. These tell you what is really taking place when a poker player wears dark glasses, a woman wears bright colors, or someone tries to control your gaze. I'll give you four ways to use body language to keep from getting a traffic ticket, the best way to meet and succeed with the opposite sex, where to sit in any room, and how to know when the time is ripe to ask for a raise. By learning to recognize nonverbal signals, and by using them to reinforce your own words, you cannot fail to get more of what you want out of every conversation.

And Still There Is More

Chapter 4, with its 12 workable ways to gather information, change minds, confirm suspicions, open purse strings, pluck heartstrings, reveal hidden emotions, discourage guessing, and recover initiatives will show you that the way you manage questions makes a powerful difference not just in your ability to communicate but in your life.

Here, you learn to pose the questions that are certain to build stronger business, social, and personal relationships.

If you intend to be successful in your dealings at home and at work you must know how to tell people what to do in ways they can accept and act on—the subject of *Chapter 5*.

Directing other people with your orders is a leadership art—one that requires skill, constant practice, and expertise. Since you cannot use force, the idea is to leverage basic communications techniques. Here I give you 11 workable ways to get people not just to carry out your orders and instructions but to *want* to go all out to achieve your goals—no matter how daunting the task.

There's always an idea, product, service, or feeling we need to sell to someone else. And selling requires persuasive communication. That's why *Chapter 6* shows you how to get others to instantly buy into your thoughts, plans, and purposes. To succeed, I give you the six trade secrets of the world's most successful salespeople—scientifically developed methods guaranteed to make your ideas their ideas, every time! I am talking about the results successful persuaders usually acquire after long years of hit-and-miss experience. My time-tested approach not only eliminates trial-and-error, it gives you skills you can use immediately—on the job, at home, even out on the town. If you are a salesperson, these cannot fail to get you the business you want. If selling is not part of your work, that's okay, too: the very same methods of persuasion are guaranteed to make you a better parent, a more considerate partner, a more respected leader in your social, romantic, and church activities.

Defensiveness, aggressiveness, dependency—I want *Chapter 7* to show you how to use conversation to deal with these and other stressful, emotionally charged situations that are part of your daily life at home, on the job, and out in the community. Whether you are a supervisor or a manager, an engineer or a word processor, a mental health worker or a janitor, laborer, attorney, physician, clerk, garage mechanic, or minister I want you to have the practical skills that will help you to defuse emotions, resolve conflicts, and work out the problems that may otherwise prevent you from getting the love and respect you want. To deal more effectively with the emotions that are so much a part of your daily business and personal life, I give you 13 workable ways to control the attitudes and emotions of anybody—tested methods, principles, and techniques that cannot possibly fail to unlock the family love you crave. An added plus, the very same methods are guaranteed to make you a better worker, a more considerate boss, a more respected leader in your business, professional, and civic activities.

And still there is more here for you.

- -

Influence People for the Rest of Your Life

Chapter 8 makes the point that every human contact involves a negotiation—for time, for space, for money, for something! That's because it is only human to always want something from others—anything from a raise in pay from your boss to a better reputation among your neighbors. Love, sex, marriage, relationships, community life, buying and selling, business, power—no matter what the focus happens to be, the job is the same: To somehow convince others it is in their interest to allow us to have what we wish for and want from them. In this chapter, I reveal the 22 secrets of professional negotiators that turn indifference into attention, conflict into cooperation, rejection into acceptance, distance into warmth, dreams into reality. Here you will find the proven methods that empower you to negotiate for anything and get it, and a step-by-step process to make it part of your life. Using practical methods and surefire techniques, you will express yourself freely and fully, get results, and strengthen relationships—all at the same time—no matter what the issues, no matter what the circumstances, business, personal, or otherwise.

Now, in *Chapter 9*, we get to one of the trickiest conversational issues of all—criticism. Here, my friend Chu Lee's painful experience at the hands of her in-laws points up the destructive force of what I call The Dirty Dozen—12 ways of behaving that give personal criticism its bad name. If criticism is the poison, the antidote is my 13 workable ways to correct the mistakes people make without criticizing them personally for having made them.

When you apply these at every opportunity, when you operate on the belief that the best way to correct the mistakes of others is to get them to *want* to make the corrections themselves, you give others a feeling of importance, a sense of personal worth, and a true feeling of friendship.

The techniques of word power, discussed with considerable detail in *Chapter 10*, show you how easy it is to crumble barriers, turn disappointments to success, convert impossible dreams into hard realities, and develop the inner confidence it takes to guide and control each and every one of your conversations—be they business or social. The 12 workable ways I give you represent the best and fastest way to put yourself across with people who count—your employer, your friends, your family. Knowing which words to use makes you more influential, gives you a greater say in the way things are done. When you are the master of your words, people listen. That's because they judge you—your background and your future—by what you say. To them, your words are you! Say memorable words . . . and you rivet and hold attention. Say persuasive words . . . and you sell opinions, ideas, products. Any way you say it, say it clearly, vividly . . . and your words sell you.

Whatever your field, whatever your goals in life and career, word power is synonymous with winning. This chapter not only gives you 191 words guaranteed to move minds your way, it also shows you the fastest, easiest, and by far the best way to steadily build your vocabulary in the most natural way possible—with no special research or extra effort on your part whatsoever.

Teacher, preacher, lawyer, or lawn doctor—it doesn't matter who you are, what you do, or what you want. One of the best ways to make your dreams come true is to put yourself across with clear and concise writing that is easy to understand. I am talking about the subject of *Chapter 11*—writing that earns you attention, respect, prestige, influence, and yes, love.

But the prospect of writing scares a lot of people half to death. The threat of facing a blank page or computer screen raises more questions than answers:

How should I open a letter or memo?

What should I say next?

Just what information do I need to include?

How do I know what to leave out?

What closing will bring the action I want?

If putting it down on paper is a problem for you as it is for so very many others, then please be reassured: If you can speak with confidence, by the time you finish *Chapter 11*, with its 11 workable ways to write as easily as you talk, and 17 model letters and memos you can use as-is or adapt, you cannot fail to win the attention, promotion, and admiration you desire and deserve.

How You Break the Ice and When to Break the Rules

I think you will agree that the ability to talk on your feet is a mighty handy business and community skill. After all, you never know when you might be called on to persuade bankers to go for a deal, motivate employees to go the extra mile, or simply inform others in your church or civic organization.

There's no end of opportunities to stand up and speak. Whatever the occasion—anything from a Sunday school class to a service club meeting—one thing is dead certain:

If you are at all normal, the first few times you speak in public are certain to mark good news/bad news milestones in your life.

The good news is that nothing raises your stock out in the community or on the job faster than making an effective speech or presentation (which is nothing more than a speech dressed up in work clothes). When you get your ideas and plans across with confidence and clarity, you can literally talk your way to anything you want—business, social, you name it.

The not-so-good news is that nothing raises personal anxieties faster than having to make one. Dry throat, sweaty palms, chest a size too small for your pounding heart—speaking in public strikes terror in nearly everyone at first.

In *Chapter 12*, Pepsi-Cola's master teacher of public speaking, Ben Dugas, shows you his personal confidence builder—a never-before-revealed secret of making a speech the practical, professional way that is as easy as one-two-three. In addition to giving you the seven secrets of platform professionals, here you also get three surefire speech openers—the actual words and phrases of billionaire Ross Perot, sex researcher Dr. Alfred Kinsey, and retired Joint Chiefs of Staff Chairman Admiral William Crowe—you can use or adapt to any and every public speaking situation. Here, too, you benefit from the secret of closing with a bang, a guide to organizing your thoughts for maximum impact, a powerful formula you can follow to get your ideas across in ways that satisfy your goals *and* the needs of your audience, and tips from the pros on such speaking-related topics as how to overcome nervousness, use visual aids, and more.

If you count yourself among the majority of people who find it difficult to break the ice with a stranger of the opposite sex, the good news in the pages of *Chapter 13* is sure to be the answer to your prayers . . . even if you are very shy, on the quiet side, or simply not the social success you'd like to be.

You see, I firmly believe that breaking the ice with a complete stranger doesn't happen by accident, mere chance, or blind luck.

Breaking the ice, like so much else about human communication, is a matter of satisfying a particular person's specific need.

That is why, with its 14 workable ways to break ice, I can guarantee that, after reading this chapter, the one you want will want you back.

- -

Turning Your Life Around Is as Easy as Turning the Page

Whether you read it from cover-to-cover or cherry-pick it, my real hope is that you find this book one you want to refer to again and again. As I said, some of it will revolutionize your thinking and get you the instant results you want and need; some will remind you of things that should never be forgotten; some will trigger questions I have not considered but, by mastering the skills in this book, a little educated groping on your own will bring you even more competence and extra added benefits.

You probably won't use everything in these pages but, used together, this collection from half a lifetime of hands-on experience will change the tide of your business, social, and personal relationships as it has mine and that of the thousands of women and men all across this country whose lives and careers benefit daily from its tested principles and surefire concepts.

Nothing in this book is untried theory.

Each of the dozens upon dozens of practical techniques, step-by-step procedures, and useful case histories I give you is the real thing— uscd by people like you in situations like yours to talk their way to the top everywhere they go. Every one of them produces spectacular results—and that's not guesswork, that is a guarantee.

Burton Kaplan

CONTENTS

Why your worst enemy is not your worst enemy • Four ways conversations backfire • How to defeat the enemy within • Two amazing benefits are yours when you neutralize the enemy within • The first benefit • The second benefit • How well do you understand yourself? • Do you bring out the worst in others? • Five conversational foot shooters • Expecting too much • What went wrong • How to free yourself from unwarranted expectations • Accept what is • Train your ego to take a back seat • Listen like your happiness depends on it . . . which it does • Understanding begins with you • Practice patience to project sincerity • The habit of bad habits • Three ways to break the habit of bad habits • Turn off your cruise control • Communicate by listening • Send in a substitute • Hurry up and wait • Seven symptoms of time-sickness • The only fail-safe way to stop hurrying up • Take a genuine interest in the lives of others • Distrust • The litmus test of distrust • Three ways to beat distrust • Stop trying to be what you are not • Stop trespassing • Try on the other person's shoes • Selective hearing • Listen to yourself first • Remember to say, "Thank you" • Once you've stopped shooting yourself in the foot, the next step is to control the conversation

CHAPTER 6
Persuasion: Six Trade Secrets of the World's Best Professional Persuaders 101

CHAPTER 7
Emotions: Thirteen Workable Ways to Defuse the Emotions That Prevent You from Getting What You Want When You Want It 127

grip of emotion • Say the five words guaranteed to encourage others to express emotion • How to stop hearing and start listening • When *not* to listen • Never fake understanding • Never say you know how the other person feels • Focus on feelings • Remember that agreement is less important than understanding and acceptance • Paraphrase to show understanding • Provide emotional feedback • Fifty verbal signs that demand emotional feedback • Look for gestures and postures that confirm what's being said • Talk releases tension

CHAPTER 8
Negotiating: Twenty-Two Secrets of Professional Negotiators That Inform, Inspire, and Persuade Others 149

The misunderstood majority: why seven out of every eight people cannot negotiate • How to make your dreams come true • Eight ways negotiation makes everyone a winner • These two spectacular benefits are yours for a lifetime • The first benefit • The second benefit • Are you able to negotiate win-win outcomes? • How to stop an argument dead in its tracks • The secret weapon every professional negotiator must possess • Three questions guaranteed to get you what you want every time • How to determine what you want • Put your own interests first • To decide what you want, examine your options • Be specific about your wants • Accept the strengths and weaknesses that make you you • How to determine what other people want • Make the first questions broad • At first, open-ended questions are best • Consent to advice • Playback your understanding of the other person's desires • When all else fails, be direct • Assume nothing • Keep hopes and fears out of listening • Three ways to listen better • Be a stranger to your friends • Empathize, empathize, empathize! • How to develop empathy • Read body language • How to find common ground • Put their case first • Build two bridges • Offer a choice • Give to get • Defuse conflict • Find something to admire • Don't make quitting an option • Stake their claim every step of the way • How to be critical . . . and get your friends to love you for it

CHAPTER 9
Correcting Others: Thirteen Workable Ways to Change What People Do . . . Without Arousing Resentment 175

Why criticism is like acid rain • Criticizing others undermines motivation to change • The dirty dozen of personal criticism • The two enormous benefits you gain when you change what they do instead of attacking who they are • The first benefit • The second benefit • Are you a Hall of Fame corrector? • Thirteen workable ways to change what people do . . . without arousing resentment • How to tell when to correct others • How to tell the difference between a mistake and a condition • Look to create solutions, not victims • Go slow to hurry up • Three times you must never correct others • Cool your jets • Put yourself on the same team • Eight shared values • Let them speak first • Build a sandwich • Four ways to put the sandwich technique to work at home and on the job • Correct one mistake at a time • When people get stuck, offer a choice • Talk body language • Close on a positive note • Praise, praise, praise • How to work miracles

CHAPTER 10
Word Power: Fourteen Workable Ways to Crumble Barriers, Turn Disappointment to Success, and Convert Impossible Dreams to Hard Realities 193

Big words are less important than effective ones • Even complex ideas need simple words • Three reasons to develop word power • Word power = winning • Two extraordinary benefits are yours for a lifetime when you make word power your personal calling card • The first benefit • The second benefit • Test your word power • One hundred and ninety-one power words that work • Activate your verbs • Make your nouns vivid and specific • Add a splash of color • Use words to create pictures • Ten vocabulary errors you must avoid at all costs • Thirteen computer words and phrases you must know to survive • Eleven business words and phrases you must know to survive • Three steps to word power: as easy as growing up • Pay attention to context • Use it or lose it • Look it up • How to succeed with words • Speak to express, not impress • Do not overstate • How to select the perfect word • Feel words work harder than think words

CHAPTER 11
Putting It on Paper: Eleven Workable Ways to Write as Easily as You Talk 213

Good writing is good conversation in print • One set of skills for all your communication needs • Two phenomenal benefits are yours when people can enjoy, understand, believe, and act on your writing • The first benefit • The second benefit • Do you know how to write as easily as you speak? • Good writing is easier than you think • Six workable ways to write as easily as you speak • Think before you write • Organize your thoughts • Fill in the outline • Draw the reader in • Write the way you talk • Be your own toughest editor • Five more workable ways to

CHAPTER 12
Public Speaking: Fourteen Workable Ways to Be as Effective on Your Feet as You Are in Private 237

CHAPTER 13
Fourteen Workable Ways to Break the Ice with the Opposite Sex . . . Even If You Are Very Shy, on the Quiet Side, or Simply Not the Social Success You'd Like to Be 257

up the courage to take the first step • The fundamental principles of romantic behavior • Love—the biggest benefit life offers—yours when you master the secrets of romantic behavior • Do you know how to talk your way to love? • Fourteen workable ways to break the ice with the opposite sex • Relax • Act instead of react • Stay vulnerable no matter what • Let your happiness show • Make the downbeat upbeat • Let the other person do most of the talking • Flattery will get you almost everywhere • Go with the flow • Stand up for your independence • Don't kiss up • Don't take the relationship's temperature • Listen like a lover • Seven ways to listen like a lover • Criticism kills desire • Give them what they cannot give themselves

THE ENEMY WITHIN

Fourteen Ways to Stop Shooting Yourself in the Foot and Start Getting What You Want

A bewildered Dan Ridgepond slumped in his chair.

Other than to say, "She's too sensitive," the 29-year-old Detroit systems manager was at a loss to explain why his older sister, Harriet, an attractive and competent woman in her mid-thirties, might be giving him the cold shoulder.

"She lost her job about six weeks after her marriage broke up. We were pretty close. I made a point of calling her two, maybe three times a week. Well, one night we were talking on the phone. She was complaining for the umpteenth time that her boss never liked her and her husband never grew up. I honestly expected a dose of reality might get her back in the game again. Harriet, I said, you gotta give up the idea it's their fault. There's nobody else to blame for the mess you are in. The next thing I knew the phone went click! I don't think we've exchanged ten words since—and that was a month ago."

Why Your Worst Enemy Is Not Your Worst Enemy

Though Dan is sadly mistaken in assuming his sister is too sensitive, the last thing he wanted was to make her recovery from her personal and career disasters more difficult than it needed to be. Quite

1

the opposite. Dan wanted her to see things in a way that got her back on track.

When he said what he said, he fully expected her to understand he had her best interests at heart. But in her distress, all Harriet could see was the finger of guilt pointed her way.

In the situation with his sister, Dan's worst enemy wasn't his worst enemy after all. He was up against a far more formidable adversary:

Himself.

Instead of making his good wishes part of Harriet's solution, the way Dan chose to express those wishes made him part of her problem.

Let's face it: When it comes to killing conversation, there's bound to be a little bit of Dan in all of us.

All of us want better results from our business as well as our personal conversations than we seem able to achieve on a day-in day-out basis. Like Dan, we're surprised when conversations backfire in our face.

For instance, here are

Four Ways Conversations Backfire

▶ With every good intention of building up another person's self-esteem we end up somehow diminishing it

▶ Out of friendship and concern we speak our minds only to trigger defensiveness

▶ Our kindness somehow provokes resentment

▶ Feelings we reveal in the hope of closeness chase others away

Obviously, if we knew what we were doing and saying wrong, we'd take steps to fix it. But it's awfully hard to fix what you can't see. After all, you can't wrestle with the devil until you've got a hold on him.

How to Defeat the Enemy Within

That's why I want this chapter to show you two very big things.

First, I intend to expose the self-defeating myth that miscommunications are the other person's fault.

You see, we are the enemy within. We are the ones sabotaging our own conversations. And our weapons are the words we choose.

Don't make the mistake Dan made. Do not blindly believe that people are too sensitive, that words don't matter, that "Sticks and stones may break my bones but words will never harm me." Words are the most powerful tools we have. They are the magic we use to create pleasure, the weapons we apply to cause pain. They endow our lives and work with meaning, warn us, and propel us.

The impressions they create put love in our souls, money in our pockets, and if we do not consider the impact of our words on others, chill the hearts of the people we most wish to affect.

I want you to see for yourself how we use words to dig ourselves into conversational traps that appear so logical and well intentioned they escape question.

Only when you recognize and understand that the impact of your words causes people to respond to you in the ways they do can you hope to find a way past your mistakes and their defenses.

But, helping you understand yourself better is only half of what this chapter will do for you. Doing something about it is the rest. I intend for this chapter to give you 14 workable ways to stop shooting yourself in the foot and start getting what you want.

By getting rid of the problems you unconsciously put in the way, you will automatically create the conditions that encourage others to respect your wishes and defer to your needs.

Family, friends, co-workers, customers—this chapter will give you the conversational skills to come out of every encounter feeling like a winner—even if there's mistrust between you, or you had a falling out.

Two Amazing Benefits Are Yours When You Neutralize the Enemy Within

People at home and on the job will want to listen to what you have to say because you know how to win and hold their favorable attention.

"If I told my son, Nathan Ralph, flat out not to hang with these kids, it would have been like micro-managing one of my employees," reports Little Rock store manager Jimmie Rob Larkee, 38. "Deep down, he would have fought me tooth and nail. So I tried what I learned on the job—appeal to the adult part of Nathan Ralph by explaining my needs to him. I know he loves us and cares what we think so I tried to

get across how uncomfortable it would make me and his mother if he
went to unsupervised parties or hung around the mall."

By searching for a way to approach Nathan Ralph, not confront
him, Jimmie was able to communicate instead of merely talk—and
Nathan Ralph did what Jimmie asked of him.

*As you perfect your understanding of communication, you will
discover more and more about yourself and your partners in conversation in less and less time. This will make it easy to more confi-
dently speak your mind in ways others will accept, believe, and act
on.*

Jay Reiser, 47, a St. Louis regional supervisor for a national hardware chain, married late. His wife, Lolette, was the mother of a pair of
high school seniors. Before the girls left on a summer camping trip
through Big Bend National Park, Jay asked his wife if she had ever spoken to them about safe sex.

Lolette replied that her girls had just begun to date and sex was not
an issue for them.

"I had a choice," Jay reports. "I could have gotten out the numbers
to prove that by the time most of the population reaches 18 they've
been approached, or I could find a way that was easier for Lolette to
accept.

"Let's see . . . the twins will be 18 on their next birthday, right?
Isn't that about your age when your folks sent you on that class trip to
Washington where you met . . . ah, what was his name?

Lolette thought for a moment. "Maybe I can find a way to open the
topic," she responded.

Learn the lesson Jay applied—to speak your mind in ways others
can accept and act on—and your ability to guide and control conversation will improve immediately. A new sense of confidence will enter
your life. Without raising your voice, creating a fuss, or harming others
you'll accomplish things in conversation most people are unwilling
even to try.

HOW WELL DO YOU UNDERSTAND YOURSELF?

I've prepared a little exercise to help you see how, and how
often, you may be working against your own conversational interests.

There are no right or wrong answers.

After you read each statement, please rate your response on a scale from 1 to 10. Try to avoid the highest or lowest rating unless you honestly feel a particular response deserves an extreme mark. When you are done, total your responses.

1. When something you care about goes haywire or someone you are really counting on screws up, are you tempted to say, "I told you so . . . ?

Never   Always

1 . . . 2 . . . 3 . . . 4 . . . 5 . . . 6 . . . 7 . . . 8 . . . 9 . . . 10

2. Name-calling isn't all bad. Some labels are really merit badges, like "kind," "dedicated," "my kinda guy." Some labels— "Egghead," "brat," "nag," "bitch"—are conversational hate-mail intended to somehow make more of ourselves by making less of the other person. You can probably think of examples of both from your experience. Compared with the hate-mail, about how often does your conversation include merit badges?

Never   Always

1 . . . 2 . . . 3 . . . 4 . . . 5 . . . 6 . . . 7 . . . 8 . . . 9 . . . 10

3. Imagine yourself as an inner-city school teacher. You hand out a quiz. One child cracks wise, asks how come he has to take a test. "Why?!," you respond, "Because I said so!" On the scale of 1 to 10, rate the likelihood of such a response to produce success.

Never   Always

1 . . . 2 . . . 3 . . . 4 . . . 5 . . . 6 . . . 7 . . . 8 . . . 9 . . . 10

4. An old friend surprises you when, after years of suffering in silence, he tells you his wife has a longstanding problem with pills. He's ready to walk. Here you have a choice: you can listen quietly, or you can advise him not to start legal proceedings by reminding him to think of the children. On the scale below, rate about how often your conversation might include the advice.

Never   Always

1 . . . 2 . . . 3 . . . 4 . . . 5 . . . 6 . . . 7 . . . 8 . . . 9 . . . 10

5. Funny thing about praise, it cuts two ways. On the one hand, it can build your confidence, but there are also times you get the feeling it is a way of being sweet-talked out of something you want.

   Instead of "Thank you," about how often do you suppose you might say something like, "Oh, it wasn't much, really," or "I could have done a lot better"?

Never   Always

1 . . . 2 . . . 3 . . . 4 . . . 5 . . . 6 . . . 7 . . . 8 . . . 9 . . . 10

6. Imagine that a popular teenager, the president of her class, is killed in an auto accident. You are called in to help the school get through the crisis. Speaking before the assembled student body, do you advise them not to dwell on the loss but to turn, instead, to something more constructive?

Never   Always

1 . . . 2 . . . 3 . . . 4 . . . 5 . . . 6 . . . 7 . . . 8 . . . 9 . . . 10

7. Day after day, people in relationships ask, "How was your day?" And day after day, their significant others say, "OK. How was yours?" In moments like these, when it seems like the trickle of sharing that goes on is ready to dry up, about how often are you tempted to ask another question or two compared with an urge to begin talking about, say, who you ate lunch with?

Never   Always

1 . . . 2 . . . 3 . . . 4 . . . 5 . . . 6 . . . 7 . . . 8 . . . 9 . . . 10

8. One of the people you supervise has a problem, and the team is up against a deadline. You know they'll figure it out, but time is of the essence. Compared with, "I know you'll get it worked out in plenty of time," about how often might you say, "Oh, that's easy. All you do is . . . "?

Never   Always

1 . . . 2 . . . 3 . . . 4 . . . 5 . . . 6 . . . 7 . . . 8 . . . 9 . . . 10

9. About how often do you think anything you do not say cannot be held against you?

Never   Always

1 . . . 2 . . . 3 . . . 4 . . . 5 . . . 6 . . . 7 . . . 8 . . . 9 . . . 10

10. You are in a room too small for the crowd that's gathered for
    the meeting. The speaker drones on. Your mind wanders. By
    the time you snap back, you've lost the thread of the speech.
    How often do you suppose this description fits your behavior?

Never   Always

1 . . . 2 . . . 3 . . . 4 . . . 5 . . . 6 . . . 7 . . . 8 . . . 9 . . . 10

Total _____

A score below 10 or above 90 suggests that your capaci-
ty for self-understanding is probably impaired, and you would
benefit from reading this chapter with great care.

A score between 11 and 89 means your communication
skills are a mix of soft spots and hard spots. Your main vulnera-
bilities are in the areas where your scores are highest. If you will
bear these in mind as we move forward, you will find workable
ways to overcome each deficient area.

Do You Bring Out the Worst in Others?

To help you discover the ways you may be shooting yourself in
the conversational foot and what you can do about it, I am going to do two
things:

First, on the theory that awareness is half the battle, I will give you
a list of the five things people unwittingly do to bring out the worst in
others.

Second, in the process of discussing each one, I'll give you tested, corrective techniques—14 concrete, specific, practical ways—guaranteed to change your life in the time it takes to read them and put them into practice.

To begin, here are the FIVE CONVERSATIONAL FOOT SHOOTERS:

▶ Expecting too much

▶ The habit of bad habits

▶ Hurry up and wait

▶ Distrust

▶ Selective hearing

Conversational Foot Shooter 1: Expecting Too Much

The sin of expecting too much is as invisible as uranium in a paper sack—and every bit as lethal.

Let me quickly prove the point. At a workshop not too long ago, I observed Julia Williams, 27, a makeup artist for a big cosmetics house, get into a scrap with accountant Dick Ensmoor, 44.

Julia complains that she is in a dead-end job. Dick takes several opportunities to tell her she makes the wrong choices.

"If I screw up," Julia finally explodes, the words bursting out of her mouth, "I don't want or need you to tell me I brought it on myself. What's the point of belittling me when I know better than anyone that I deserve the blame . . ."

"But . . . "

"Just because the sign reads 'Kick Me' doesn't mean you have to!"

WHAT WENT WRONG

They expected too much of each other. Julia expected unconditional support and Dick expected her to be more like him—a realist.

Of the two, Dick was the guiltier. He expects life to be a certain way come hell or high water.

Folks like Dick come with a hidden agenda, a secret and predetermined schedule for the way life is supposed to be. Their conversations are likely to be peppered with "ould've"—"*should* have," "*could* have," "*would* have."

They think giving voice to their unwarranted expectations does you a favor. After all, if they didn't, you might never recognize your shortcomings and work to overcome them.

They are motivated by a strong sense of right and wrong. Though it is neither always in plain sight nor correct in its assumptions, deep down it is there.

So strongly do they believe theirs is received truth, they make it their life's secret mission to enlist you in their process. This leads them to the most unwarranted expectations of all—they expect you to behave as they might, and think as they do!

Look, if you figure there are basically two kinds of people in this world—the ones who memorize life and the ones who live it—people harboring unwarranted expectations are definitely to be counted among the memorizers.

They seem to have mental pictures of outcomes well before events take place.

HOW TO FREE YOURSELF OF UNWARRANTED EXPECTATIONS

Technique 1:Accept What Is

Acceptance is the invisible shield that prevents you from acting on your unwarranted expectations.

Acceptance does not equal agreement. It means allowing others to be themselves and not carbon copies of us. It is an idea that says a lot and implies even more. It implies that before we can accept others we need to be able to accept ourselves and our own personal imperfections.

Psychologists say expecting too much of others comes out of inner feelings that we are not the people the world presumes us to be. Deep in our personalities, we know we've got our faults:

Where the world sees flowers we see more thorns than roses.

But we are reluctant to let these show because, if we act naturally, our imperfections will somehow make others think less of us. We make offense our defense and, with our perfect understanding, keep others at bay. So, when we say to others, "Hey, you should have read the signs better . . . ," what a trained clinical psychologist might hear is, "I'd like you to believe I am in better control of my life than you are of yours."

Of course we are not.

And each go-no-place conversation—each frustrated hope of friendship or involvement or respect—proves the point.

When you can accept others without necessarily agreeing with them—allow them to be them—magic comes into your life. You are less tense communicating with others and, because you relate to them as an equal, they feel less tension interacting with you.

Technique 2: Train Your Ego to Take a Back Seat

The very next time you are tempted to set someone else straight by asking them to meet your expectations,

▶ Concentrate entirely on what you can say to make them feel good

▶ Pay them a compliment by talking to their need for recognition

By doing just these two things sincerely, you automatically train your ego to take a back seat.

The responses you get in return are certain to be the ones you want, and others will think of you as a natural communicator.

Technique 3: Listen Like Your Happiness Depends on It . . .
Which It Does

By listen I mean concentrating all of the intensity and awareness you can possibly command on everything the other person has to say.

I know what you are going to say: Everything they say isn't worth the effort. True, but some of it is. The problem is separating the wheat germ from the wheat.

Back in the 1900s, merchant John Wanamaker was one of the first to use advertising in a big way, and it paid off. Someone asked how he decided what to spend. He acknowledged half of every advertising dollar was wasted but, until he could figure out which fifty cents, he said he would go on spending it all.

Do the same about listening and you will be every bit as successful as Wanamaker was. Train yourself to get a hundred cents return on every dollar's worth of listening, and your gains are sure to exceed your losses. Among the responses you get will be many if not all of the ones you want.

Technique 4: Understanding Begins with You

When we give the other person a solution to their problems—"If I were you I'd _____," we open the door to misunderstanding.

It happens not because what we say is necessarily so wrong but because advice can be a vote of no confidence, an insult to the basic intelligence of the other person. And as for the haughty and arrogant moralizing that seems to come with prescriptions—oh, please!

Instead of telling people what to do, instead of judging their behavior, the next time you are tempted to give advice:

▶ *Listen to what they are really saying*, not what you think in response to what they are saying. Put more of your attention on what they are groping with than on what you can do about it.

▶ *Echo their concerns*. Hold a mirror up to their thoughts by showing them, with your words, you get the picture. For instance, when a friend says they are confused, and they really don't know what to do next, you say, "Sounds like you are stumped."

Technique 5: Practice Patience to Project Sincerity

As you engage with others you need to remember that the important thing is not whose ideas are better but how to find ground that is as comfortable for them as it is for you.

That takes patience.

Here are two techniques you can employ immediately to create the right impression:

▶ *Take two deep breaths* before each response you make. A pause gives you time to consider your reply, and contributes to the impression of thoughtfulness you need to convey.

▶ *Never interrupt*. When temptation strikes, take an extra breath and exhale slowly. Allow the other person to complete their thought whether you agree with them or not.

In no time at all you will project a new air of sincerity. You won't have to fake anything or butter up others because deep down you will be practicing good human relations.

Conversational Foot Shooter 2: The Habit of Bad Habits

Habit, the triumph of experience over good sense, is what you do when your mind is on cruise control.

▶ Someone calls your name and you respond. That's a habit.

▌ You always say please and thank you. That's a habit.

▌ You have a track record of success. Even that is a habit.

But so is

▌ A short fuse

▌ The inability to recognize gender difference as more than a matter of human plumbing

▌ Teary responses to stress

▌ Complaining there is never enough time to do things right but always finding enough time to do them over

▌ Excessive truth telling and/or lying

▌ Always asking the advice of others before making a decision

▌ Excessive worry

▌ Blocking things from happening

Habits—and the ones I've listed are just a beginning—are the unseen baggage we schlep through life. Silent, invisible—they influence our every thought, feeling, and action, from the side we part our hair to the way we get annoyed over little things that crop up; from our taste in clothes to our hunger for victory that leads us to think we have to win every time.

What makes a habit a habit is more than repetition. We cling to certain ways of thinking and feeling not just because we've always done it that way but also because we get something out of it.

Now what in blazes could you possibly get out of habitually asking advice of others, or thinking that people are selfish and can't be trusted?

It's hard to pinpoint why people feel these ways without knowing them. But psychologists say too little confidence in our own judgment drives the habit of always asking someone's advice before acting. It makes us feel more secure. Selfish people have a habit of wanting more than they have a right to expect. When they don't get what they want they call others selfish. Otherwise, they would have to face the unpleasant fact that, really, what is selfish is their demands.

Good, bad, or indifferent—our habitual responses are independent of what is going on at the moment, and they often prove lethal to conversation.

If the habit of bad habits is one of the ways you victimize a conversation, here are three tested techniques guaranteed to turn things around:

THREE WAYS TO BREAK THE HABIT OF BAD HABITS

Technique 6:Turn Off Your Cruise Control

If you do nothing but stop taking others for granted and start taking them for what they really are, two things will happen.

First, you will immediately break the chain of habit.

And second, improve the chances of getting the satisfaction you want out of your business and personal conversations.

Here are two steps you can take immediately to prevent yourself from operating on cruise control:

▶ *Express fresh interest in your fellow human beings.* Mentally treat each encounter as if it were the first encounter. This instantly eliminates conversational hang-ups and contributes to, rather than detracts from, the other person's pleasure in engaging with you. This alone will make you popular and well-liked wherever you go.

▶ *Play things as they lay.* Do nothing more than nothing to change the nature of things and I guarantee you will never make another enemy—not even accidental ones.

Technique 7:Communicate by Listening

Because no one ever teaches us how to listen, people develop bad personal listening habits. There are four major symptoms:

▶ Eyes wander,

▶ Fingers fidget,

▶ Interrupting,

▶ Asking too many questions.

If you see yourself committing any of these on a fairly regular basis, it is a pretty safe bet the habit of bad listening is part of your problem.

The good news is that by making four simple actions part of your everyday face-to-face contacts, you will automatically train yourself to listen with all you've got.

- Make eye contact and hold it.

- Lean towards the other person with an expression of concentration on your face. Keep your body still.

- Don't interrupt or jump to conclusions. Wait until they have spoken their piece.

- Resist asking too many questions by putting more effort into actually listening than into trying to figure out ways to argue against what the speaker is saying.

Listen like you mean it—in person or, with obvious adjustments, on the phone—and others will regard you as a person genuinely interested in the well-being of your friends, your family, your neighbors, and your colleagues.

Technique 8: Send in a Substitute

One of the best and fastest ways to break bad habits is to put good ones in their place.

- If your habit is to be untrusting, experiment with trust in small, safe ways: start by not counting the small change the next time you go to the store. Gradually build up from there.

- If truth is your flail, speak a little less of it.

- If you are habitually pressed for time, try rearranging your schedule and/or priorities.

- If you always seek the advice of others, make at least one small decision by yourself everyday.

- If you are gender blind, start thinking that men and women see life from different perspectives.

Don't worry about faking these things on the grounds that they do not reflect the real you. Do them often enough and they will become part of the *new* you—someone others enjoy being with and respect.

- -
Conversational Foot Shooter 3: Hurry Up and Wait

A famous quarterback, Bart Starr of the Green Bay Packers, married on a Tuesday morning at eleven.

A sports reporter asked him why so early.

"Well, if the marriage doesn't work out," Starr replied, "I don't want to blow the whole day!"

It may be a dumb story but it makes the point: the hurry-up state of mind we generate for things worth having comes at the expense of things worth being.

As people, we suffer badly from time-sickness.

We judge candidates on five-word sound bites.

The nightly news gives us fires that consume entire neighborhoods in the time it takes to show the flames. We demand computers work faster (though their speed is already beyond human comprehension), cars accelerate quicker (though speed limits above 55 are rare), microwaves defrost food in less time (even though we take many, if not most, of our meals out).

SEVEN SYMPTOMS OF TIME-SICKNESS

Can anyone doubt that the time sickness we suffer is affecting the way we think, behave, and act? Or the unconscious ways we think, behave, and act are frustrating our desire to be in close and warm contact with others?

Here are the seven signs of time-sick people:

) Hurry or interrupt the speech of others

) Eyes blink rapidly, fingers tap, knees jiggle—sometimes no matter who is speaking

) Faces and, often, bodies, show tension

) Speak rapidly, slur or drop the ends of sentences

) Cannot sit and do nothing, often do two or more things at once

) Dislike intensely waiting in line

) Walk fast, eat fast, and no dawdling after dinner

THE ONLY FAIL-SAFE WAY TO STOP HURRYING UP

Jonathan Swift, author of *Gulliver's Travels* wrote, "Whoever is out of patience is out of possession of his soul." I promise you a way not only to regain possession of yours, but to win the hearts, minds, and souls of those whom you mean most to affect—your friends, neigh-bors, colleagues, and family.

The first thing you must do . . . the only thing you must do, is this:

Technique 9: Take a Genuine Interest in the Lives of Others

Since you are the very (and only) reason you are in a hurry-up state of mind to begin with, the whole idea is to tear your mind away from self-absorption. This makes room for a broader view that embraces the concerns and cares of those around you, too.

"He knew I had a career to attend to—you know, meetings, travel, the whole nine yards—so I couldn't get to the hospital. If Avery needed help, I'd've given it to him if he asked," Dick Snell, 37, a rising man-ager in a financial publishing house, admitted. "But Avery never asked. He died of cancer and it was only a year later I came to realize how cold and insulting I must have seemed to him to be more concerned over my career issues than over him or his family—and I was."

It takes a conscious effort to shift the focus from inside to outside but millions of people have done it and so can you.

Here are four ways:

▶ Let's say the woman you had lunch with today spoke of her son's job hunt, her mother's move to a nursing home, or her brother's new car. This evening, take a moment or two to reflect on what you heard. Allow yourself to wonder how things are turning out. The next time you speak with her, express interest about these matters.

▶ Get up 10 minutes earlier so you can experience breakfast as a pleasure.

▶ Every afternoon around three, give yourself a five-minute break to daydream or meditate.

▶ Do one thing at a time. Don't, for example, sign checks while speaking on the phone to your best friend, or brush your teeth while showering.

Each of these prescriptions (and others you may think up) force your mind to shed a few activities and thoughts. Do enough of them and you slow down automatically.

As you begin to take a real interest in what your friends and acquaintances think, hope, do, and experience, they are likely to show as much interest in you.

This will create a fresh, healthy basis for communication and others will think of you as a new and better person whose friendship they value and cherish.

- -
Conversational Foot Shooter 4: Distrust

I was seated at a table just inches from a couple of well-turned-out young men in their thirties—lawyers, I guessed. Even if I wanted to I could not avoid overhearing their conversation. They were talking about their love lives, and I have to admit I was fascinated.

"You know how it is," one young man was saying to the other, "the right woman can't say anything wrong . . . "

"And the wrong one," rejoined the second, "can't say anything right!"

"You got it," replied the first with a wink and a leer.

Sound pretty harmless?

It might—if your idea of harmless is a .357 Magnum aimed straight at your big toe!

You see, labels—"right" and "wrong" are just two of many—reflect the fundamental distrust with which we greet life. They are the means we use to deny reality, and—here's the bad news—they hit with a double whammy. They prevent us from knowing not only others but ourselves as well.

Apply a label—be distrustful—and what we get is not our honest appraisal of the other person, not pluses and minuses to be weighed in the balance, but the reflection of our own built-in bias.

What I am talking about here is not necessarily the sort of bigotry that labels Jews "hymies" and Asian Americans "gooks" but the bias born out of a more subtle form of distrust—call it closet bias because it is so well hidden even you may not be aware of it.

Let me prove the point.

Have you ever labelled a thoughtless individual "jerk," tagged a well-built man a "hunk," or described a nasty child as "brat"? These are some of the characterizations we use to blind ourselves not just to what is happening but to what may be possible.

Here's the problem. The labels we apply make it seem like we know the other person when, in fact, all we have caught is the shadow and not the substance. In the mental half-light we create, our judgments loom overly large and we tend to place more credence in them than they deserve.

And who is the victim of our distrust? All concerned! Label the right person the wrong way and they are diminished; brand the wrong person the right way and you are.

Either case creates a win-lose proposition that makes true communication—shorthand for the relationship that bridges the biggest gap of all, the one between two minds—impossible.

My point is to show you that communication is fostered or hindered as much by the unconscious distrust we bring to each encounter as it is by the words we and others may speak.

THE LITMUS TEST OF DISTRUST

Here's a quick way to take your own pulse on the issue of distrust. Imagine you meet someone who stirs your love interest, but you are having second thoughts. Sure, you come from similar backgrounds and share values and interests. But the person you're attracted to doesn't always see things the way you do, doesn't react in ways you expect. In fact, the person's reactions often catch you by surprise.

The question is, do you see these differences as a problem or an opportunity? Generally speaking, people who see differences as more of a problem than an opportunity need to give some thought to the possibility that distrust is an issue in their lives.

THREE WAYS TO BEAT DISTRUST

I think reasonable skepticism is useful in some situations and a life saver in others. I do not intend to suggest you give it up entirely. But I do mean for you to give up the part that gets in the way, and here is why. If distrust, bias, labelling—call it what you will—remains your stock operating procedure you are condemning yourself to the worst of all possible hells—the one we call boredom.

Wherever you find yourself right now will be where you stay for life. People like the ones you engage with today will remain your clique forever. So long as you persist in your distrust, the only people you attract will be those who are willing to share or tolerate your distrust. You will never be enriched by others or grow to become the person you want to be—the one who wins the love and admiration of a wide and satisfying circle at home, on the job, and in the community.

My tested methods are geared to help you find a better way to serve your interests in the least possible time.

Technique 10: Stop Trying to Be What You Are Not

Trying to create a false front is a case of the dog chasing its tail: the more you pose the more secretly worried you become others will see through the false front. This prompts you to try even harder and, before you know it, even you can't tell who is the real you and who is the Memorex®.

To prevent this, I want you to draw a line down the middle of a piece of paper. Label one side with a plus sign, the other with a minus sign.

 ▶ On the plus side, note one of your positive characteristics—for example, "good parent."

 ▶ On the other side, enter one of your negative traits—say, "short temper."

Do not enter a positive without also entering a negative.

 ▶ Enter only one pair of offsetting attributes per day.

 ▶ Keep this up for 14 consecutive days.

At the end of two weeks two things will happen. First, you will have a more balanced picture of who looks back at you in the bathroom mirror. And second, you will automatically start to become the person you see.

As others begin to experience you as more genuine, someone who no longer hides behind labels of distrust, your influence will grow.

Technique 11: Stop Trespassing

The very next time you are tempted to characterize another person with a label, think about the label they might wish to put on you.

By training yourself to do this as often as situations demand, you will create an environment that invites others to be forthright and forthcoming without fear of getting stuck with an ugly label. As their comfort level increases, more of the respect that is at the heart of mutual understanding will be yours.

Technique 12: Try on the Other Person's Shoes

The very next time you are rankled by what someone says or the way they look, I want you to try this experiment. Imagine what it might be like to say and do the things they say and do. You do not have to agree with their actions, condone them, or even sympathize—just get a feeling for how it might make sense to say what they say.

Psychologists call this empathy.

They say it is the most effective agent for fostering communication with others.

Follow the three techniques I have given you to overcome distrust—practice them daily until they become as much a part of your life as breathing—and I guarantee:

▶ If you are a parent, your children will respond to you in more positive ways

▶ If you are a teacher, you will immediately begin to foster greater student achievement

▶ If you are a doctor or a nurse, you will facilitate your patients' return to health

▶ If you are a manager, your employees will be more motivated to perform

▶ If you are a salesperson, your customers will grow more satisfied and your sales results are sure to reflect the difference.

- -

Conversational Foot Shooter 5: Selective Hearing

My friend Michael, a successful suburban dentist, can be the life of the party. But Mike has a way of making jokes at other people's expense. A couple of weeks ago I was the designated target of his needling. To be honest, it got on my nerves. I took him aside and explained gently that making less of me to make more of himself left me feeling diminished—maybe even a little abused. Next time we got together it was as though Mike never heard me.

I stopped calling Mike.

He phoned the other day to ask why I had become a stranger.

Mike's not a rare breed. People like him are as old as the Bible: It was Jesus who said, "Thou hearest in thy one ear but the other thou hast closed."

The fact is, most of us listen more attentively to what we wish to hear than to what we don't. Yet, like Mike, the stuff we turn a deaf ear on often proves the very thing we need most to hear.

If the poison is selective hearing, the antidote is to listen.

Earlier, I gave you five techniques to communicate by listening. I'd like you to bear those in mind as I add two more:

Technique 13: Listen to Yourself First

For the next 10 days, I want you to make a list of things you do not want to hear.

Here's the step-by-step plan:

▶ Tape a piece of paper to your bathroom mirror.

▶ Every day, note one item. For instance, if you are short and hate Napoleon jokes, put it on the list; if you are fat but don't want others to talk about your weight, write it down.

Be as honest as you can.

By the tenth day, an amazing phenomenon will take place in your life. Things that seemed crushingly important at first will be less important. And, without any further effort on your part, you will begin to shed a lot of the sensitivity that prevents you from hearing what others might have to say.

Technique 14: Remember to Say, "Thank You"

There will be times when the things people say touch one of your hot buttons.

Here is what to do the next time this happens:

▶ Recognize that what upsets you is probably not the person but what the person says. This realization in no way implies you agree with what they are saying.

▶ Since they are doing you a favor by giving you an opportunity to perfect your communication skills, the right response is to say, "Thanks."

It is as simple, and as difficult, as that.

Each and every time you hear something you prefer remained unspoken, thank them for sharing their thoughts with you. As your thanks grow from a mechanical response to an ingrained habit, people will find that you are easier to talk with and your conversations with them will grow deeper and more meaningful.

To rid yourself of the enemy within, let me summarize what has been covered in this chapter.

To free yourself of unwarranted expectations,

- Accept what is

- Train your ego to take a back seat

- Listen like your happiness depends on it . . . which it does

- Understanding begins with you

- Practice patience to project sincerity

To be rid of the habit of bad habits,

- Turn off your cruise control

- Communicate by listening

- Send in a substitute

To shed a hurry-up-and-wait attitude,

- Take a genuine interest in the lives of others

To discard distrust,

- Stop trying to be what you are not

- Stop trespassing

- Try on the other person's shoes

To overcome selective hearing,

- Listen first to yourself

▶ Remember to say, "Thank you"

- -

Once You've Stopped Shooting Yourself in the Foot, the Next Step Is to Control the Conversation

To get the respect and cooperation you want from others, when you want it, without fuss or argument, you don't have to make things perfect.

But you have to make an effort to stop sabotaging your own conversations.

Follow the techniques I have given you faithfully and two things will happen: You will, I promise, stop shooting yourself in the foot. The moment that happens, you are ready to learn the surefire secrets every successful communicator uses to press the levers and push the buttons that control conversation.

All you have to do is turn the page.

CONTROLLING CONVERSATION

Twelve Workable Ways to Press the Levers and Push the Buttons That Get You What You Want . . . When You Want It

"I want you to wear your boots today, Frankie, not your sneakers."

"Why?"

"Because I love you and don't want you down with a cold."

Frankie thinks of his last cold.

No school. Every time he wanted something, somebody brought him juice or a Twinkie. He got to watch his programs. No homework. Uncle Roger and Aunt Shelley came over with a new computer game.

Hmm, maybe being sick isn't so bad.

"Hey, anybody see my sneakers?"

- -
How to Avoid Being Dissed, Dismissed, and Dumped On

Even if you've never found yourself in a precisely Mom-and-Frankie situation, I am confident you know how it might feel. Chances are, you've been in encounters where you have offered the very best you've got to give . . . only to get dissed, dismissed, or worse, dumped on.

For instance,

▶ You work your heart out but, somehow, when you use your track record as a basis for asking for a raise, your boss doesn't pay it much mind

▶ You love your heart out but, somehow, when you ask the family to do something out of care and concern, they look at you like you're the loved one from hell

And you are left to wonder: Did they hear you? Did you say the right words?

The Five Most Powerful Words in the English Language

Ninety-nine times out of a hundred you can be sure they hear you. The reason you are getting rejected has nothing to do with what you are saying you want. It has to do with what they are listening to.

And what they are listening to more than anything else is not you—it is themselves.

It is a well-established fact that people listen to themselves more than they listen to you or anybody else.

If what you say doesn't jibe with what they are telling themselves at the moment—for instance, you ask for a raise when they tell themselves to cut back on costs—what you've got is a failure to communicate.

Everybody—you, your preacher, the boss, the company, friends, children, clerks, even your cat!—acts out of self interest. We filter the world through our secret needs. If what you happen to want somehow fulfills their most pressing need at the moment, Bingo!—you are certain to get it. And if it doesn't, you can be just as certain you won't.

Spoken or hidden, the headline on everybody's personal agenda is the five most compelling words in this or any other language:

What's in it for me?

The what's-in-it-for-me? state of mind both complicates and simplifies communication.

It complicates it because a person's deepest needs are almost always hidden and never static. That means just to get the other person's favorable attention—nothing more, mind you, than a simple mental glance our way—we have to somehow figure out what to say right now that is more interesting to them than they are to themselves!

And simplifies because the quickest way to grab a person's attention and hold it is to appeal to their self-interest.

Let me give you a quick example of exactly what I mean.

When we left Frankie, he was tuned-in to his own thoughts. Now,
I want you to pay careful attention to how these might be used to get
Mom what she wants:

Suppose that he had been going to the recreation league try-
outs.

They announced they'd pick the first squad at the next meeting. He talked about it all week, couldn't wait for Saturday morning. Now when Frankie asks why he should wear boots, Mom says,
"Well, Frankie, if you get your feet wet and catch cold, you can't go to
practice and see who makes the starting lineup."

The Secret of Every Great Communicator

What makes a person willing to engage in a conversation with
you is not your ideas or your language or even your tone of voice—
though all of these count. No, the critical element is the feeling of self
importance you instill within them.

To give them this feeling instantly, what you want to get across
first and foremost is not what you *expect* from them but what your
conversation will *do* for them!

How to Get People to Do What You Want When You Want It

I want to use this chapter to give you 12 workable ways to
find out exactly what other people want so that you can help them get
it. For it is only by concentrating entirely on what you can do for them
that you guide and control the conversation to get what you want when
you want it.

To be able to do that, you've got to get inside a person's head, find
out what makes them tick—discover the secret motivators that drive
their every thought and action.

Then, when you understand why they say and do the things they
do, you can press the emotional levers and push the psychological hot
buttons that guide the conversation toward your goal.

THE TOP TEN HUMAN NEEDS

All human behavior becomes instantly understandable when you realize that secret needs drive people. Everything a person says and does is intended to satisfy their most pressing needs and desires.

If you can show people how to gain their desires by going along with what you say, they will gladly do whatever it is you may ask of them.

It is up to you, of course, to find out which desires are dominant at the moment. You've got to identify these so you can direct the conversation your way.

Psychologists tell us there are 10 basic drives at work in everybody all of the time. They say the drive for power and need to feel important are the most motivating forces. That means you can almost always appeal to a person's need to feel superior or to be in control to influence the outcome of a conversation.

But there can be—and often is—more to human need than power and control.

Here are the 10 secret needs that, alone or in combination, motivate normal people:

▶ Affection

▶ Ego

▶ Esteem

▶ Excellence

▶ Greed

▶ Liberty

▶ Power

▶ Privacy

▶ Recognition

▶ Security

HOW TO MAKE YOUR INTERESTS THEIR INTERESTS

Communicating effectively depends on a sympathetic grasp of the other person's most driving need. Once you know the deep needs and pressing desires that cause them to say and do the things they say and do, you can easily match your intentions to their interests.

For instance:

▶ When you know that one of the hidden reasons people ask for a raise is to satisfy their inner need for recognition, and a budget crunch has you by the short-and-curlies, you might fill part of their need with better benefits or an extended vacation.

▶ True, spiritual generosity drives most charitable donations. Still, the wealthiest people in the country send their money to causes—the arts, Yale and Harvard, and the like—that benefit rich people more than they do poor. Knowing this about the well-to-do empowers you to talk about your private-school fund drive in ways that are consistent with their ego needs.

If you will simply think more about what they need to hear than what you want to say—see things from their angle as well as your own—you cannot help but fulfill their needs. When you do,

Three Magnificent Benefits Are Yours for Life

When you understand the secret forces that drive people to think and act as they do, you've got the leverage to actually make things happen. Others will find it easy to identify with your ideas, thoughts, and views and they will do what you wish as you wish it.

"I was late on a car payment," reports Harry Dern, 28, who lost his job building nuclear submarines at a Connecticut shipyard. "I called, apologized for causing the finance company so much bother, told them I was ashamed, but hey, the defense cut-back made times tough. The bill collector said my call was making his life easier—deadbeats never return calls. Then he said he would be glad to accept partial payment now and asked me to come in so we could work things out in a way we could both live with."

Harry sensed the bill collector had a strong need to feel like a winner. He played to it by opening with an apology—an act intended to make the bill collector feel superior. Of course, it worked. And Harry, meanwhile, got the relief he needed.

The better you are at understanding secret human needs, the more effective you will become at work and at home, and people will

appreciate your thoughtful approach to things. This will attract new customers and harden the loyalty of the ones you already have.

"This stranger pulls up on a cherry Harley, Electra-Glide 1200. It was more than just a good bike—it was his ego on wheels," reports Wilbur Quinones, 34, who owns an antique motorcycle repair service in Palo Alto, California. "I told him it was the best candy-apple yellow I had ever seen. That was three-and-a-half years ago. He's still a pretty good customer."

Understanding the self-image of others will uncover hot buttons that will help you protect and enhance their interests. This will lead others to want to be part of whatever it is you seek.

"My daughter wanted to sell Girl Scout cookies in the bank lobby downtown, so she put on her uniform and went to see the president," reports Wilma Barrent, 37, a Pawling, New York freelance writer. "She told him she knew he never allowed people to set up a table in the lobby but her mother had said he did a lot of charity work for children. He gave her an order for six boxes, and made arrangements for her to set up on Saturdays between nine and noon."

AN INSTANT PROFILE OF THE NEEDS THAT MAKE YOU YOU

As you begin to explore the fact that everybody is driven by inner needs, and that their needs are the key to getting what you want, there is something useful to be gained from taking a private look at your own.

To help you create a personal profile, I have prepared an exercise I think you will both enjoy and learn from. So sit back, unfasten your seat belt and take a look at my list of top 10 needs. Beneath each is a scale from one to ten. I want you to read each need and to think about it. Then, I want you to wait at least thirty seconds before you rank its importance.

Just circle the number that, in your judgment, reflects how important this particular need is to you *at this moment.*

The lower the number you assign, the weaker the need is within you. The higher the number, the stronger the feeling. Try to avoid the highest and lowest numbers unless you believe a particular need deserves an extreme mark.

Take as much time as you need. If you want more than 30 seconds to think about the importance of a need, by all means give yourself a break and come back to it later. But try not to use less than 30 seconds.

1. Power: a desire for superiority

Weak   Strong

1 . . . 2 . . . 3 . . . 4 . . . 5 . . . 6 . . . 7 . . . 8 . . . 9 . . . 10

2. Ego: a sense of personal pride

Weak   Strong

1 . . . 2 . . . 3 . . . 4 . . . 5 . . . 6 . . . 7 . . . 8 . . . 9 . . . 10

3. Excellence: a feeling of winning

Weak   Strong

1 . . . 2 . . . 3 . . . 4 . . . 5 . . . 6 . . . 7 . . . 8 . . . 9 . . . 10

4. Security: a hunger for protection from threat

Weak   Strong

1 . . . 2 . . . 3 . . . 4 . . . 5 . . . 6 . . . 7 . . . 8 . . . 9 . . . 10

5. Recognition: a need for personal worth

Weak   Strong

1 . . . 2 . . . 3 . . . 4 . . . 5 . . . 6 . . . 7 . . . 8 . . . 9 . . . 10

6. Privacy: a craving to protect personal space

Weak   Strong

1 . . . 2 . . . 3 . . . 4 . . . 5 . . . 6 . . . 7 . . . 8 . . . 9 . . . 10

7. Liberty: an urge to be in control of personal destiny

Weak   Strong

1 . . . 2 . . . 3 . . . 4 . . . 5 . . . 6 . . . 7 . . . 8 . . . 9 . . . 10

8. Greed: a longing for more than a fair share

<u>Weak</u>   <u>Strong</u>

1 . . . 2 . . . 3 . . . 4 . . . 5 . . . 6 . . . 7 . . . 8 . . . 9 . . . 10

9. Esteem: a passion to be admired by others

<u>Weak</u>   <u>Strong</u>

1 . . . 2 . . . 3 . . . 4 . . . 5 . . . 6 . . . 7 . . . 8 . . . 9 . . . 10

10. Affection: a yearning to belong

<u>Weak</u>   <u>Strong</u>

1 . . . 2 . . . 3 . . . 4 . . . 5 . . . 6 . . . 7 . . . 8 . . . 9 . . . 10

Now that you have completed the exercise, simply note the need you ranked highest. Follow that with the next highest and so on until you have completed all 10.

What emerges is a profile that ranks your needs. It shows you exactly which ones press hardest right now.

Later, as time permits, take the exercise again. Don't be surprised to discover your results are not the same. You might want to share this exercise with a friend or a loved one. Or, use it to profile the inner needs of someone you may want to get to know.

Thirteen Workable Ways to Press the Levers and Push the Buttons That Get You What You Want . . . When You Want It

Technique 1: Find the Motivating Need

Needs that are satisfied will not produce action.

Attempting to fill them further is no more likely to succeed than overfilling a glass to get more water to your lips. Only unfilled needs—what a person wants most right now—are powerful motivators.

It is up to you to discover which of the 10 human needs press your listener hardest at the moment. Only then can you pitch your ideas in ways they can accept and act on. Sometimes they freely supply the information you want. Other times you have to draw it out or deduce it any way you can.

Gillian Brisbane, 33, from Louisville, was called in for an interview with one of the big distillers. As she entered the VP's office, he was tacking up a cartoon on the bulletin board behind his desk. It showed a pair of vultures. One was saying to the other, "Patience, my ass! If we don't get some action soon I'm going to kill something."

"When I saw that cartoon it was like a curtain lifted," reports Gillian. "I knew exactly what made him tick—power. So I imagined what I might want to hear if I was on his side of the desk. I told him that, when I was starting out, one of my bosses kept heaping my desk with work. One day I complained. I said, "Why don't you give some of this to people who are less busy?" She told me the best way to be sure something gets done is to give it to the busiest person. At first I thought it was unfair. It took me a while to get the message. Ever since, I really enjoy meeting the challenge of impossible deadlines."

In the end, Gillian reports, the VP thought she was perfect for the work—the company offered her the job.

Gillian's experience makes it easy to see how important it is to discover the motivating need. In her case, she was lucky—the interviewer showed her. But what happens when people are not as forthcoming?

Technique 2: Get Others to Talk About Themselves

The best way to discover a person's inner workings is to get them to talk about themselves. The subjects they choose, the words they use, their body language, the things they leave out—all of these open windows on what is really going on inside.

"I say something. He'd say how it reminds him of the merchant marines. Then I say something else and he'd say how it was like being on a boat," reports Luke Pursell, 35, a fleet dispatcher for a trucking company in Richmond, Virginia. "You ask me, he'd be better off working as part of a team because the need to belong seemed a lot stronger than the need to work independently."

When you get other people talking, they reveal their deepest needs.

CHAPTER 2

TWO FOOLPROOF WAYS TO OWN THE CONVERSATION

Whether you are dealing with the folks you lead, the folks you follow, the folks you love, or anyone in between, the ideas people find most important are invariably their own.

Appeal to these and you own the conversation.

How do you do that?

1. Make an effort to understand their needs and slant your ideas accordingly

2. Say what you would want to hear if you were the listener

Technique 3: Ask Open-Ended Questions

What's an open-ended question? One that cannot be answered with a fact, a "yes," or a "no."

An open-ended question often begins with one of five w's:

▶ *Who?* "Can you give me some background on who's who around here?"

▶ *What?* "It would be helpful if you could tell me in detail, What took so long for the order to arrive?"

▶ *Where?* "I heard you talking about the Napa Valley. I'm going there and I wondered, Can you let me know where your favorite restaurants are?

▶ *When?* "Can you give me the context—everything going on when you walked in the door?"

▶ *Why?* "Why do you suppose things turned out the way they did?"

Technique 4: Talk in Terms of the Other Person's Interest

Sure, it sounds easier to talk about our thoughts and plans in the ways we ourselves think about them. But that is like leaving the landing lights on for Amelia Earhart. Let me give you an illustration of what I am talking about:

Visitors to President Lyndon Baines Johnson's office never got talked into anything. Quite the opposite. Johnson set it up so he never had to talk about what he wanted because he knew others could care less about the aims and goals he brought up. Instead, he leveraged their interest in ways that got them to talk themselves into what he wanted.

Whoever they were, wherever they came from, Johnson knew just what to say to get results.

To one Georgia senator whose vote he needed on a farm bill, LBJ talked about an out-of-the-way barbecue pit, The Georgia Pig. It was just outside of Brunswick, the senator's hometown. That of course, started a long conversation on the merits of Texas beef barbecue versus Georgia pork.

Eventually, the senator himself turned the conversation around to agricultural supports. This gave the President the opportunity to talk up his bill in terms of its impact on the senator's constituency.

On his way out, the senator, who left promising to vote with the President, asked when Johnson had last visited the Brunswick restaurant.

"Some friends of mine rave about it but to tell you the truth, senator, I never set foot in the place," Johnson confessed.

What the President did not confess was this: the White House staff spent most of the previous night finding out what particularly interested the Senator, and prepared a memo with detailed talking points for the President.

Follow the powerful example set by President Johnson—talk about things the other person treasures most. The new knowledge that emerges from your interest will widen your horizons, enlarge your life, and you will come out of each conversation with exactly what you want.

Technique 5: Listen Like you Mean It

When it comes to filling the unsatisfied needs of others, bad listening is certain to produce bad results.

I know people, and I am sure you do too, who occupy expensive offices, furnish them well, embrace all the latest technology, but who hire staff who neither understand how important it is to listen properly nor care much about their shortcomings in this area. I am talking about folks who interrupt, argue, irritate—people who give communication in the workplace a bad name.

If you find yourself in this crowd, it would be well for you and your people to review the recommendations I made in Chapter 1:

- Concentrate intensely on the other person

- Focus on what they say, not what you think in response to what they say

- Be alert to gestures and body language

To get what you want out of conversation, one of the goals of your every encounter must be to create a listening experience for the other person such as they have never known before.

Technique 6: $N = B \rightarrow C$

When you know which hidden need presses hardest for satisfaction, you must use it to leverage the power of your idea—show them how a feature of your thinking satisfies their need.

The "leverage" is a formula—an easy way to remember what must happen if you are to get what you want,

$$N = B \rightarrow C$$

If you will commit this simple formula to memory, if you will use it without fail in every conversation you have from this moment forward, I guarantee it will produce exactly the business and personal results you want. No ifs, and, or buts: It will work no matter what the circumstances—every time, without fail.

I say this with unshakable confidence. I know from years of research and close personal experience that whether you are proposing marriage, arguing with your children, or writing a love letter, when the BENEFITS you offer equal the NEEDS they possess, the result is COMMUNICATION.

Let me put the formula into a real-life context. In training, sales people are taught buyer's have needs. For instance, many car buyers want power, many want value, and even more prefer both.

Filling those needs gets shoppers to purchase.

Sales trainees are asked to describe a product feature. For the sake of argument, let's say it is a powerful 24-valve engine.

Then they are instructed to convert that feature into a benefit—a reason that will get buyers to buy.

Now they reshape their description so the product appeals to the buyers' interests:

Our 24-valve engine delivers more horsepower, yet costs less to run, than Honda.

In the same way America's most successful salespersons translate a feature into a reason to buy, the N = B → C formula takes your idea and works it up into a benefit—a way that satisfies the other person's most pressing need.

You might say at this point that you are not a sales person. I grant you that. But the purpose of most conversation is to swing another to act or think or do or believe something: to vote up or down, take out the trash, play a game of Horses, do the chores, share a frozen yogurt, or maybe just listen. So bear with me, it will do you good to learn something about selling.

You have to sell them on what you want. N = B → C does the selling for you.

Technique 7: Speak of What You Want in Terms of What They Want

Wisconsin OSHA inspector Rick Percey, 37, needed to convince a sawmill operator to change over to a new type of safety system on the green line.

"I could have talked about job safety standards and made it stick, but that would have gotten me the usual back talk. I would've been tied up for an hour explaining what he already knew and didn't like. So all I said right off the bat was that several other mills like his had done it and the new system paid for itself in lower insurance premiums."

Percey makes it seem easy to talk with others by talking like others . . . and it is.

Don't tell them about how you benefit because they don't really care about the ways you gain. Tell them how they will gain, what the gain means to them in concrete and specific terms. Tell them what is in it for them. For instance,

▶ "When you take the course in statistics, I'll be able to upgrade your job description and get you the raise you've been after."

▶ "That color is perfect with your complexion."

▶ "Here's a chance for the two of us to do something for the kids' future and it won't cost anymore than we are spending now."

Spare no effort to play to their interest. Lose no time in telling them they have a stake in listening to your thoughts. Get their interest early and hit it hard.

Technique 8: Make Their Problems Your Problems

Hickey Brown, 41, a Utah aerospace worker, volunteered to man the phones for a union welfare-fund drive.

"This morning, " Hickey said to one fellow unionist, "I lost my job. Now how do you suppose it feels to tell your family? I can tell you it felt low.

But I am not alone in this. What happened to me today happened to one out of every four people in our local. Nobody wants that kind of change but I am afraid it is here in spades and who knows who is next: You? Somebody in your car pool? "

Almost every call Hickey made that day resulted in a contribution. Follow his lead and you will be as successful in attaining your objectives as he was with his. Just remember, if your words do not relate to the people you are speaking with, the people you are speaking with will not relate to your words.

Technique 9: Inject Emotions Whenever You Can

It is fine to marshall all of the facts and statistics to prove the logic of your thinking. But you must bear in mind that many things are brought about by emotional reasoning.

Some appeals that tweak emotions include these:

▶ Material gain: *I want to show you a way to save . . .*

▶ Romance: *The boys will ring your phone off the hook*

▶ Health: *Jog with me for a week and you'll hit the golf ball two miles, and straight*

▶ Prestige: *It's sure to get the votes you need*

▶ Domestic happiness: *The kids will know how much we love them*

Technique 10: What to Do When They Won't Go Along

There will be times when you are met with resistance to your thoughts. More often than not, it is because you have failed to do something. Before you take any corrective action, the very first thing you must do is to mentally ask yourself six critical questions.

SIX-POINT CHECKLIST

▶ Did you let them know immediately what was in it for them?

▶ Did you speak of what they wanted, not what you wanted?

▶ Did you convince them it was in their interest to listen?

▶ Did you use the right appeals?

▶ Did you make your points in terms they understood?

▶ Did you make emotions as important as facts?

Assuming you have followed my procedure to the letter, try to recall that nothing happens for nothing.

There has to be a reason why you aren't being given what you want.

If you can dig that reason out and find a way to satisfy it, you'll stand a very good chance of getting things your way.

When people object to anything in the ordinary course of life, there are usually two reasons: The first is the reason that sounds good. And the second is the real reason—the secret need—that is kept hidden. Your job is to find that real reason, get it out in the open where you can deal with it.

Technique 11: Draw Out Their Defenses

Ask them to explain their objection. When they reply, ask them, "Is there anything else?" When they answer that, follow it up with another question, "And in addition to that?" Eventually, when what strikes you as the real reason surfaces, move immediately into my next technique.

Technique 12: Test the Answer

There's only one way to be sure you are not being okey-doked, and that is to determine the level of conviction behind the words.

You do it with a question.

"If I can show you how my thinking really links up with yours, will you go along?"

If the answer is no, keep the conversation going by inquiring, "How come?"

When the two of you reach agreement, move immediately to my next technique.

Technique 13: Demonstrate the Fact

Tell them exactly how your thinking and theirs dovetail.

Now, to put the finishing touches on the subject of controlling the conversation, let's go over the key points in this chapter:

1. There are two foolproof ways to own a conversation

▸ Make an effort to understand their needs and slant your ideas accordingly

▸ Say what you would want to hear if you were the listener

2. Always heed the logic of self-interest

▸ Think about your keen interest in your own affairs

▸ Contrast that with your mild concern about anything else

▸ Accept the fact that everyone else feels the same way about themselves

3. Three benefits are yours when you appeal to their self interest

▸ Others will identify with your thoughts and they will do what you wish

▸ As the number of people who accept your views grows, your circle of influence will spread

▸ As you win the hearts and minds of others your self confidence will grow and your ability to be outgoing will increase

4. Secret needs make us us

Minds meet when your thoughts fill a need that motivates them. The top 10 needs of most people are:

▶ Power: a desire for superiority

▶ Ego: a sense of personal pride

▶ Excellence: a feeling of winning

▶ Security: a hunger for protection from threat

▶ Recognition: a need for personal worth

▶ Privacy: a craving to protect personal space

▶ Liberty: an urge to be in control of personal destiny

▶ Greed: a longing for more than a fair share

▶ Esteem: a passion to be admired by others

▶ Affection: a yearning to belong

5. To discover which of these needs press hardest at the moment, draw people out.

▶ Ask leading questions to get revealing answers

▶ Talk in terms of the other person's interests

▶ Listen like you mean it

6. Once you know the needs that make them say and do the things they say and do, use the formula $N = B \rightarrow C$:

▶ Tell them immediately how they are going to benefit

▶ Speak of what you want in terms of what they want

▶ Convince them it is in their interest to consider your point of view

▶ Use the right appeals

▶ Make your points in terms they understand

▶ Inject emotions wherever you can

7. To overcome objections, you've got to apply three surefire techniques. You must:

▶ Draw out their defenses by asking them to explain their objection

▶ Test the answer

▶ Demonstrate how your thinking matches theirs

You know, when all is said and done, the fact remains that we cannot become the communicators we wish to be by remaining what we are. I say that because I believe that the process of communication is really the process of opening up . . . to ourselves as well as to others.

By turning inward first, by searching our own feelings, our empathy with others grows. We become better and better at understanding not just what they say but why they say it.

But what about the part of us that communicates in ways that do not require words? What about body language and other forms of nonverbal communication? Do these play a vital role in making us well liked and popular, or is this body language stuff a lot of hype?

The next page tells all.

CHAPTER 3

NON-VERBAL COMMUNICATION

Sixteen Workable Ways to Listen with Your Eyes

When American Express won a Malcolm Baldridge Award from the Department of Commerce, Mickey Van Vechter, 41, said the New York office was "walking on air." Twenty-six year-old Harold Chennowith, a Salt Lake City systems specialist, "jumped for joy." Consuelo O'Brien, 34, in customer service at Fort Lauderdale, reported her boss "swelled with pride."

What is astonishing about all of this is not their evident and well-deserved pleasure. No, what truly amazes me is that, having said what they said, none of them claims to know anything about body language. Quite the opposite. They think of themselves as nonverbal illiterates.

But, like them, and without being aware of it, most of us are board-certified experts in nonverbal communication.

- -

If You Understand These, You Can Read Body Language

Popular figures of speech, things that you and I often say and always understand, prove the point.

▶ *Freeze* in terror

▶ *Tremble* with rage

▶ *Lift* an eyebrow in disbelief

▶ *Grit* our teeth

▶ *Stiffen* our upper lip

▶ *Flush* with embarrassment

▶ *Rub* our nose in puzzlement

▶ *Shrug* our shoulders in indifference

▶ *Wink* one eye to convey intimacy

▶ *Clasp* our arms to protect ourselves

▶ *Tap* our fingers in impatience

▶ *Slap* our forehead to indicate forgetfulness

Quick as we are to pick up on and repeat these signals embedded in our culture, we also miss a lot. And no wonder.

Sometimes nonverbals are so clear you would have to be blindfolded to misinterpret them.

The meaning of other nonverbals—a certain sideways glance, for instance, or the position of a hand, or perhaps a subtle eye-hand gesture—may be harder to read, but they are no less subject to meaning, interpretation, and consequence.

LISTENING WITH YOUR EYES

The legendary French beauty, Juliette de Raoul-Ponsot, was the object of Gaul's most dashing, ardent, and determined lovers. But, after just one meeting, an aging Victor Hugo, the famous French novelist, won her heart for life.

"When a woman is speaking with you, monsieur," Hugo revealed in his memoirs, "listen to what she says with your eyes."

Juliette's voice might have been telling one story but her body was saying something else.

The point is this: when you listen with your eyes you hold the key to controlling one of life's most complex events—a face-to-face encounter with another human being.

I want this chapter to give you 16 workable ways to listen with your eyes and act on what you see.

Here you will learn the unspoken signs to watch for in conversation, signs that are invariably better indicators of what is really going on than words alone. By learning to recognize these when someone uses them on you, and by using them to reinforce your own words, you will get more of what you want from every encounter. The unique power of communication that will be yours is certain to change your life for the better.

HOW TO USE WHAT YOU SEE TO GET WHAT YOU WANT

It is a scientific fact that people's facial expressions, tone of voice, and postures and gestures give away their true intentions. Much more human communication takes place through these than verbally. Psychologists say as much as 70 percent of our understanding comes to us visually as we pick up and transmit subtle body movement—often unconsciously.

Here, you will learn to decode the secrets of nonverbal communication and understand the *true* meaning of

- An arched eyebrow,
- An itchy nose,
- The wink of an eye,
- Knuckle biting,
- Drumming fingers, and
- Even a flabby handshake

You'll know what is really going on when

- Poker players wear dark glasses
- A woman selects certain colors and scents
- Someone tries to control your gaze
- The time is ripe to ask for a raise
- Conditions permit you to take control of a job interview

And, you will understand how to leverage body language:

- Four ways body language keeps you from getting a traffic ticket

▶ The best way to meet and succeed with the opposite sex

▶ Where to sit in any room

And more.

- -

Four Far-Reaching Benefits Are Yours When You Learn to Communicate Without Words

You establish yourself as a desirable conversational partner—a quality most people like and find easy to respond to.

Take the mating game: Lovers look deeply into each other's eyes without really knowing why. Body language explains it. When someone is aroused, their pupils grow, unconsciously, as much as four times normal. Somehow, we are equipped to decode this signal without being aware we are decoding it. As we do, it sets our own hearts thumping.

"When I learned about the eye thing," reports Nicole Garmisch, 23, who repairs electronics in Madison, Wisconsin, "I tried it. The first date we hit it off nice. I suggested dinner at a really cute little country place where the only light is from the fireplace and candles. I guess it worked—we've been seeing each other for four months."

Nicole's knowledge of nonverbal communication put her in the driver's seat as far as how and how fast the relationship was going to develop. Without it, she might never have chosen a dimly lit place where shadows encouraged her pupils to open.

By affecting your behavior, bearing, and manner, nonverbal strategies and signals get your self-confidence across to that certain someone.

This encourages them to take you and your approach seriously.

Blowups are short-circuited and you can head off a bad situation before it explodes.

Without a word, just through body position, you can put down a revolution at home or on the job and get things back to normal a.s.a.p.

"I heard on the grapevine that one of my people was stabbing me in the back," reports Chip Alton, 46, political worker in La Jolla, California. "So I just walked into her office, sat on the corner of her desk, looked down at her, and said I wanted things to be more comfortable between us. By entering her personal space, I staked a claim to leadership she had to acknowledge. Ever since, it's been quiet on the western front."

Other people have no choice but to show you what is really on their minds, and this knowledge gives you a big leg up on success.

Terry Berman-Browne, 36, an Atlantic City tennis club pro, won't play poker with anybody wearing dark glasses.

"Poker is a game of small edges," he says. "People don't realize it but with each card their mood swings. So I watch their eyes. When they get bigger it means they've probably got a good hand. So I bet conservatively. That's an edge. When they wear dark glasses, it erases my edge."

Whether you are working on your game or a big deal, asking for a raise or for a hand in marriage, when you know how to read another person's body language you not only know their secrets, you are actually inside their mind.

They won't need to tell you what they are thinking; you'll know it—often before they themselves are totally aware of it.

You approach life in a more disciplined way, a way that is intensely focused on achieving not just your immediate goals but your complete potential.

Pete Metcalf, 30, a board member of a Shaker Heights, Ohio church, tells about an experience trying to hire a professional fund raiser.

"On paper, the guy was made for the job. In person? Well, when I met him, he shook my hand with a knuckle buster. That told me he was over aggressive. He confirmed the impression when he hung his other hand on my shoulder like we were long lost buddies. I knew right away the Arnold Schwarzenegger routine wouldn't go down with conservative people in our community."

In the opening of any conversation, when the parties size each other up, their words may play it safe but, as Pete discovered, their body language is a dead giveaway. Crunching another person's hand is the nonverbal trademark of the aggressive tough guy. Pete was wise to feel suspicious about the job candidate's ability to fit in with the long range success of his congregation.

DO YOU LISTEN WITH YOUR EYES?

I spent this morning at a shopping mall. I sat on a low wooden bench with trees and a water fountain at my back, and all of humanity before me. For 15 minutes, I watched what went on as people met, interacted, and went their various ways. I'd like to share those observations with you.

Beneath each description you will find a scale from 1 to 10. On it, I want you to circle the number that, in your judgment, reflects your personal position on the interpretation offered. The lower the number you circle, the more you agree with the interpretation; the higher the number, the stronger your disagreement. Try to avoid the highest and lowest numbers unless you believe a particular interpretation deserves an extreme rating.

There are no right and wrong answers, and you are not under any particular time pressure.

1. An older man, face etched with worry lines, meets a young girl. They kiss. They speak. His frown vanishes. It returns as they part.

   Interpretation: whatever she said was powerful enough to erase—even if for only a moment—a lifetime of worry. It was probably the most important part of the encounter.

   <u>Agree</u>   <u>Disagree</u>

   1 . . . 2 . . . 3 . . . 4 . . . 5 . . . 6 . . . 7 . . . 8 . . . 9 . . . 10

2. A couple of smiling younger men, mid-twenties, eyeball-to-eyeball—and nobody's blinking. The feet of neither man points directly at his listener. As they part, they punch each other in the arm.

   Interpretation: none of the moves mean anything by themselves but, taken together, they suggest a context. Hard gaze, mildly aggressive punching—these say neither one was as friendly as a first glance might suggest. The confirming gesture is the position of feet. Their bodies are showing where their minds want to be.

Agree   Disagree

1 . . . 2 . . . 3 . . . 4 . . . 5 . . . 6 . . . 7 . . . 8 . . . 9 . . . 10

3. She: very attractive, twenty-something, pinstriped suit, Ferragamos. He: mousy. She adjusts the waistline of her skirt. He polishes his left shoe on the back of his right trouser leg.

   Interpretation: the sexuality she communicates through her look and her moves make him extremely uncomfortable. The shoe-shine gesture signals his desire to end the encounter.

Agree   Disagree

1 . . . 2 . . . 3 . . . 4 . . . 5 . . . 6 . . . 7 . . . 8 . . . 9 . . . 10

4. A man and a woman, thirty-ish, take seats in the food hall. They sit at either end of a table.

   Interpretation: when two people are in a love relationship, their unconscious desire is to draw close. By choosing to sit opposite each other as opposed to occupying a corner, they are signalling theirs is a business encounter.

Agree   Disagree

1 . . . 2 . . . 3 . . . 4 . . . 5 . . . 6 . . . 7 . . . 8 . . . 9 . . . 10

5. Two women push baby carriages. As they converse, their heads tilt toward each other. One woman scratches the side of her neck. They stop, face each other, continue speaking.

   Interpretation: in response to what she was hearing, the woman who scratched her neck used body language to say, "I am not sure I go along with you on that."

Agree   Disagree

1 . . . 2 . . . 3 . . . 4 . . . 5 . . . 6 . . . 7 . . . 8 . . . 9 . . . 10

6. From a distance, a man and woman come into eye-contact. She takes a deep breath, he fiddles with his bow tie. They pass like ships in the night.

Interpretation: though neither acted upon their feelings, each was momentarily attracted to the other.

<u>Agree</u>   <u>Disagree</u>

1 . . . 2 . . . 3 . . . 4 . . . 5 . . . 6 . . . 7 . . . 8 . . . 9 . . . 10

7. Uh-oh, Dennis The Menace. Two steps forward, one step back, he approaches the person next to me. They make eye contact. The boy puts his hands on his hips, lifts his chin.

Interpretation: part of him, he of the halting step, is a kid who has been told not to talk with strangers. Another part, Mr. Hands-On-Hips, wants to appear big enough and tough enough to handle the situation.

<u>Agree</u>   <u>Disagree</u>

1 . . . 2 . . . 3 . . . 4 . . . 5 . . . 6 . . . 7 . . . 8 . . . 9 . . . 10

8. A speed-walker approaches a charity fund raiser holding out a coin box. He frowns, shoots her a sideways glance. She backs out of his path.

Interpretation: depending on the situation, a sideways glance can mean attraction or repulsion. His frown was the confirming gesture: it communicated suspicion, hostility, and a critical attitude.

<u>Agree</u>   <u>Disagree</u>

1 . . . 2 . . . 3 . . . 4 . . . 5 . . . 6 . . . 7 . . . 8 . . . 9 . . . 10

9. A mother and her teenage daughter. The mother looks like she is having a bad-hair day. She shakes a finger at the girl. They walk, the girl rubs her palms.

Interpretation: the child expects the shopping trip to be a big success.

<u>Agree</u>   <u>Disagree</u>

1 . . . 2 . . . 3 . . . 4 . . . 5 . . . 6 . . . 7 . . . 8 . . . 9 . . . 10

10. An older couple are deeply engaged in conversation. He speaks with his legs wide apart, spreads his arms, turns his palms toward the woman.

Interpretation: he is telling the truth.

<u>Agree</u>   <u>Disagree</u>

1 . . . 2 . . . 3 . . . 4 . . . 5 . . . 6 . . . 7 . . . 8 . . . 9 . . . 10

Now that you have completed the exercise, simply add up your ratings.

A total of 50 or more indicates that the subject of body language is something of a new frontier in your life. If this is the case, this chapter may be the most important in the book for you. Please continue reading until you have completed it. Then, my advice is to put the book aside for a day or so. Later, return to this chapter and read it once more.

A total of 49 or less suggests a developing but perhaps imperfect ability to listen with your eyes. Your blind spots are probably in the areas where your ratings are the highest. If you will bear these in mind as you continue reading this chapter, you will find surefire techniques to strengthen your nonverbal skills.

Sixteen Workable Ways to Listen with Your Eyes

Technique 1: Concentrate on Main Signals

The average encounter between two people is an exercise in information overload.

Overwhelming numbers of clues come at us from four different sources:

▶ Facial expression

▶ Tone and pace of voice

▶ Posture and gestures

▶ Specific words

FACIAL EXPRESSION

"When you are taking depositions, you pay attention to more than what the witness says," reports Victor Sammons, 32, a Denver paralegal. "It is the face that tells the truth."

A number of trustworthy scientific studies support Sammons' point of view. These say facial expression most accurately reveals what a speaker is feeling.

TONE AND PACE OF VOICE

Number two in importance is tone and pace of voice.

"After 24 years on the job, you learn to read subtle changes in voice and tempo," reports Miami elementary teacher Jefferson Powell, 49. "They could blindfold me and I would still know that a slow monotone says the kid is bored, and a fast, rising tone means she is surprised."

POSTURES, GESTURES, ACTIONS

Third is posture, gestures, and actions.

"When my boss wants to close a meeting, she searches through her desk," reports Washington, D.C. Pepsi-Cola route salesperson Harold Beck, 30. "Sometimes she says she is looking for a memo, other times a Kleenex. No matter what she says, it translates to she wants out."

By concentrating on the main signal, you leverage your nonverbal skills to reveal the point where your efforts are likely to do the most good.

Technique 2: Pay More Attention to Patterns than to Isolated Events

Behaviorists say when we cover up our bodies we are defending our psychological selves. However, someone at a chilly football game with crossed arms and legs, and chin pressed down, is more likely to be cold than to be defensive.

The interpretation of a nonverbal signal depends on what is happening at the moment, where that moment happens, and between whom.

Give the crowd a V sign in America, for instance, and you're visualizing victory. Do it in Australia and you are giving your audience the finger. Change any of the conditions—event, environment, or personalities—and the meaning shifts. Because that is true, your success depends on paying more attention to nonverbal patterns than to isolated body moves.

Technique 3: Be on the Lookout for Inconsistencies

When words and body language are at odds, both messages are important: words tell you what is on their minds, body language what is in their hearts. Of the two, trust body language. It is the truer barometer of what's really going down.

"I pulled a real airhead move once," reports Paula Yagjian, 28, a Haverill, Massachusetts word processor. "So I said to my husband I hoped it didn't make him angry. His face got red. You could just see him boiling, his fists got all balled up. He said he was not angry but I was more convinced by what he looked like than by anything he said."

When nonverbals don't confirm spoken language, your best bet is to follow Paula's lead: search body language for meaning.

Technique 4: Feedback the Feelings

As you come to be more observant of nonverbals, you will begin to notice that you respond mentally to what you observe physically.

If someone signals boredom, you'll see it, if they're tense, you'll hear it. This gives you the opportunity to do two things at once: First, to get a reality check on your assumptions. And second, to get across the idea that you are an accepting and sensitive conversational partner. You do these simultaneously by verbally feeding back to the other person the feelings you yourself experience in response to them.

"Once upon a time, I might have pushed the whole thing away, put a smiley on it, and sent my son up to bed," reports Zipporah Weiss, 37, a librarian in Wilmington, Delaware. "This time something in his voice made me feel sad for him. His lip was trembling. So I said I was feeling a little glum, too, and wondered why he felt so unhappy. He explained the whole thing and we both felt better."

Technique 5: Respect the Geography of Human Interaction

People's need for certain amounts of space is so basic there must be a chromosome for it. Like all higher animals, humans are territorial. That is, we follow an unwritten law that establishes our needs for personal space. It controls the size of invisible capsule we require to feel safe in any given situation. Although these vary based on our upbringing, there are recognizable patterns that regulate the way we handle space and distance.

Most of us operate within four zones. While the size of these are determined by culture—Japanese tolerate closer contact than, say, Americans—these zones can be generally defined as

▶ Intimate

▶ Private

▶ Social

▶ Public

The *intimate* region, from 6 to 18 inches in the United States, is whispering distance, open to those who are emotionally close. It is the only space we are prepared to defend.

The *private* space, from one-and-one-half to four feet, is where most Americans prefer to speak quietly to others at the office.

The *social* area, 4 to 12 feet, is the distance from which Americans address strangers.

The *public* circle is, in this country, anything beyond 12 feet.

When people violate these boundaries, even if they are from different cultures, it makes us uncomfortable, and our discomfort shows up in unconscious movement of ourselves or the things that belong to us.

"When a stranger crowds me at the cafeteria by sitting too close," reports Devon Jeffries, 19, a student at the University of Arkansas, "I move my chair or tray away from them."

"I want to be able to say that all the news about sexual harassment in the workplace makes them respect women more," reports Quad Cities shop steward Harriet Sheeran, 40. "Nowadays, you don't see so many men barging right in close where they are not invited."

If you want people to be comfortable with you, heed the meaning in Harriet's words: keep the distances between you appropriate both at home and at work.

Knowing this, you will quickly see that it is not a good idea to put your arm on the shoulder of someone you just met socially or on the job. They may smile, but the chances are they will feel their personal boundaries have been violated. One way or another, this feeling eventually will affect your ability to create a meeting of the minds.

As we enter, move through, and exit spaces of various kinds we are both sending and receiving body language.

▶ The way we *move* toward or away from others reflects how we feel about what may be, has been, or is yet to be said.

▶ The way we *sit* speaks volumes: we lean forward to show interest, lean back to put distance between ourselves and what is being said.

▶ The way we *walk* indicates to others the way we feel—everything from good to happy to cheerful to gloomy to tired to dejected.

▶ *Posture* is critical: we tend to relax our bodies when we are with people of equal or lower status, suck in our bellies and tense up in the presence of people we regard as more powerful or sexually attractive.

HOW TO USE BODY LANGUAGE TO AVOID A TRAFFIC SUMMONS

It is a good idea to remain quietly in your car when you are pulled over for a traffic infraction. The police are aware the space immediately adjacent to your car is part of your intimate zone. They violate it on purpose when you are pulled over. Safety considerations aside, it is to establish control of the situation.

Any move to exit the car is a potential threat. It heightens the officer's inner tension and often provokes cops to write a ticket. To prevent that, all you have to do is *absolutely nothing.*

That's right!, no provocations, no copping a plea, no arguments, and nothing terribly more than no sir or yes ma'am. The less you say the better.

"One night I was doing 52 in a 40-mile zone," reports Sally Le Van, 29, a Hartford restaurant hostess. "My daughter was sick and I needed to get home. I turned on the dome light, rolled down the window and waited. When the officer asked if there was any special rush, I simply said I work in a restaurant downtown and my daughter in Waterbury was down with a fever of 102°F. And I swear that was all I said. He let me go with a written warning."

Sally's successful body language experience doesn't guarantee you will always avoid a summons, but do the four things she did and you could get lucky.

1. Do not say or do anything to provoke a buildup of tension.

2. Remain inside the vehicle with your hands on the steering wheel.

3. At night, be sure to turn on your interior lights to get across the idea that you have nothing to hide.

4. Speak only when spoken to.

> ### Technique 6: Check Out Clothing, Grooming, and the Environment

"It is amazing how much people tell you without ever even opening their mouths," reports Bureau of Indian Affairs health worker Robert Thunderheel, 41, a Four Corners resident. "A circle worn in the right-hand back pocket of their jeans says they chew snuff, which puts them at risk for mouth cancer. Boots worn at the outer edges of the heels says they've got fallen arches and probably don't get enough exercise because their feet hurt too much."

Thunderheel makes an important point: Be it business or pleasure, the way we look and the way we live and perform in our chosen environments tell the world who we are, where we stand in life, and what we think about ourselves.

Even if you feel people like you should not be judged by their clothing, grooming, and environment, these say something about you.

- Bright colors suggest youthful vitality, grays and deeper shades a more sedate mood.

- Intended or not, suggestive clothes and cosmetics deliver a sexual message.

"When women wear bright lipstick and nail enamel," reports Rae Bittinger, 31, a Tulsa department store cosmetics consultant, "they're calling attention to themselves. When they put on a floral fragrance like *L'Air du Temps* the impression they want to create is one of innocence; when they wear *Shalimar*, it is to draw attention to their womanliness."

Hairstyles, jewelry, attire, and furnishings help us understand the people with whom we engage. Their desk might be clean or cluttered. Chins could be shaved or five-o'clock-shadowed. Clothes can be anything from chic to schlock.

Any of these things—no, all of these things!—are messages to the world.

It is useful to remember that we almost always react to others in terms of the messages we see. It is even more useful to keep in mind that so do they.

Technique 7: Be Especially Alert to Head Moves

Head moves tell you in a glance the feelings, emotions, and reactions that really count.

"When a job interviewer tilts his head towards you, he is telling you he is tuned in on the point you just made," reports Hickey Berwin, 39, a human resources trainer from Birmingham, Alabama. "By concentrating on and developing that point, you gain complete control of the session. But when he leans away, he's saying the opposite. This is the time to change your tack."

Some head actions are deliberate: you smile at a friend to show approval, raise an eyebrow to indicate surprise, frown to show dissatisfaction.

Others are unintended.

"During staff meetings, when I hand out work assignments, I try to keep my eyes on their postures," reports Bob Schnee, 34, a legislative assistant at the Delaware State House. "When I see someone brace up, sit up just a little, I can pretty much count on their cooperation."

Technique 8: When Eyes Talk, Listen

TV closeups have helped make facial expressions an important part of communication—especially the eyes. They weep, twinkle, glower, mourn . . . and a whole lot more. What about shifty eyes, beady eyes, bedroom eyes, the evil eye? Two things make the eyes important.

First, with all of their conscious movement, they are an obvious focus of interest.

And second, because the pupils expand and contract unconsciously in response to attitude and mood, they are true indicators of what is really going on inside. Prostitutes in Paris put drops of belladonna in their eyes: it dilates their pupils to make them appear more desirable.

There's no doubt eyes tell you what people may not be able to put into words. That is why it is vital to make eye contact in a face-to-face encounter. By carefully monitoring the eyes of others, you get real-time feedback on the impression you are making.

Technique 9: Manage Eye Contact

To build rapport, your gaze should meet the other person's about 60 to 70 percent of the time. Any more and you may be issuing a non-verbal challenge; any less and you may unwittingly suggest you have something to hide.

Technique 10: Control Your Focus to Control Theirs

Under most circumstances, the focus of your gaze determines who you control and for how long.

"To get a buyer's full attention when I'm asking a premium price," reports Phoenix citrus broker Felton Weatherup, 47, "I control their gaze by focusing on the triangle between their eyes and a point just a little above the bridge of the nose. I make an effort not to look away until the transaction is finished."

On the job, a tip like Felton's may prove especially useful next time you ask for a raise. At home, you can use it to control a difficult personal situation.

Technique 11: Pay Attention to Culture

How to look, how long to look, and where to look are affected by your upbringing.

African and Hispanic Americans are taught not to look into the eyes of elders, but the white middle class demands it. Safe areas for unlimited gazing in all cultures are above the neck and below the knees. It is more acceptable for your boss or a superior to stare at you than for you to stare at them. Matching them look-for-look may put you at risk of appearing insubordinate.

Technique 12: Look for Rapid Eye Blinking

During a conversation, when their eyes blink more than the normal six to eight moves per minute, you can be sure what you just said won't work.

Technique 13: Hand Signals Tell Gripping Truths

People's hand and arm movements are especially revealing. Consider, for instance, the palm. The open palm speaks of honesty, truth, and submission to higher authority. After all, when we swear an oath, the palm is held up for all to see.

Ken DiPietro, 30, who runs a Nashville employment agency, says he is a palm watcher. "Hidden palms," he reports, "suggest a job candidate may be holding back on something."

Shake hands palm up and you are signalling willingness to be submissive. Turn your palm down when you grip somebody else's and you establish an early impression of strength.

A limp handshake leads us to the often mistaken belief we are dealing with a wimp. Let me put it this way: If you were a concert violinist, for example, or a brain surgeon, would you risk your livelihood on a knuckle-cruncher?

Rubbing your palms or your fingers says you expect to benefit. Clenched hands communicate frustration.

Meanwhile, steepled hands project power. Steepling is often used by physicians, judges, and people in superior positions to suggest dominance.

"When I make a presentation to my boss I know I've gotten his attention when he makes a steeple with his hands," reports Dona Curtis, 27, a Charleston marketing assistant. "It tells me he is mentally searching for a way to take over, to make my idea his idea."

We often talk about getting a good grip on ourselves, which explains why people trying to remain in control unconsciously fold their arms to grip a hand, wrist, or perhaps their other arm.

Folded-arm gestures come in several forms. Whether you clasp your biceps, grip hands behind your back, or adjust the band on your watch, qualified psychological investigators say you are somehow protecting yourself. You may feel comfortable doing these things but they invariably create negative feelings in the eye of the beholder.

Carole Wattreau, 38, a Baton Rouge social worker, has a trick to break any folded-arm gesture."I just hand the person something—a pen, a piece of paper, chewing gum—anything to get them to let go a little bit. Things usually loosen up after that."

If you have ever picked up a hitchhiker you know thumbs make signals you can rely on and be guided by. When they protrude from a pocket or hook on a belt or coat, the message they deliver is one of superiority.

"Sometimes, it backfires!," reports assistant Cook County court clerk, Joanna Brinkowczi, 44. "When a lawyer approaches a jury with his head back, gripping his lapel with the thumb visible, you can bet the jury will come back with a verdict against him. That thumb gives them a feeling of haughtiness, you know, insincerity."

Technique 14: Watch Out for Hands Touching Faces

When your listener's hand supports his head, it generally means he is bored. It would be useful to back off from whatever you said to provoke such a reaction.

A more serious signal comes across when people put their hand to their mouth or nose.

"Growing up, my folks gave me a little statue of three monkeys—See No Evil, Hear No Evil, Speak No Evil," reports Rick Savander, 38, a Boston printing broker. "Maybe that is why, when people put their hands to their noses or mouths, I get the feeling they are trying to hide a lie."

Conversely, when we hear a lie it is not unusual for us to rub our eyes or ears.

Fingers in the mouth tell another story.

"Whenever I am under pressure," reports Regina Mills, 26, a Boise administrative assistant, "I find myself biting my knuckles."

Hand and arm movements and gestures create situations where very little needs to be said to communicate a lot. They make it easier for others not only to be influenced by your thinking, but to enjoy your company.

Technique 15: Give Leg Movements Low Priority

Leg movements and postures are generally less certain indicators of mood and intention than foot signals.

By themselves, for instance, crossed legs may hold no special meaning. But when a seated person crosses arms and legs, they are signalling feelings of threat or deep displeasure, and a desire to withdraw.

"Lately, I've noticed that people who sit by my desk and cross their arms and legs rarely turn into buyers," reports Adena Zervoulakis, 27. She sells cars in Pittsburgh. "On a busy day with the showroom full, I try to ease away from people like that and steer to the ones who look more open to buy."

When the same crossing leg-crossing gestures occur in a standing position—you've seen a lot of it at big parties where people don't know each other—it signifies a sense of aloneness. Next time you find yourself at a party, look for people standing with their legs crossed. If their feet are pointed in your direction, the body language says eye contact is in order.

Placing an ankle—usually the right one—on the knee may or may not be a way simply to take pressure off the spine when in a seated position. But when a hand is placed on that selfsame ankle, assume you are being met with combative intent and a show-me attitude.

Technique 16: Where You Sit Says Who You Are

"Where I sit depends on what I want," reports Osman Turkovich, 30, a Seattle meeting planner. "The boss takes the chair at twelve o'clock. If I want to cooperate, I'll sit at eleven or one. If I want to show him I am really behind what I say, that I am willing to slug it out verbally, take the heat, I go for the chair at six. But I never sit at four or eight o'clock—it says I don't want to interact and, at a crowded table, it makes engaging with him one-on-one impossible."

Here's a way to make your awareness of seating strategies payoff instantly in practical terms that will affect your life.

Just take a few seconds to think of your favorite chair—at home or on the job, just visualize it for an instant.

Now, I want you to ask yourself two questions: Am I getting what I want from others when I sit here? Would I get more satisfaction by changing things?

Most of us are creatures of habit. We take a lot for granted, including seating arrangements. Simply by making active choices about where we sit, we leverage body language to develop favorable impressions in the minds of others.

Before this chapter on nonverbal communication comes to a close, I want you to have a recap of the major points.

1. Listening with your eyes is the key to reading and understanding nonverbal signals and body language

   ◗ unspoken signals indicate what is going on
   ◗ learning to recognize and use them changes your life

4. Communicating without words benefits you four ways

   ◗ makes you a desirable communication partner
   ◗ you head off trouble before it explodes
   ◗ what other people reveal gives you an edge
   ◗ you achieve your potential not just your goals

5. Sixteen workable ways to listen with your eyes:

   ◗ concentrate on the main signals
   ◗ pay more attention to patterns than to isolated events
   ◗ look for inconsistencies
   ◗ feedback the feelings

▶ respect the geography

▶ check out clothing, grooming, and the environment

▶ be alert to head moves

▶ when eyes talk, listen

▶ manage eye contact

▶ control your focus to control theirs

▶ pay attention to culture

▶ beware of rapid eye blinking

▶ be alert to hand movements

▶ hands touching faces are danger signals

▶ give leg most leg movements low priority

▶ where you sit says who you are

BODIES SPEAK LOUDER THAN WORDS

Ever since the Tower of Babel, words have often proved masks.
Bodies, on the other hand, never lie.
Unfailingly, they transmit the mind's truest intentions.
That's why, when it comes to nonverbal communication, you can safely say that bodies speak louder than words.

Your interest in learning to read body language reflects your willing orientation to others. Each experience is an opportunity to imagine what drives others to speak and act as they do, and to forestall the difficulties that might otherwise arise out of behavior.

The point I make here is one that looks both forward and back.

Back in the sense that the information you gain from reading body language shows you their humanity, their needs. These can and should be plugged in to the needs/benefits formula developed in Chapter 2.

And forward because your new understanding will shape the kinds of questions you will need to ask from here on out.

As you embark on the next chapter, you, like my friend Dara, will discover that questions themselves are often the answer. Because no one ever asked her the right one, Dara paid a price. Read all about it, about the fateful day her car was broken into not once but twice!

CHAPTER 4

QUESTIONS

A Dozen Workable Ways to Gather Information, Change Minds, Confirm Suspicions, Open Purse Strings, Pluck Heartstrings, Reveal Hidden Emotions, Discourage Guessing, Recover Initiatives . . . and More

Remember the *Pink Panther* films?

French policeman, Inspector Jacques Clouzot—the kind of guy who goes to the men's room, opens his vest, takes out his tie, and wets his trousers—harumphs his way to the front desk of a Swiss inn.

There, coiled in anticipation, a large dog tenses.

Clouzot lifts a pen.

A growl rumbles out of the animal.

Clouzot signs in.

The beast bares its fangs.

Clouzot lifts an eyebrow.

"Does your dog bite?"

"My dog?" the indignant clerk responds. "Monsieur can be certain my dog does not bite!"

Clouzot swaggers to his baggage.

The dog lunges.

"I thought you said your dog doesn't bite!" Clouzot next bellows from a slippery perch on the mantlepiece, pants legs in tatters.

"That's not my dog!" replies the clerk.

Questions Are the Answer

A silly story? Perhaps. But it makes a point about questions. We pop them, beg them, even put things beyond them.

They help us change minds, confirm suspicions, open purse strings, pluck heart strings, reveal emotions, discourage guessing, recover initiatives, and much more.

What it comes down to is that we need and use questions to get information. And here we have a choice.

We can ask the wrong ones and, like Clouzot, put ourselves up a conversational tree. Or, by asking the right questions, get the road map we need to steer any encounter to our goals.

This chapter will show you that the way you manage questions makes a powerful difference not just in your ability to communicate but in your life. Here, I am going to give you 12 tested ways to get the reliable information you need—to pose questions that encourage your listeners to let you in on the facts and feelings you need to build stronger business, social, and personal relationships.

When these powerful, tested techniques become part of you, your automatic response to life,

You'll Gain Three Enormous Benefits

Questions help you understand the gripes and complaints of the people you work with and through. Your growing appreciation of what other people really want, can accept, and will act on will lead you to solve problems in ways that win the recognition of your superiors, the regard of your co-workers, and the business of your customers.

"I develop a Misery Index before every sales presentation," reports Haskell Luce, 29, a Wyoming office automation specialist. "I cold call to ask what they hate most about their present equipment. Their answers help me match the benefits of my line to their needs."

Effective questions empower you to resolve problems and create greater understanding between yourself and your family and friends— people whose personal good will you cherish most in life. When your questions give others a feeling of self-importance, you come across as being interested in their needs, and they cannot fail to respond to you in the ways you want.

"My stepdaughter, Dara, used to be hard-headed," reports Marty Brickman, 44, a New Jersey housewrecker. "Elinor, her mother, warned her not to park in the street. The kid is 17, she thinks she's bulletproof. When she comes out the next morning, somebody's forced the lock on her trunk. Well, Dara comes home that night and where does she park? And what happens? I convinced Ellie that Dara needed some professional guidance. The counselor saw her several times and it was like day and night. I asked him if he used some kind of magic pill to straighten kids out. He said no, he used a question to get the child to feel she was responsible for her behavior: Tell me, Dara, what are you going to do to turn this situation around?"

Other people's questions reflect their secret emotions, fears, and dreams. Being able to decipher these helps you recognize what they want. Helping them achieve their goals makes you an important person in their lives, someone who deserves thoughtful consideration.

"My mother, who is 83, is not what you might call easy to get along with. The other day I got her on the phone and she said to me, What's the matter, Bernard, did you have a bad dream about me?," reports Bernard Portman, 50, a Pennsylvania typographer. "I knew right then she needed to get something off her chest so I put aside my agenda to listen quietly. When she was done I made a little joke and we laughed."

POWERFUL QUESTIONS = EMPOWERED OUTCOMES

The fastest and the best way to improve the quality of our interactions at home, on the job, and out in the community is to improve the quality of the questions we raise.

Habitual questions produce habitual answers.

Q. How are things going?

A. Fine.

Questions like this cannot possibly yield the knowledge we must have to produce the business and personal results we are looking for.

Better questions always yield better information.

Q. How is your department coming along with the new procedures?

A. We're getting some static from the people in accounts receivable. They're asking for a little more fine tuning.

More powerful questions empower us. They lead us to what has to be done or said or considered next to produce the outcomes we want.

In a moment, I'll give you an even dozen workable ways to improve the one part of the communication process you can never afford to misuse. Step-by-step, I am going to give you the tested techniques guaranteed to breathe new life into your work and personal relationships.

But first, let me ask you something:

ARE YOUR QUESTIONS DOING MORE HARM THAN GOOD?

In this self-analysis, you are going to be the proverbial fly on the wall.

First-hand, you will see Akron's Vadim Hruska and Elena Petrov, both 35, through 10 relationship situations.

The outcome of each turns on a question.

But what's the right question, one likely to contribute to loving?

Beneath each situation is a rating scale—1 to 10.

Please use it to circle the number that, in your judgment, reflects the strength of your personal feeling about the recommendation you just read. Bear in mind that each recommendation is one of a number of possible approaches.

It is not offered as the only answer. Rather, it is meant to be an appropriate one.

The lower the number you circle, the more appropriate you believe the recommendation to be; the higher the number, the stronger your disagreement with it. Try to avoid the highest and lowest numbers unless you believe a particular recommendation deserves an extreme rating.

There are no right and wrong answers, and there is no deadline.

Just read the descriptions and recommendations and rate your feelings.

1. When tragedy strikes—Elena's father died a year ago, her mother two years before that—Vadim is loving, caring, and unusually thoughtful. But Elena reports that, over the last 10 years, he has never once remembered their anniversary. She is tempted to ask, "Why do you seem to be more sensitive to my grief than my joy?"

Recommendation: Elena might be surprised by an honest answer to the question she mentally poses: "Because grief is so out-of-the-ordinary." A more empowering question might be, "Are you as sensitive to my needs as I need you to be?"

<u>Appropriate</u>   <u>Inappropriate</u>

1 . . . 2 . . . 3 . . . 4 . . . 5 . . . 6 . . . 7 . . . 8 . . . 9 . . . 10

2. "Vadim's always making a joke when things get grim," Elena reports. "Sometimes I get the urge to ask him, 'Is humor your way of dealing with stress?'" Vadim says, "Elena laughs in all the right places but I get the feeling that whatever she feels, she feels alone. Sometimes I want to ask her, How come I never hear you laugh in a crowd?"

Recommendation: Because there is a certain sense of personal longing within the questions each of them raises—an unfilled wish—a better question might be: "Do we trust each other's laughter?"

<u>Appropriate</u>   <u>Inappropriate</u>

1 . . . 2 . . . 3 . . . 4 . . . 5 . . . 6 . . . 7 . . . 8 . . . 9 . . . 10

3. On the really important issues, both Elena and Vadim appreciate the effort the other makes to communicate. But she wonders, "How come we talk more easily about life insurance than about what's for dinner tonight?"

Recommendation: Elena might broaden her questions in ways that involve Vadim more personally: "Can you think of anything that might prevent us from having all kinds of conversations together?"

<u>Appropriate</u>   <u>Inappropriate</u>

1 . . . 2 . . . 3 . . . 4 . . . 5 . . . 6 . . . 7 . . . 8 . . . 9 . . . 10

4. Every once-in-a-while, Elena thinks about the strength of Vadim's commitment. "If I get sick, will he be there?" she wonders.

Recommendation: Elena might better raise a broader question: "Can I count on you?"

<u>Appropriate</u>   <u>Inappropriate</u>

1 . . . 2 . . . 3 . . . 4 . . . 5 . . . 6 . . . 7 . . . 8 . . . 9 . . . 10

5. Vadim tries to understand that she can be moody or depressed or just plain batty. Still, he sometimes steps out of line. Elena's you-just-kicked-me-in-the-belly responses make him think, "Hey, lady, where is it written that I have to be more perfect than you?"

Recommendation: The strength of a relationship is directly proportional to the ability of the partners to tolerate personality differences. Instead of the provocative question that occurs to him, one certain to put greater attention on that which separates them, Vadim would get more useful information from, "What can we do to deal with the things that seem to set us apart from time-to-time?"

<u>Appropriate</u>   <u>Inappropriate</u>

1 . . . 2 . . . 3 . . . 4 . . . 5 . . . 6 . . . 7 . . . 8 . . . 9 . . . 10

6. Only a fool would deny that some people are more socially inclined than others, and only a fool would deny that, over the long run, this can benefit both sides of a relationship. But there are moments Vadim feels left out, moments in which he thinks, "How come you need to spend so much time with other people? Is it because there is something wrong, something you don't want to tell me?"

Recommendation: While personal independence enriches a relationship, it needs to be anchored by an overall sense of common interest. Vadim might find a more constructive question: "What interests—church, movies, redecorating the house—can we pursue together that would make us both more comfortable?"

<u>Appropriate</u>   <u>Inappropriate</u>

1 . . . 2 . . . 3 . . . 4 . . . 5 . . . 6 . . . 7 . . . 8 . . . 9 . . . 10

7. Some of Vadim's friends don't seem to like Elena as much as she would like to be liked. This makes her wonder, "Why can't your friends be my friends, too?"

Recommendation: The question on Elena's mind is likely to open a door that is better left closed. If she wants to be part of a shared circle of acquaintances, she might better ask, "What can we do to make mutual friends?"

Appropriate   Inappropriate

1 . . . 2 . . . 3 . . . 4 . . . 5 . . . 6 . . . 7 . . . 8 . . . 9 . . . 10

8. Mention a Grateful Dead concert and Vadim is off and running. He buys the tickets, calls the babysitter, reserves a table for dinner—the whole nine yards. On the other hand, when friends are coming over, Elena is a one-woman catering service—she does all the calling, shopping, cooking, and serving. They both wonder, "Through a lack of interest in what concerns me, is he/she trying to tell me something?"

Recommendation: The mental question they raise is certain to get them no place fast. Each would honestly deny a hidden message in their actions. Since what seems to be missing is shared excitement, a better question might be, "What can we plan together that we would both enjoy?"

Appropriate   Inappropriate

1 . . . 2 . . . 3 . . . 4 . . . 5 . . . 6 . . . 7 . . . 8 . . . 9 . . . 10

9. Looking at the big picture, Vadim and Elena think of themselves as a contented couple. But, after 10 years of marriage, each suspects the other of waning sexual interest. Neither wishes to hurt the other's feelings so each wonders privately, "Is there something wrong about the way I make love?"

Recommendation: It would be more useful to frame the question to refresh and encourage intimacy: "Are you hesitant to talk about what satisfies you sexually?"

Appropriate   Inappropriate

1 . . . 2 . . . 3 . . . 4 . . . 5 . . . 6 . . . 7 . . . 8 . . . 9 . . . 10

10. Both Vadim and Elena sometimes feel that being in love with each other is the craziest thing either of them has done. The questions they share but do not speak: "Is love really like this? Is it right for me?"

    Recommendation: People who are madly in love sometimes find it difficult to sort things out. Better to content themselves with the belief that, if they feel they are in love they are in love! Instead of asking for a definition, both would be enriched by a question that asks, "What can we do to enjoy each other even more?"

    <u>Appropriate</u>   <u>Inappropriate</u>

    1 . . . 2 . . . 3 . . . 4 . . . 5 . . . 6 . . . 7 . . . 8 . . . 9 . . . 10

Now that you have completed the exercise, simply go over your ratings—but pay special attention to any rating greater than five—the recommendations you felt were inappropriate.

Each of these represents a soft spot in your questioning technique—an area in which your questions may be doing you more harm than good. Your most pressing problems are likely to lie where your disagreement with the recommendation is strongest.

If you will bear these in mind as you move forward, you'll discover concrete, specific, and practical ways to perfect your Q & A skills.

A Dozen Workable Ways to Ask Empowering Questions

Questions are laser lights. They burn through to priceless nuggets of knowledge, information we must have if we expect to get any place at all with and through others.

With that in mind, I am going to give you the tested techniques guaranteed to produce the results you want and need, right from the get go.

Read them, participate in the exercises, and I am confident you will come out a winner two ways:

First, you will pose questions that encourage your listeners to give you the information you need. And second, as your skills grow, you will start to respond to questions in ways that invite others to make your goals their goals.

Automatically, you will stop asking the disempowering questions that limit happiness in your life and career.

And just as automatically, start asking the ones that unleash your potential to take what is and make of it all that it can be.

Think of these as a battery of ideas to jumpstart your thinking.

Apply the lessons they demonstrate, practice their techniques for the next several weeks, and see for yourself the changes they make in your life. You will be amazed at how willing people will be to share their information and points of view with you.

Technique 1: Don't Ask for Information if You're Not Prepared to Listen to Answers

When you use questions to get information, you must be prepared to listen attentively to the responses they provoke . . . or risk finding yourself worse off than ever.

"The secret around here is that to go fast you've got to work slow," reports Department of Labor interviewer Janice Onnerbee, 29, who operates out of the courthouse in Kansas City, Misssouri. "Folks are uptight to begin with so if you diss them by not listening to their answers, well lookit, better it takes a little longer and gets done."

When you ask a question but don't listen to the answer, the person being questioned is certain to feel trying to talk with you is like trying to row up a waterfall.

Technique 2: Make the Q & A Process Enjoyable

Your questions should convey a sense of appreciation for the information the other person makes available to you. Even though you may be impatient to get to the heart of things, give the other person's response the time and attention it deserves.

Here are four ways to show your interest:

▶ Comment on what he says. "I wish I had known about that before. I could've saved a lot of trouble."

▶ Express sympathy with his point of view. "In times like these, its not easy to put aside a few dollars."

▶ Share a similar experience of your own. "My kids, too—it seems they all want to grow up faster than we did."

▶ Give him some information in return. "Oh, really? I'm in advertising too. I've spent most of my career in an agency—Byrd, Seed & Fieder."

Technique 3: Make Questions Easy to Understand

Phrase questions in language everybody understands. Use them to cover one point at a time. Avoid asking two questions when one will do.

"It's a least-common-denominator kind of thing—the people in my department aren't dumb. They speak five different languages perfectly. It's just that none of those five happens to be English," reports Sam Anastas, 28, a south Florida production supervisor. "When I need to ask them something I try to use simple words and terms they know."

Technique 4: Start with Questions That Are Easy to Answer

Everybody enjoys giving answers they know are right. That's why your first question must be one you are confident he can answer effortlessly, e.g., "What time did the accident occur?"

Make your second question easy, too. The idea is to build his trust in you, e.g., "Where were you standing when it took place?"

Technique 5: Follow with Questions That Can't Be Answered with a Fact

Once answers are flowing easily, frame your succeeding questions to get the other person to talk at length about the topic at hand rather than provide a simple "yes" or "no."

For instance,

"Why do you suppose things turned out as they did?"

"Can you tell me how you see it?"

"What do you suppose went on?"

Technique 6: Let the Other Person Know What You Are Hearing

As the conversation develops, feedback to the other person your understanding of what he is saying. Structure the feedback in question form. For example, "Am I right in saying that you think the root cause was worn tires?" If he agrees, move on to the next topic. If he disagrees, allow and encourage him to give you more information by prefacing his key thought with the words, "What about," as in "What about the weather?"

SIX WAYS QUESTIONS MAKE A DIFFERENCE IN YOUR LIFE

1. They trigger positive emotions when you are feeling down, put you in a better frame of mind instantly.

2. They keep people focused on your priorities.

3. They uncover people's hidden needs and motives.

4. They help you cultivate the one personality trait common to successful people.

5. They make you a hero when you are only half right.

6. They keep people from ignoring or interrupting you.

> *Technique 7: How to Use Questions to Trigger Positive Emotions When You Are Feeling Down, and Put Yourself in a Better Frame of Mind Instantly*

We usually don't give much thought to the need to know how to explore issues with others. We give even less to the idea of exploring issues within ourselves.

Yet, like it or not, the information we need to get the most out of living is almost always contained in our own minds. Sometimes, we are forthcoming about what we think.

More often, it is a seam of emotional pay dirt deep in the geology of our lives: We need the help of questions to haul it up to the surface.

Questions define us to us. They shape our view of ourselves and what we believe our capabilities to be. They control everything about us, including our moods.

Simply by learning to control the questions you ask yourself, you can trigger positive emotions when you are feeling down, and put yourself in a better mood instantly.

"I came back from work to find my kids complaining about the baby sitter, my husband bellyaching about a note we had gotten asking us to help raise church funds, and a list of phone messages," reports

Nancy Hulce, 34, mother of three and a New York retail services manager. "The first question that came to me was, Why don't they leave me alone? Then I realized my frustration was going to make things harder on me. So I said to myself, What could be good about coming home to this? It made me stop and think. Ten years ago, all I dreamed about was having a career and a family. Right away I began to feel better. There were so many people who wanted my attention, it was nice to feel wanted. So I started to think about how I could make time for everyone by making some changes in the way I schedule things."

Because Nancy asked a question guaranteed to empower her in the situation, she had an instant reason to feel better about life. The question led her to think in more positive terms about what she really wanted, and made her a happier person, a better wife, a more giving mother.

Technique 8: The Best Way to Keep People Focused on Your Priorities

In Chapter 2, I gave you my needs/benefits formula, $N = B \rightarrow C$. To refresh your thinking, let me sum it up: When the benefits you offer match the other person's needs, minds meet.

I left it up to you to discover the best way to deliver those benefits, to use them to persuade others to share your enthusiasms and priorities. There's no end to the possible routes of delivery you might try. You can make a speech. You can tell a funny story with a point. You can even make an announcement.

But by far the best way to deliver the benefits they want most is in the form of a question that promises to reward them just for sharing your priorities.

It works every time without fail—and that is not a matter of opinion, it is a matter of evidence. Even the brattiest child is unlikely to be immune to a question that asks, "How would you like a raise in your allowance?"

Here are some other examples:

▶ How would you like to get a promotion?

▶ If I could show you a way to cut labor costs in half while increasing output 10 percent, would you be interested?

▶ Wouldn't you feel more secure if you were the low-cost producer in the marketplace?

▶ How would the congregation feel if we could get the extra classroom we need and still save money?

▶ If I could show you how to clean up your room in ten minutes flat, that would give you time to get to the ball park, wouldn't it?

No matter who you are, whether you are at home, on the job, or out in the community, use questions to deliver benefits and others will tune in instantly.

"When interest rates drop, my bank puts on a campaign to refinance existing mortgages, but some people don't like the idea of fluctuating interest rates," reports Dubuque telemarketer Ed Pierson, 30. "So I worked up a way to get them involved. I ask them, "How would you like to lower your cost of living for the next year, guaranteed, without having to change where you are living? That gets me in the door because they always answer, Yes!"

Here's why Ed's question worked.

First, because it promised a relevant benefit, the question immediately pointed the other person in the direction of Ed's top priority. Second, it established the basis for a meeting of the minds because it identified the common ground between them: the customer wants lower costs, the bank wants to sell more mortgages. Third, it put the other person in a "yes" frame of mind. This sets up a positive mood that makes agreement with your priorities easier to obtain.

Technique 9: The Best Way to Uncover People's Hidden Needs

Like most people I am something of a creature of habit. Every morning I head to the bakery for a cup of coffee. And every morning, when the clerk rings up my order, he asks, "Is that all?"

Invariably, I answer, "Yes, thanks."

As I left home today, it occurred to me that I needed a loaf of bread. But when the clerk asked, "Is that all?" I simply answered out of habit, "Yes, thank you," and went on my way, breadless. Here's my point. Most people take other people's needs for granted. Then, they build these assumptions into their questions. The clerk assumed all I needed was coffee. That prevented him from discovering my need for bread.

Imagine the impact on yearly sales if he asked every customer, "Is there anything else I can get for you?"

Here are some other examples of questions that uncover people's hidden needs:

❯ Do you feel you have been treated fairly?

❯ Why do you suppose most people would disagree?

❯ May I show you our policy on that?

❯ Do you think it might be a good idea if I drove on the way home?

Remember, a question is supposed to bring you news. You use it to find out what somebody really wants.

The whole idea is to uncover hidden needs so that you can satisfy them on a timely basis using the N = B → C formula.

"At an alumni function, I was talking with one of our most loyal givers, an African American who had come up the hard way," reports Dick Durfee, 35, a fund raiser for Hobart College, Geneva, New York. "He was saying that his education gave him everything he got in life, so, sure, he would make his regular donation. But then he said that, even after all the years since he graduated, the place still looked lily white. So I asked him, If you were to make an additional gift to the school, how would you set it up to be certain we attracted more minorities? Not only did he give me answer, he called several of his friends and they chipped in to set up a grant for inner-city kids."

Dick's question succeeded because it focused immediately on the alumni's hidden need to run the show. It offered the donor an opportunity to express a hidden desire for control in a proud and useful way.

Technique 10: The One Trait Common to Successful People—and How to Cultivate It in Yourself

Ever notice how people on the automobile showroom floor never start a conversation by asking which specific model you are interested in? Or how insurance salespeople, no matter how rushed, never start by asking how big an estate you intend to leave to your heirs? Or how college and business recruiters who have just 10 minutes to make up their minds never open an interview with a specific question about your background?

Before they get down to the nitty gritty, people who ask questions for a living take you through a warmup. Their apparently aimless questions cover family, sports—everything but the topic you are meeting on.

Don't be deceived by appearances. People who make their living through persuasion always have a mental plan of attack. First, they talk about things that will make you feel comfortable.

Then, when they sense you are at ease, they build questions on the information you reveal about your needs. These turn your mind to the thing they want to get across.

"My daughter left her soccer gear in my office," reports Roanoke broker Lesley Joplin, 39. "This customer notices it and says his sons are soccer crazy. Tells me all about where they play, how many goals they average. I listen, make a comment here and there, and when he is done talking I say, Are you in the market for good value in a family house with a big enough yard for a soccer field? Oh yes, he says. He ended up with the Horganwiller place—great buy!"

Use the secret of successful people: use your questions to bring hidden needs to the surface and you cannot fail to get what you want from others.

Technique 11: How to Be a Hero When You Are Only Half Right

"For crying out loud, Danny, how many times do I have to ask you not to leave your jacket on the front hall railing?"

"Me? Who do you think you are, Mr. Clean? What about the cassettes you leave all over the coffee table every night?"

It happens to all of us. Oh, sure, the words are different. And the times, places, and subjects, too. But can't you see yourself in the sort of situation bedeviling Danny Orten, 26, and his companion, Rick Seelig, both Los Angelinos?

The natural impulse is to fight or flight. Let me save you a lot of time. Ignore your natural impulse. Neither choice works.

For one thing, it is certain to be one of the few sparring matches to produce two losers. And as for heading for the nearest border, it makes a repeat performance an eventual certainty.

You are better off to do three things:

▶ Stay put

▶ Stay calm

▶ And, difficult as it may seem at first, focus more on solutions than on problems.

The whole idea in these situations is to understand people better than they seem to want to be understood!

Here's Rick's approach:

"Gee, Danny, you're right. I do leave tapes lying around," Rick said. "I am sure that bothers you as much as your jacket bothers me. I'll tell you what, I'll do a better job picking up the tapes, and if I come across your jacket I'll just hang it up. Can I count on you to do the same for me?"

"Well . . . what the hell, why not?"

Rick recognized that the way to be a hero when you are only half right is to ask a question in an understanding way . . . a way that attracts cooperation.

Technique 12: How to Keep People from Ignoring or Interrupting You

About the only thing more toxic to conversation than being interrupted every 10 or 15 words is the dead silence of being ignored. The antidote for both is to keep people involved in what you have to say. So involved, in fact, they become part of it.

Here, questions can be show-stoppers. They break the patterns of either neglect or interruption so that you can get things back into focus. In these situations, you want your questions to appeal immediately to whatever need drives them to behave as they do.

"I was presenting the bimonthly figures but I couldn't seem to complete a sentence. One manager kept interrupting," reports Phoenicia Drell, 26, an account manager in a Chicago public-opinion polling company. "I was at my wits end and I just had to break the chain so I asked him, Bob, this next slide's right up your alley. Since its in your field, would you mind giving us your comments? He did, and those were the last things he said for the rest of the meeting."

Phoenicia's question instantly broke the pattern of interruption. It appealed instantly to Bob's need to express his personal power, leaving Phoenicia in complete charge.

As you approach the end of this chapter, let's take a minute to review the major points.

1. We use questions to change minds, confirm suspicions, open purse strings, pluck heartstrings, reveal emotions, recover initiatives. Most important, we use them to get information.

2. How we manage questions makes a powerful difference not just in our ability to communicate but in our lives.

3. The secret of controlling our encounters is through questions that make your thoughts their thoughts.

4. Learning to ask the right questions will make you a winner twice over.

> ❯ You will get the information you need, and

> ❯ You automatically learn to respond to questions in ways that invite others to participate in your goals

5. Questions empower us by leading us to what has to be done or said or considered next.

6. You gain three enormous benefits when your questions are empowering.

> ❯ Questions help you gain recognition and success by deepening your understanding of the needs of people with whom you work.

> ❯ Questions help you nurture understanding between yourself and the people you cherish most.

> ❯ Questions help you come across as an interested person who deserves consideration.

7. There are 12 workable ways to develop your skills as a questioner:

> ❯ Don't ask for information if you are not prepared to listen to answers

> ❯ Make the Q & A process enjoyable

> ❯ Make your questions easy to understand

> ❯ Start with questions that are easy to answer

> ❯ Let the other person know what you are hearing

> ❯ Follow with questions that cannot be answered with a fact

> ❯ When you are feeling down, change the questions you ask yourself and your mood will change instantly

> ❯ When you want others to focus on your priorities, ask a question that promises an immediate benefit just for listening

> ❯ The best way to uncover people's secret needs is through questions that appeal to what they most want out of life

> ❯ To be a hero when you are only half right, you must ask a question that reflects your complete understanding

▶ When you are being ignored or interrupted, break the toxic pattern with a question that requires the other fellow to act in your behalf

- -
The Oxygen of Human Interaction

Imagine a world without questions. It makes a grim fantasy, don't you think? Deprived of the millions of questions they bombard us with, children would probably never learn what things mean and what they should do.

Cut off from any opportunity to grow, adults would probably find themselves on the brink of extinction—stuck in place, alone and destined to remain so.

Questions, you see, are the oxygen of human interaction.

They're so basic to lively conversation we hardly notice their presence. Yet, what are the first things they teach us in a foreign language? Where is the toilet? How much does it cost? When does the plane leave?

Questions! Choke them off and you strangle communication. Use them intelligently and you make any and every encounter come alive.

If there is a way to put your new skills to work, to use the information your questions produce to issue orders and instructions that others will accept and do their very best to carry out, would you want to know about it?

Well, there is and you can.

See for yourself what happens when a right-handed quarterback throws a left-handed pass.

CHAPTER 5

ISSUING ORDERS AND INSTRUCTIONS:

Eleven Workable Ways to Say What You Mean, Get What you Want . . . and Make People Like You for It

No more timeouts. Less than a minute left. The score was tied. Illinois had the football on their opponent's 5-yard line. The coach sent in a play. It was an option to the left. Spotting the open receiver, the Illinois quarterback started rolling to his left.

There was just one little problem: The quarterback was right handed. You see, a six-foot four-inch, 275-pound tackle was hanging on his right shoulder.

Without a moment's hesitation the quarterback switched the ball to his other hand and threw the only left-handed pass of his life . . . for a game-winning touchdown.

The crowd went gaga. Everyone on the sidelines jumped up and down. Everyone, that is, but the coach. Finally, he turned to a hovering sports writer.

"Now that's what I call following orders!"

- -
They Won't Just Do It, They'll *Want* to Do It!

If you intend to be as successful in your dealings at home and at work as the Illinois coach, you must know how to tell people what to do in ways they can accept and act on.

Directing other people with your orders is a leadership art—one that requires skill, constant practice, and expertise. Since you cannot use force, the idea is to leverage basic communications techniques. These win the willing cooperation of others. Get them, like the quarterback, to want to go all out to achieve what you want—no matter how daunting the task.

This chapter gives you 11 workable ways to give personal directions and issue business orders that will always be carried out without fail. As you develop your ability to translate your thoughts, feelings, and desires into instructions others can respond to, follow, and be guided by,

THESE TWO PRICELESS BENEFITS ARE YOURS FOR A LIFETIME

People on the job will act more quickly, work better and to greater effect, and there will be no wasted effort or false starts. This will lead to the results you want: If you are in your own business, it might be increased profits; if you are employed, we are talking promotion.

"I don't subscribe to the theory that bosses know it all and workers have to do it all," reports Otta Flashbein, 34, who owns a small market research business in Minneapolis. "I tell my people the results I want, and when it needs to be done. I never tell them how to do it. The process of figuring it out gets them involved, forces them to take personal ownership of the order and hold themselves accountable for fully carrying it out."

In your personal life, the ability to clearly and precisely communicate with your friends, your family—even perfect strangers—is certain to work like magic for you. Because people always understand what you want, they will take confidence from your strength of purpose, invariably defer to your requests and suggestions, and look to you as a born leader.

"Do this! . . . Don't do that! . . . I am always amazed when some of the most prayerful people in our church issue so many orders to their kids," reports Rosser Osborne, 36, who is in the waterproofing field in Birmingham. "If they'd bother to check Scripture, they'd see that the whole idea is to be simple, clear, and easy to understand. In Mathew, for example, Jesus said, 'Follow me,' and 'Mathew arose and followed Him.'"

ARE YOU LEADERSHIP MATERIAL?

Whether it is an order or an instruction, telling others what to do requires communication skill, expertise, and constant practice.

To get a picture of where you stand right now when it comes to issuing personal and business orders and instructions, I've prepared an exercise.

Below you will find 10 questions. After you have read each one, you will be offered a choice of responses. Please select the one you think is correct.

1. Your daughter screwed up and something has gone dreadfully wrong. She is crying her heart out. You know exactly how to correct the problem. Is this the right time to issue an instruction?

   ❏ Yes
   ❏ No

2. Arnold doesn't appreciate most of the people in the department he manages, which is alright with most of the people in the department: they don't appreciate him, either. If he confines his orders and instruction strictly to business—keeps his personal feelings out of it—should he expect full working cooperation?

   ❏ Yes
   ❏ No

3. There are several new faces in your work group. To make sure things go smoothly, is it a good idea to call a meeting of all hands to go over routine orders?

   ❏ A good idea
   ❏ Bad timing

4. When you are dealing with top-flight people, you don't want to insult their intelligence. But you still need results. To get the output you want, is it better to issue general orders or make them as concrete and specific as you can?

   ❏ Specific orders are better
   ❏ Smart people prefer generalities

5. The people under you know that you are the boss and that, in the end, they must comply or risk trouble. Does it soften discipline to use a carrot instead of a stick to encourage full compliance with your orders?

   ❑ Softens discipline
   ❑ Doesn't soften discipline

6. The kids will have to start doing three things if life around the house is to approach sanity. Is it a good idea to put forth your instructions one at a time over a period of days, or all at one sitting?

   ❑ Over a period of days
   ❑ All at once

7. To keep performance at peak levels, you issue frequent orders and instructions. You follow up on these in writing. Ninety-nine times out of a hundred, are the written follow-ups working for you or against you?

   ❑ For you
   ❑ Against you

8. Whether you are dealing with adults or children, smart people or dummies, at work or at home, is it a good idea to double check their take on your orders and instructions?

   ❑ Depends on the situation
   ❑ Always

9. By the time you get to the meeting you called to issue an order, only a few seats are open. Which is the right one for you?

   ❑ Middle of table
   ❑ Head of table
   ❑ Off to the side

10. If you ask most people, they'll say an order consists of three things:

   ▶ What is to be done

   ▶ How it is to be done

   ▶ Expected results

One of these is wrong. Which one?

❏ What
❏ How
❏ Expected results

Now that you have completed the exercise, simply compare your responses to this list of correct answers:

1. No 2. No 3. Bad timing 4. Specific orders are better 5. Doesn't soften discipline 6. Over a period of days 7. Against you 8. Always 9. Head of table 10. How.

Each incorrectly answered question indicates a soft spot in your ability to issue orders and instructions in ways other people can accept and act on. If you will bear these in mind as you read on, you will find a number of useful and workable ways to strengthen your leadership skills.

YOU WILL NEVER AGAIN SETTLE FOR LESS THAN YOU'RE WORTH

By the time you are done, this chapter will give you nearly a dozen proven techniques you can use individually or in a step-by-step program to tell anyone what to do in a way they can accept and act on.

If you are in business, these will help you

▸ Take instant control of difficult people trying to get their way at your expense

▸ Avoid conditions that force you to settle for less than you are really worth

If you are not in management—perhaps not employed outside the house—that's okay, too. Learning to use my techniques is guaranteed to help you steadily increase your value to the people you love and cherish.

WHAT EVERY LEADER MUST KNOW BEFORE ISSUING ORDERS OR INSTRUCTIONS

Leadership, which is the business of issuing orders, is one of those amazing things that defy simple definition.

For me, it is as much about attitude as it is about style.

Further along in this chapter, you will come to 11 tested and proved ways to develop a leadership style—a style of issuing orders and instructions.

For now, though, I'd like to explore the attitude thing.

Now, if you are especially antsy—perhaps you've got a problem and want to get my views on the best ways to issue orders now—maybe you ought to jump ahead. You'll find everything you need to issue orders that are carried out with enthusiasm, beginning on page 92.

FOUR ELEMENTS OF HUMAN LEADERSHIP

A leader

▶ Delivers the one thing all human beings need

▶ Uses his or her most valuable hidden asset to fill needs

▶ Practices the three As of human satisfaction

▶ Uses a secret catalyst to multiply the power of his or her words

I want to go over each of these with you in terms of how human beings act and react. Then, once you know why people behave as they do, you'll have the perfect grounding for my eleven techniques.

THE ONE THING EVERY HUMAN BEING NEEDS

Everybody is an individual. Yet there is one factor that is as true of males as it is of females. As much a part of goldenagers as it is of teenagers. Yes, as characteristic of lawyers and doctors as it is of laborers and debutantes, as defining of homebodies as it is of the homeless.

This common denominator is the ever-present need for self-esteem. When self-esteem is high, people are responsive to your orders. They are willing to listen, contribute, and execute because they feel secure about who they are.

However, when self-esteem is low, they are afraid to open their minds to hear you in the way you mean to be heard. They fear they will be somehow embarrassed or, perhaps, found wanting.

That is why, in addition to physically achieving the things you want done, your orders must somehow work to build the self-esteem of the people you lead.

How do you go about that?

Leaders Tune in to Build the Self-Esteem of Others

People are like television towers: they're always sending out signals about the status of their self-esteem.

But before you can make sense of these, you've got to receive what they are transmitting—you've got to tune them in.

To sharpen your ability to tune in, get yourself a sheet of paper. Then, rule it down the middle. Headline the left column "Person" and the right one "Reason."

Each morning for a week, put down the names of two people you came in contact with the previous day, one from your personal life, one from your job. Next to each, put down one good reason they should like themselves. The first couple of entries will be harder than the last. My advice is to stick with it. Do so and two things will happen.

First, you will have 14 fresh, compelling, and strong ways to reach and affect people you lead on a daily basis. And, second, you will develop the instant ability to size-up the self-esteem needs of anyone anywhere. As you will soon see, the ability to understand the needs of others is an important skill.

Why Hidden Emotions Are Important to Self-Esteem

Leaders are alert to the emotions of others, especially the hidden ones that press most for expression.

They reveal what the other person will not openly say—the thing that they need most for self-esteem.

Discover these, speak to these, leverage these to pump up the other guy's appreciation of himself, and your orders will be accepted and carried out with confidence.

"One of my employees—I'll call her Maggie—needed an AIDS test," reports Horace Kinnock, 30, a Vermont weaver. "She was anxious. I thought about instructing her to get right to the hospital. But I don't think she would've heard me. Instead, I got her to tell me how she felt about it."

There's a big lesson to be gotten from Horace's thoughtful approach: Before you issue orders and instruction, give the other person a chance to relieve the emotional tension, to feel better about herself.

HOW TO USE YOUR MOST VALUABLE HIDDEN ASSET TO SATISFY THE NEEDS OF OTHERS

"No man," wrote poet John Donne, "is an island unto himself."

It is a line of thought as old as Adam and Eve. It means nobody is, was, or will be 100 percent anything. Human beings arrive incomplete and we remain so for the rest of our lives.

There's always something we need, one priceless commodity that is the key to all human happiness. Hoard it, deprive people of it, dole it out stingily, and you make them hard to get along with. Spread it around lavishly and you cannot fail to influence people with your leadership wherever you go. Here's the curious part: Though we can never receive too much of it, leaders can never run out of it. That's why a leader gives away as much of her hidden wealth as she possibly can.

After all, it costs nothing, you can never use it all up, and it creates a climate that leads others to accept and act on your orders. This millionaire status I am talking about is your inborn power to satisfy other people's need to feel important.

R$_x$ LEADERSHIP: TO MAKE YOURSELF IMPORTANT TO THEM, MAKE THEM IMPORTANT TO YOU

Because people are hungry—sometimes even starved—for the affirmation that comes only from outside themselves, making the other person feel important is crucial to getting your orders carried out promptly.

"My faculty adviser says that most strikes aren't over money, they happen because management fails to give workers the recognition they need," reports Ibrahim Nabbia, 20, a labor relations student at New York's Cornell University. "Take a simple thing like suggestions about how to improve work throughput; failure to give credit where it is due says the boss doesn't value the employee's contribution enough. Sure, they go out over money but a lot of times it's just a cover up. They feel left out."

Ibrahim's point is this: the more you feed people's sense of importance, the less likely they are to risk losing you as a source of good will.

The greater the goodwill between you, the better your orders are executed.

HOW TO DEVELOP A LEADERSHIP ATTITUDE ABOUT PEOPLE

▶ Think about the three most important people in your life right now. These could be your boss, your mate, your children, the credit manager at a store you want charge privileges, the dentist who is going to squeeze you in on an emergency basis to relieve a toothache . . . you name it.

⟩ Write their names down.

⟩ Opposite each name, write two things:

1. What they could say to you that would make you important in their eyes;

2. What you can say to them to make them important in yours.

The Three A's of Good Human Relations

1. LEADERS PRACTICE SELF ACCEPTANCE

Ever notice how wrong the old idea is—that it is lonely at the top.

I've been dealing with the CEOs of some of the biggest companies in the country for quite a few years.

Let me tell you—these are not what anybody might call lonely. On the job you expect them to be surrounded. But what's true of their careers is equally true of their social lives. Net conclusion: Leaders like people. And here's why. Because they like themselves, and accept themselves.

You see, it is a proven psychological fact that you can't accept others until you can accept yourself. You can't accept yourself until you are willing to acknowledge the somewhat inadequate human being that from time-to-time stares back at you in the mirror. When you learn to accept yourself as you are you will automatically accept others.

Notice, I did not say when you accept yourself you will like others. I said you will accept them—allow them to be them and you to be you.

HERE ARE THREE WAYS TO BE MORE ACCEPTING OF OTHERS

⟩ Don't set up rigid behavioral standards other people need to meet before you will accept them.

⟩ Stop insisting people have to be perfect before you can accept them.

⟩ Even if your heart is not really in it, start acting like you accept others for who and what they are. Don't worry, your heart will follow soon enough.

2. LEADERS PRACTICE APPROVAL

Accepting someone's words means allowing them to be; approval means finding something in them—perhaps even only the tiniest of details—you can think well of.

"I am running a company of 10 people, half of whom I really don't like," reports Front Royal, Virginia small businessman Herb Kittle, 36. "But each of them does something good for the business. I try to remember that. It keeps me from letting my personal feelings get in the way."

I want you to grab a piece of paper now. Rule it down the middle, label the left side "Who" and the right column "What."

Every day for five days running I want you to list the name of a person you dislike under the left column. A colleague, someone you once dated, a bill collector—you name it. Each day for five days just come up with the name of someone you'd hate to be stuck in a lifeboat with.

Next to each name, under the right column, I want you to write down one thing about this person you can approve. It can be anything from, "He wears nice ties," to "She has a lot of respect for older people."

At first, you may have some trouble thinking of things to like about people you don't. Don't worry about softening your standards. I'm not asking you to like the person, just approve of something about the person. At the end of five days what you will have learned is this:

Despite your overall feelings, there is at least one thing about anybody—even your worst enemy—you can approve of.

Do as much in every leadership situation—but especially when you issue your orders and instructions—and people will go out of their way to give you the results you want and need.

3. LEADERS PRACTICE APPRECIATION

To appreciate is to raise in value. When people appreciate you, it says you are important to them.

▶ When the manager of your department informs you he will see to it personally that your harassment claim is taken seriously, you feel appreciated.

▶ When the manager of your love life says you've got the kind of body that looks good in dramatic clothes, you feel like someone waved a magic wand of appreciation.

One of the most important things people seek from leadership is a sense of being valued, being appreciated. And I am not talking about insincere flattery. I am talking about being able to honestly value something about another human being, something that makes you feel good for thinking of it and them feel special for your having taken the trouble to do so. It can be as simple as treating other people's time as valuable as yours and never keeping them waiting, if you can help it. Or as complicated as a negotiating a contract to buy a house or lease a car.

No matter, if you will make appreciation of other people an active part of issuing your orders and instructions, you can count on others treating your orders and instructions with special care.

SIX WAYS TO SHOW YOUR APPRECIATION OF OTHERS

1. *Inject their names into your conversation.* As you do, make brief eye contact. Caution: personalizing a conversation to show how much you value the other person is a little bit like mustard—some heightens flavor, too much kills taste.

2. *Deal with individuals.* Avoid lumping people by age, occupation, geography, and so on. Avoid sweeping a person into such generalities as, "All women are alike," or "Lawyers! You can't live with them and its against the law to kill them." Talk to and about individuals.

3. *Spread your light.* When you are in a business or community group, pay as much attention to the leader as you can, but do not fail to take notice of others when you are talking.

4. *Don't cut others out.* When you meet with a couple, make sure you pay at least some attention to both, but don't overdo it.

5. *Be attentive.* When a child acts up, psychologists say it is usually because they are not getting the attention they want—for instance, refusing to eat or even bed wetting. More of your attention makes them feel calmer.

6. *Little things count.* In a love situation, failing to notice a new hairdo or a change in fragrance or a birthday means you do not consider these—and the person they concern—important enough to pay special attention. Feelings are certain to be hurt less often when you appreciate the little things that go on daily in a relationship.

Use these techniques to let people know they are worth your interest and you will have the goodwill a leader needs to succeed. Wall Street says a rising tide floats all boats. The same can be said of appreciation.

By raising the value of others—by showing appreciation—your wishes become more valuable to them.

THE SECRET CATALYST THAT MULTIPLIES THE POWER OF YOUR ORDERS

Here's my entry for the title of Most Sweeping Generality:

Nine-and-one-half out of every ten times you are treated discourteously, it is because you yourself asked for it.

Look, I am not saying that your words say, "Kick me." I mean your tone of voice and your body language are saying it!

"I hate to admit it but walking in to that Manhattan restaurant alone, I expected the maitre'd to give me grief," reports Peggy Termeer, 40, a senior product manager, from Boise. "I mean the guy was so puffed up he looked like Michelin Man. I approached him with my fists mentally clenched. And you know what, I was right: he made me wait 40 minutes for a table. Where did I end up? Next to the kitchen!"

Peggy's mentally clenched fists suggest the tension she may have been feeling. She knew that, among restaurateurs, businesswomen travelling alone are thought to be the world's worst tippers. But they imply even more. They suggest she walked in with a chip on her shoulder, some kind of need to protect herself.

Moral of the story:

Leadership with a mental chip on its shoulder never gets what it wants.

Ever notice how the President of the United States clears away a space at his place to expand the limits of his personal territory? That's part of the body language that makes people accept his leadership. Be as smart as the president. Because people tend to respond to you in the ways your nonverbal signals suggest, make careful use of body language part of the process of issuing orders and instructions. It won't guarentee success but it will make success more likely.

ELEVEN WORKABLE WAYS TO GIVE ORDERS THAT ARE ALWAYS FOLLOWED

Technique 1: If You Don't Need an Order, Don't Issue One

Unless there's something new, or you plan to make changes in the routine way things are done, there's no need for orders.

"One of the things you've got to watch out for is the new corporals and second lieutenants," reports Gunnery Sergeant Dan Thrapp, USMC, 36. "They make the mistake of thinking they have to issue orders to prove who is in charge. So they tell the troops to do what the troops are already doing. It leads to a breakdown in respect for leadership. In battle, that can cost lives."

Technique 2: Orders Are Needed Under Two Conditions

If it is in the best interest of your work or personal life, do not hesitate a minute to issue orders for what needs to be done.

"I used to avoid giving people orders because I wanted people to like me," reports Maurine Locherby, 24, who works in insurance in Omaha. "The longer I waited the worse things got. The worse things got the less they liked me. It was awful to have to do it the first time, but things started to get better as soon I did."

By keeping the focus of your conversation on the activity as opposed to the person, feelings are less likely to be hurt. On the off-chance that they are, try to remember that it is nothing personal—issuing orders is part of your job.

HOW TO TELL WHEN AN ORDER IS NEEDED

Here is a litmus test you can apply to determine if and when an order is in order.

Orders apply in only two specific situations:

▶ When you want to start, stop, or change something

▶ To fix a mistake

If an order is not needed, forcing one makes you look power-mad. On the other hand, if it is needed, don't procrastinate.

Technique 3: Orders Are Specific and Unequivocal

If you are not sure what you want your order to accomplish in the way of results, it is a pretty safe bet no one else will either.

Until your thinking is specific, concrete, and unequivocal, you are not ready to issue an order.

"Ever notice how tightly focused highway billboards are—Eat this! Drink that! Buy X!," reports Boone Brown, 41, who teaches organizational management at a New England university. "That's what I want my orders to be like—fully understood in the time it takes to flash past at 55 miles an hour."

To shape to the specifics of your order, just answer two questions:

▶ What results do I expect from this order?

▶ Who needs to do it and why?

Technique 4: Feed Their Interests

Sure, some interests are better camouflaged than others but I do not know a soul, my clergyman included, who does not confront a new situation without wondering, What's in it for me?

If they don't speak the words you can be sure they think the thoughts.

So it stands to reason—even when they do not ask, you must let other people know how implementing your order works to their good.

"If I just tell the children to do something, period, the best I'm going to get is a bare minimum response," reports Jan Boone, 41, who works in commercial real estate outside Philadelphia. "If I tell them doing it is going to get them something they want, it gets more attention."

Technique 5: Stroke Their Ego

It is a proven scientific fact. Job for job, relationship for relationship, people who feel recognized for the human contribution they make to their work and their families get higher performance ratings than people who feel overlooked.

That being the case, your orders are more likely to be zestfully carried out when they come with praise for the individuals whom they affect.

"New policies came down from headquarters. We had to put in some changes overnight. I called my people together," reports corporate sales promoter Ian Ashley, 32, from Gary, Indiana. "I said it was going to be tough to implement but I couldn't imagine a more helpful bunch to do it with. We got done faster than I thought."

Here are three more ways to stroke egos while you are issuing orders:

▶ Tell people what makes their roles important to the success of the whole group

▶ Explain how much you personally need them

▶ Express how happy it makes you to know they are part of you because you feel you are part of their success

Technique 6: Don't Confuse Planning and Orders

Let's make a distinction here between plans and orders. Extremely complex plans are implemented by simple orders.

"We were going to realign the organization to serve customers better," reports executive Rusty Reuff, 46, who works in Frito-Lay's Dallas HQ. "The plans took months to work up. They called for a total upheaval of the organization—facilities, job descriptions, schedules. But in the end, all those people, all those changes, were set in motion with a one-page statement."

Reuff's point is an important one: no matter how complex your planning, the order that goes out should be reduced to as few words as possible.

Technique 7: Simple Is Better

Even the most educated person wants instructions to be as clear as possible. To avoid mistakes and misunderstanding, your best bet is to use concise language to express a single point.

"You can't bog your people down in details when you want action," reports Blake Struller, 29, a shop foreman in Tarrytown, New York. "Let's say we're going to make a line changeover for a new model. I don't go around telling my people about the engineering trivia and parts comparability. I tell them that at such a time and such a date, we're going to start building another model. The line supervisors can fill in the details to their subordinates. That's what they get paid for."

If your orders are too complicated, people will lose sight of what you want. Keep them simple and you'll get full compliance.

Technique 8: Talk It if You Can

You save time and speed understanding when you make your orders verbal rather than written.

"I'm walking through the office, I spot a problem that can be fixed with a few words, what am I supposed to do, write a book?" reports David Ashley, 30, who works in customer service, in Pendelton, Washington. "First of all, I don't have time, and second, I try to avoid written orders because it makes people nervous to get a piece of paper whereas they can take what I say in stride."

Unless you are dealing with changes in established routine, there's really no point in taking time out of your busy schedule to issue a written directive. Ninety-nine out of a hundred times you can get the results you want with an oral order.

Technique 9: Double Check Understanding

An order is only as good as the understanding it creates. If people don't understand it, your order will not produce the results you want. Because people interpret words differently, you must make it a hard and fast rule to double check understanding each time you issue an order.

Method number one is to ask the recipient of the order to repeat it.

"When I give an order, even if it is to my children, I ask the person to repeat it. I tell them it is to be sure I don't leave anything out," reports Ilana Benitez, 34, who works for an airline in Sioux Falls, Montana.

The second check method is to raise questions whose answers tell you how well the orders have been received.

Questions that begin with "Do you see . . . ?," "Do you know . . . ?," and "Do you understand . . . ?" work best.

Here is a sample of each. Feel free to modify any or all of them to meet your particular situation:

▶ "Do you see why X goes first?

▶ "Do you know why we've changed your password on the network?

▶ Do you understand where the customer fits in the new marketing equation?

Technique 10: Don't Be Too Bossy

Nobody likes to feel pushed around—not family, not co-workers, and certainly not your friends. That's why it is always a good idea to present your orders and instructions in ways that get the other person to think of them as their own.

"The whole idea is to get the other person involved," reports Stephen Laski, 25. He's in the paper industry in Dayton, Ohio. "I want to tell my wife to stop smoking this minute, but I know it won't work. So I am going to ask for her input. I hope we'll talk about it, and maybe by the time we're done it will be as much her idea as it is mine. Then I'll know for sure she is going to follow through."

FIVE WAYS TO MAKE YOUR ORDERS THEIR ORDERS

Here are five highly effective approaches to get others involved in your orders:

1. "What do you think about A?"

2. "Is it possible we can do B and get C if we . . . ?"

3. "When do you think D will be ready?"

4. "Should we try it with E or is F going to be better?

5. "Can you think of a way to G?

Technique 11: Body Language Leverages Orders

When you deliver your orders, the nonverbal signals you make are every bit as important as the words you express. Think of your clothes, your posture, your gestures, your tone of voice in terms of the kind of impression you wish to create. The most important thing is to come across with a high degree of personal confidence.

That means the clothes you choose should look like the clothes of a leader.

"I use my boss as the template for my dress-for-success approach," reports Blake Struller, 29. He's an electronics manager in Topeka, Kansas. "He's got the job I'd like to get. If management gave it to him, it means they think he dresses appropriately. So, if he's wearing well-fitted business suits in very small patterns and dark colors, so will I."

Blake's point is this: When you make your orders known, dress to show the confidence your boss would have if he were in your place.

Now, turning to posture, the key thing is to be as settled and as comfortable as specific business conditions permit.

If your orders are coming out in a formal standup meeting, then you must be sure to project alertness and energy with your chin up, your head leaning slightly towards your audience, your shoulders back.

If the setting is less formal, say a lunch meeting, you can still use your posture to exert a firm and steadying influence. First, take a seat at the head of the table. Sit upright in your chair, keep both feet flat on the floor. Square your shoulders, lean slightly towards your audience, make your movements slow and deliberate.

There's no middle ground about gestures: They either build confidence or detract from it. The safest course is to make as few of them as possible.

For instance, you don't want to cover your mouth when you are talking because it tells people you think something about your order is fishy. Nor is it a good idea to fidget with the waistline of your skirt when you speak, since that suggests personal discomfort with the very thing you are telling others.

People who wear glasses must be particularly vigilant. When you chew on the frames as you speak, it is like a baby sucking its thumb. It says you need reassurance.

No matter what your gender, your tone of voice needs to be as deep and as resonant as you easily can make it. Pitched too high, it leads people to suspect uncertainty. On the other hand, the deeper it is pitched, the more it communicates a cool and calm presence of mind. One of the ways to control tone of voice is to control its speed. You see, the average person speaks about 120 words a minute. As the verbal pace increases, tone goes up. To get your voice more resonant when you are issuing an order, simply speak 100 words a minute or less.

Before this chapter on issuing orders and instructions draws to an end, let me give you a brief recap of the points that deserve your closest attention.

1. When you issue orders and instruction people can accept and understand, you benefit two ways; you command acknowledged leadership on the job, and the respect of your family and friends.

2. Leadership, which is revealed in orders and instructions, has four elements.

▶ It delivers the one thing all human beings need.

▶ It uses your most valuable hidden asset to fill needs.

▶ It practices acceptance, approval, and appreciation.

▶ It employs a secret catalyst to multiply the power of words to command action.

3. The prescription for leadership is this: To make yourself important to them, make them important to you.

4. Eleven workable ways to give orders that are always followed:

▶ If you don't need an order, don't issue one.

▶ Orders are needed to start, stop, or change something, or to correct a mistake.

▶ Orders are specific and unequivocal.

▶ Feed the interests of others.

▶ Stroke their egos.

▶ Don't confuse planning and orders.

▶ Simple is better.

▶ Talk it if you can.

▶ Double check understanding.

▶ Don't be too bossy.

▶ Use body language to leverage orders.

HOW TO FIND THE LEVER IN LEADERSHIP

The ability to issue orders and instructions others can accept and act on is the lever in leadership leverage. But there's another side of winning the cooperation of others that has nothing to do with commands and everything to do with persuasion.

When you turn the page, I will be wearing the emperor's clothes. In less than a minute an unlikely stranger shamelessly persuades me to do something unthinkable.

Here's the best part:

I walk away a hundred times happier for doing it.

Now *that's* what I call persuasion!
But don't let me get ahead of you here.
When you are ready, turn the page and read on for yourself . . .

C H A P T E R   6

PERSUASION

Six Trade Secrets of the World's Best Professional Persuaders

The other day, as I was walking along New York's Madison Avenue, a florid man approached. He wore no socks and three sweaters. Even from a certain distance it was evident that bathing was not high on his list of personal priorities.

"Pardon me, your grace," the derelict said with the serenity of a nun holding five aces. "I was wondering, governor, you looking so well-cut and all, could you find it in your heart to spare ten dollars for my evening aperitif?"

Ten dollars?!

Despite my best efforts to hide it, I felt a smile come on. The man's unbridled nerve somehow appealed to something within me.

"You see, your dukeship," the observant wretch glibly continued, "contrary to the opinion of obstetricians, of which I was one once, nothing happens overnight. Now in my own case . . . "

Against my better instincts I listened to the man's troubles. Every fact and detail raised more questions than it answered. In the end, I lost my grip on truth, as I was meant to do.

He was still talking as, $10 lighter, I dodged traffic to reach the tall shining office tower where I was to attend a meeting.

The Secret That Makes Your Ideas Their Ideas

I tell you this story to make the point that, in one way or another, everybody—I don't care who you are or what you do (or don't do) for a living—is persuading someone to do something:

- ▶ My homeless friend, by means of outrageous malarkey, persuaded me to part with money.

- ▶ A baby, by means of crying, sells mother on the idea of feeding time.

- ▶ A standup comedian, by means of one-liners, persuades the audience to applaud.

- ▶ Your assistant, by means of extra effort, sells you the idea of a pay raise.

There's always an idea, product, service, or feeling we need to sell to someone else. And selling requires persuasive communication.

I want to use this chapter to show you how to be more persuasive. I want you to be able to instantly get others to buy into your thoughts, plans, and purposes. To do that, I will give you the six trade secrets of the world's most successful salespeople—scientific methods guaranteed to make your ideas their ideas, every time! I am talking about the results successful persuaders usually acquire after long years of hit-and-miss experience. My time-tested approach eliminates trial-and-error. It gives you skills you can use immediately—on the job, at home, even out on the town.

If you are a salesperson, these principles cannot fail to get you the business you want. If selling is not part of your work, that's okay, too: the very same methods of persuasion are guaranteed to make you a better parent, a more considerate partner, a more respected leader in your social, romantic, and church activities.

Apply these surefire techniques wherever you go, and you'll gain these three never-ending benefits of effective persuasion.

The ability to persuade others is the indispensable key to making your dreams come true. Imagine the rush of confidence that comes with knowing you can turn your fantasies into realities; the powerful thrill of knowing you are a really special person—someone whose plans for success at home, out in the community, on the job, and in love are certain to bear fruit.

"Being right is one thing. Getting others to agree is something else," reports Philadelphia's Ursula Bongiove, 32, a recently promoted print production manager. "I could dream up the best idea since sliced bread but if I don't persuade my boss, it might as well be the worst for all the good it will ever do me. So I put as much time into figuring out how to get him to take my proposition as I do on developing the idea in the first place."

Persuasion works on tough bosses, obstinate customers, pesky children, reluctant lovers, stubborn bureaucrats—anyone who stands between you and what you want.

The fear of failure will never haunt your mind again. You will approach problems with an infectious "Yes-I-can" attitude, to which nobody is immune. This guarantees others will always end up doing what you want them to do.

"I used to take 'No' for an answer and let it go at that," reports Lamar Thorpe, 29, a Muscle Shoals recording contractor. "I was amazed to learn that 'No' doesn't always mean 'No.' People have two reasons for not going along. The first one, the one they tell you, usually sounds good. The other is the secret truth. Now I know it sounds almost too simple but trust me on this: Whenever I help people bring the hidden reason out into the light, they end up persuading themselves to go along with my thinking."

By employing the techniques of persuasion I will give you—the very ones Lamar Thorpe uses daily—you won't eliminate roadblocks before they start. But you can be 100 percent certain you can leverage objections in ways that get others to change their minds.

The sooner the techniques of persuasion become part of your daily life the easier it will be to make new friends and win the hearts and minds of men and women you can admire now only from a distance.

"I used to be fearful about new people because I imagined they were in control, but I am much more confident now," reports Aspen condominium manager Parker Moran, 23. "When I go to a party I can talk with anybody in the room and feel sure I can persuade them to like me at least well enough to make small talk."

Persuasion, like love, is one of those truly amazing phenomena: It feeds on itself.

Here's the best part: The more it eats, the bigger it gets.

Put my six secrets of persuasion to work in your life and you will find that others will think of you as cooperative—a team player. That will make it even easier for you to continue to persuade them.

The Difference Between *Have To* and *Want To*

There's a big difference between doing something because you want to and doing something because you feel pressured into doing it.

Most people think the art of persuasion is getting other people to do what you want them to. That's true as far as it goes. It just doesn't go far enough. True persuasion is getting them to *want* to do what you want.

Have you ever heard a person say, "I'll do it, but my heart isn't in it"? Sure you have, and what they are saying is this: the moment you stop looking over their shoulder they will stop doing whatever it is you ask of them. The reason? You have failed to activate the hot button that turns grudging participation into the whole-hog commitment. Once you learn how to push that button they will not only do what you want, they'll keep on doing it—not because you tell them but because they tell themselves.

Here's a for-instance:

People who don't know better rely on logic and common sense to get a person to take a certain action. If you've ever tried that on a willful child, a reluctant date, or a selfish colleague, you know how rarely it works.

The same is true of inexperienced real estate agents. To sell prospects, they rely on the economic advantages of owning a house. But taking this approach appeals only to the customer's logical mind.

Master persuaders, on the other hand, add a wrinkle. They tailor their pitch to both the mind and the emotions of the potential buyer. In addition to talking about the financial advantages of owning a house, they talk also about lifestyle benefits of owning a home in the particular subdivision they represent—things like status, security, neighborliness, community spirit, and so on.

They invariably close more deals than the johnny-come-lately crowd because their appeal blends both logic and feeling. The prospect leaves with dreams of a whole new and better way of life in his mind.

In effect, he persuades himself that it is in his own interest to go along with what the realtor says.

My point is simple: no matter what you wish to persuade people to do, people need to be convinced at two levels—head and heart—before they will go along completely.

At the risk of being redundant, let me repeat what I just said because it is the principle behind every great persuader who ever was or will be:

To win a person over completely, you must appeal to their heart as well as their mind.

If you do nothing more than remember this one thought as we move forward, your success as a powerful persuader is guaranteed. I say that because this is the key my clients—thousands of America's brightest and most ambitious rising managers—use daily to unlock the respect of their peers, the regard of their superiors, and the business of their customers. Over the course of 25 years of close personal observation I have never seen it fail any of them yet.

In a moment, I am going to give you my six-step plan to get anybody to willingly do anything (within reason)—even if they've said "no" once.

But to put these into the right framework, let's first agree on some basic ground rules.

Communication takes place—minds are persuaded—when the benefits you offer match the needs of the other person.

"By encouraging the customer to talk about her feelings and opinions, I start the process of selling her the car she wants," reports Marlen Kantor, 34, award-winning sales manager at a Provo auto dealership. "Discovering the things that are important to her sets me up to deliver the automobile with the benefits she wants, the one that is going to fill those needs she has."

Throughout this book I've stressed that to communicate—in other words, to persuade—you must uncover and satisfy the secret needs and desires of others. The whole idea is to bring to the surface deep desires that can be satisfied by a benefit of your thinking.

Just in case you need a reminder, let me recap the three secret cravings that drive most people: Every normal person wants to:

▶ Win respect, regard, and admiration

▶ Earn fame, save money, or gain status

▶ Get or stay healthy

It is up to you, of course, to discover which of these the person you are talking with wants most of all so you can be the one to help him get it.

Which brings us to, the second ground rule

By making others feel important, you lead their interest to yours.
"The quickest and surest way to persuade is to pay others the attention you yourself would appreciate getting," reports Germane Trommer, 44, on the guest relations staff at Cleveland's Stouffer Inn. "Helping them open up by asking questions gets them to talk freely about themselves. Listening carefully enables me learn what they most want."

Ms. Trier's message is one you would do well to heed:

First, pay complete and undivided attention to everything the other person says. This encourages him to pay attention to you. And second, ask questions—preferably ones that promise or imply a benefit just for listening.

Here are some quick examples of the kinds of benefit questions Germane uses:

Have you heard about our free room upgrade program?

If I could save you money on your next visit, would you be interested?

Would it be okay if I arranged a room on the executive floor for the same price as one of our more affordable singles?

I think you get the idea—lead others to your point of view by asking questions that grab their favorable attention.

ARE YOU AN EFFECTIVE PERSUADER?

▶ Parents need to persuade children on doing homework

▶ Doctors persuade patients on using a prescription drug strictly according to directions

▶ Lawyers persuade juries

▶ Managers persuade workers

▶ Lovers persuade each other

▶ And, of course, salespeople persuade buyers.

Whenever we get someone to think or feel or do something he might not otherwise do, we are persuading. The trick is not to pound your idea in from the outside but to get the other person to grasp it in from within so that he does your bidding not because he has to but because he wants to.

With that in mind, I've prepared a little exercise designed to give you a reading on your persuasive strengths and weaknesses.

In each of the six questions below, you will find a choice of answers.

I'd like you to select the response you think makes the most sense.

1. The people you engage with have certain requirements or needs. Your product, service, or idea has certain characteristics or features. To persuade other people you must:

❏ A. Tell the other person what his needs are.

❏ B. Show the other person how the features of your thinking can meet his needs.

2. A person will be more receptive to your offering if you mention a general benefit likely to spark interest before you speak about your product specifically. Suppose you are selling No-Nick razor blades. Which of the following statements would you make first?

❏ A. Our blades are made of several steel alloys.

❏ B. Your customers will want a razor with a safety feature.

3. Your child says, "Well, that's not what I had in mind, Mom." The garage mechanic says, "Listen, I had too many complaints." And your pastor says, "There's something about this that bothers me." In each of these situations, the other person offers very little in the way of information. To bring about a meeting of the minds in encounters like these, persuaders should:

❏ A. Ask questions.

❏ B. Introduce all the features they want to get across.

4. A key to persuasion is to let the other person know you under-stand what he is saying, and that what he is saying is as impor-

tant to you as it is to him. To achieve this, the persuader must listen carefully to the other person's remarks, then:

❏ A. Agree with remarks that allow him to introduce features that fit the other person's needs.

❏ B. Disagree with the other person each time he says something negative.

5. "Now, Mrs. Jones, we've agreed that Norfolk's miracle fibre content and special manufacturing process make the carpet more durable and better looking. And you feel our direct-to-the-customer delivery system will get you the carpet you want when you want it. Shall I arrange for delivery this week or would it be better after the first of the month?"

The attitude of the persuader is an important factor in winning commitment. Throughout the statement above, the persuader is:

❏ A. Assuming the sale has already been made.

❏ B. Trying to overcome an objection.

6. People often say "no" before they say "yes." When an objection to your thinking arises, you must:

❏ A. Answer the objection directly or rephrase it in the form of a question that confirms your understanding of what the other person really wants.

❏ B. Recap all the benefits in a way that makes the other person feel there is more that is right about your thinking than is wrong.

Now that you have completed the exercise, simply compare your responses to this list of correct answers:

1. B 2.B 3.A 4.A 5.A 6.A

A total of less than six correct answers suggests an imperfect ability to persuade others. Your most pressing problems are likely to lie in areas where you made the wrong response. If you will bear these in mind as you move forward, you'll discover concrete, specific, and practical ways to perfect your persuasion skills.

WHY HARD SCIENCE GETS BETTER RESULTS THAN SOFT-SOAP

Ever since The Serpent—the first, and most compelling, persuader of all—sold Eve, the world's tried every which way to sell apples.

Probably more books have been written about persuasion than almost any subject you can name—with hundreds of new titles coming on the market every year.

Ever wonder how come there are so many? After all, if even one of them lived up to its hype nobody would need anything else, and a lot of trees might be spared.

But they don't. And the reason they don't is this: They are more guesswork than hard science.

That's what corporate giant Xerox discovered in a pioneering study. You see, once upon a time, Xerox owned about 90 percent of the copier business—which is the same as saying it owned 90 percent of the problems and breakdowns those copiers suffered.

In the early days, Xerox machines were pretty unreliable. People complained, they threw fits, went bananas every time their copier crapped out. A lot of them said they'd never buy another Xerox product again.

The thought of teeing off the very people they were counting on to buy the next generation of copiers gave a lot of executives in the higher echelons the uncomfortable feeling they might be slowly choking themselves to death. They knew they needed to get ahead of the curve on this one a.s.a.p.

They decided to train their 5000 service people—the only point of direct contact between the unhappy customer and the worried company—to keep the customer sold *after* the sale had been made.

They tested every persuasion program on the market. None gave the consistent success they were looking for. So they commissioned a team of university-accredited behavioral scientists—Harvard, Yale, the whole nine yards. The big idea was to come up with the best way to teach the *skills* of effective persuasion.

Now notice, I didn't say "teach the formulas of effective persuasion." I said, "teach the *skills* of effective persuasion." There is a big difference between an alphabet-soup formula and a fundamental skill:

Formulas are quirky—always rigid and often irrelevant. How can you hope to paint-by-the-numbers when you find yourself in an uncharted scene?

Skills, however, once learned, work all the time, for everyone, under any and every circumstance, no matter how fast things change, or what else is going on. The possibilities are unlimited.

The professors observed more than 100,000 interactions between customers and service representatives. And since they were out to scientifically discover the skills of persuasion—the techniques that time-after-time-after-time proved the critical difference—that is exactly what they came up with.

Beyond a shadow of doubt, the work established the factors that were always present in successes, always absent when a Xerox representative struck out. In total, six crucial skills met the tests of science.

What works for thousands of people at Xerox is guaranteed to do as much for you if you will but master these same six powerful skills.

So critical do I believe these to be to your day-in day-out success, I want to give them to you now as fast as I can. A few already may be part of your unconscious M O, others may take a little time on the learning curve. Plenty of examples you can follow and be guided by amplify the fuller discussion of each that follows:

SIX STEPS GUARANTEED TO PERSUADE ANYBODY TO DO ANYTHING

1. Make an Initial Benefit Statement.

2. Ask questions.

3. Support the other person.

4. Ask for what you want.

5. Overcome objections.

6. Ask for it again.

- -

Step One: The Initial Benefit Statement

It may surprise you to learn that, in at least one way, persuading someone and training a mule are more alike than you might realize.

You've probably heard the story about the old mule skinner. He was a mild and kindly country gent whose animals loved him, followed him everywhere. But one visitor was shocked to observe a training session. It began with the trainer clobbering the jackass right between the eyes with a two-by-four. "Thing with mules," he later explained, "'fore you can train 'em you got to be sure you got their full attention."

Attention is what the Initial Benefit Statement is all about—the kind that comes instantly when you let the other person know right off the bat your sincere desire to help them get what they want and need the most.

Remember, successful persuasion is based on the need-benefit approach.

The other person has certain needs. He agrees—he is persuaded—when you uncover those needs and satisfy them with a benefit of your thinking or product. The whole idea is to filter your goals through their desires. For example, you might talk on and on about this or that benefit, but unless these satisfy the specific needs of the person to whom you are talking, you might as well save your breath.

YOUR MENTAL TWO-BY-FOUR

Well then, how do you uncover needs?

The first step is to use what you already know, or sense, to make an IBS that will get or keep the other guy talking—for it is only through conversation backed with intelligent questioning that you discover what you must know to persuade his thinking.

While there are as many different ways to make an IBS as there are people multiplied by ideas, the primary objective is always the same: To introduce you or your idea in a way that is logical from the other person's point of view.

"If I sense a farmer's big drive is a need for respect, that is the hot button I push, right from the start," reports Jackman, ME agricultural extension service agent Brawley Bates, 43. "He could be tilling four acres with a horse and still I say something like, Some of the tidiest farmers in the county are saying the same thing—they are looking for . . ."

Brawley serves his community by satisfying the needs of others. He succeeds by showing them the instant recognition and respect the other person craves. Think of the IBS as your mental two-by-four. Use it to get the other person to pay favorable attention to the point you wish to get across.

HOW TO CREATE, AND WHEN TO USE, THE IBS

The IBS begins with a *general* expression of benefit and concludes with a *specific* reference to your idea, product, or service.

The general benefit can be a discussion of

▶ Need

▶ Problem

▶ Desire

▶ Value to the other person

▶ A difficulty they may or will encounter.

On the other hand, the specific benefit must refer to something about yourself, your product, or the organization you represent in ways that promise

▶ Satisfaction

▶ Solution

▶ Right choice

▶ Answers

▶ Ability

▶ Correct approach

An IBS should be made at the beginning of a discussion, when the other person indicates the time has come to get down to business. However, it works just as well as a pivot point later in the conversation—for instance, when you want to introduce a completely different topic.

Let me show you the IBS at work with a few quick examples:

Example 1: "Most of our customers are retired people on fixed incomes," reports Bremmerton travel agent Melanie Wyndoe, 40, "so every penny counts. Trip cancellation insurance is something they rarely think about until I mention it by saying something like, 'Naturally, you want to get the most out of every travel dollar. That's why I recommend Argo trip cancellation insurance. No matter what happens, Argo covers you 100 percent for every penny you have laid out so that a canceled charter flight or even an earthquake doesn't mean you have to give up your vacation.'"

Melanie unveils the general benefit by addressing what she correctly assumes to be the widespread need among her clients for economic security. She says, "Naturally, you want to get the most out of every travel dollar." She completes the Initial Benefit Statement with a specific reference to the benefit of Argo's plan —"No matter what happens, Argo covers you a hundred percent for every penny you have laid out so that a canceled charter flight or even an earthquake doesn't mean you have to give up your vacation."

Example 2: "My job is to introduce smaller food stores to the new products my clients make," reports food broker Harry Burling, 37, operating throughout the Deep South from a base in Gatlinburg, Tennessee. "A typical way to get down to business? I might say, 'Mr. Schmitz, our studies tell us that your customers are more likely to buy a product when they know and respect the brand name. You'd be able to increase sales of salsa-and-cheese-dip because people associate the Heinz brand with unmatched quality.'"

Harry's approach works because the general benefit addresses the need for sales appeal (" . . . our studies tell us your customers are more likely to buy . . . ") and ends with a specific recommendation for the brand he is selling (" . . . people associate the Heinz brand with unmatched quality.").

Example 3: "When a friend's son, Hank, was in high school, he had his heart set on going to a Pac Ten college," reports Boise guidance counsellor Utta Dunnicht, 44. The news both delighted and worried her: she was pleased to see Hank aiming high, but concerned his language and mathematics skills might prevent him from earning a place in a freshman class at a school like Berkeley or UCLA. She explained the importance of high scores on the Scholastic Aptitude Test. "Hank, to get into the school of your choice you need to do as well as possible on the SATs. Several of the test preparation centers can help identify problem areas and drill you on what you need to know faster than if you did it on your own. The Omega centers seem to be about the best— they offer one-on-one tutoring for any deficiencies you may have in English or math."

Utta's powerful IBS began by referring to Hank's known desire ("Hank, to get into the school of your choice . . . ") and concluded with a specific solution ("The Omega centers offer one-on-one tutoring . . . ").

TWENTY-FOUR WAYS TO POWER YOUR IBS

To give you a leg up on building powerful Initial Benefit Statements, I want you to have a dozen different sample openings you can use (as is, or modified to meet your special circumstance) to make a general statement. I'll follow these with twelve more examples to specifically refer to your idea, product, company, or service.

INITIAL BENEFIT STATEMENTS

TWELVE SAMPLE OPENINGS . . .

1. "It is my understanding, Mr Jones, that you . . . "

2. "A number of people have been saying . . . "

3. "I hear you've got a problem in the area of . . . "

4. "What most people want . . . "

5. "The inconvenience and lost time many people face . . . "

6. "If you could get better results for less money . . . "

7. "There is always a problem when . . . "

8. "Let me see if this is your situation . . . "

9. "One of the major problems with . . . "

10. "Lets outline the things that can be done to . . . "

11. "We've found that many people are looking for . . . "

12. "Mrs. Jones, if what you are looking for is . . . "

TWELVE WAYS TO INTRODUCE SPECIFIC BENEFITS

1. "The 'X' approach is not only . . . "

2. "This is why a lot of people have . . . "

3. "You get the best of both with . . . "

4. "'X' works especially well when . . . "

5. "We have a reputation for . . . "

6. "In other words, you are looking for . . . "

7. "My thinking ties into these needs by . . . "

8. "Their flexibility allows you to . . . "

9. "We can do the job faster than . . . "

10. "Here is how 'X' does the job for you . . . "

11. "'X' is your best bet to satisfy this need . . . "

12. "In situations like yours, 'X' is the solution because . . . "

If you want to persuade anyone to do anything, or if you want to be admired for your ability to influence your customers, peers, and superiors—everybody!—the IBS is the place to start.

- -
Step Two: Ask Questions

Okay, you've made your IBS. Now, because he is the sole source of everything you've got to know, the second step is to **probe the other person's mind with questions that elicit the information about his needs that you want and only he can deliver.**

"There are times it is obvious what's on a person's mind but I find it is always better to make sure," reports Dicky Dunne, 26, who works at the membership desk of a fitness center in Vallejo, CA. "A young guy inquired at the desk last week. I asked, Work out much? He said he had just gotten out of a rehab center following a heart attack. Imagine, a heart attack at age 29! That gave me an opening to talk up our doctor-recommended cardiac fitness programs and our certified exercise physiologist on staff."

Remember, every other step in my equation of persuasion rests on your ability to discover relevant hidden information—get it into the open where you can address it.

WHEN QUESTIONS ARE THE ANSWER

Questions are obviously in order when the other person gives you little or no information about the way he feels toward you and your thinking.

But there are other situations which also call for intelligent probing. For instance:

▶ Questions are necessary to clarify objections to what you say. Once you understand where these negatives are coming from, you can go on to handle them.

▶ If your idea is entirely new to him, probing will help you and the other person locate areas of dissatisfaction with the status quo that you can then use to further your point of view.

"The most amazing thing happened the other night. I bought something over the telephone. I usually don't trust those fast-talking telemarketers," reports Passaic, New Jersey municipal clerk Nello Milkening, 30. "I said I didn't need it and she said, 'How come?' So I explained and she asked, 'Why?' She never made a spiel, she just kept asking me questions. Somewhere along the way I saw that I really did need what she was selling so I bought it sight unseen."

Nello's experience makes an important point: intelligent questions get people not only to reveal their needs but to reconsider them in the light of what you have to offer.

TWO KINDS OF QUESTIONS: LIMITING AND OPEN-ENDED

In addition to knowing when to ask questions, I want you know the most effective way to probe in any given situation. Generally speaking, there are two kinds of questions we need to concern ourselves with.

The first is the one you use whenever you want the other person to give you a specific response such as "yes" or "no." This is called a limiting question because it limits the other person to make a specific—and often fact-based—answer. It gives you tight control over the conversation since you choose the topic and ask the customer to respond appropriately.

How to Create A Limiting Question

Creating a limiting question is a three-step procedure:

1. Mentally choose a benefit that you think might satisfy the other person's need.

2. Raise a question that will direct the other person to that benefit.

3. When the other person answers with information about his needs, agree and develop the benefit further.

Let me crystallize things with some quick examples that show you how to direct the other person to the topic of your choice:

"Then you've received complaints about your son's behavior in school before?" is an example of a limiting question: in limiting the parent to a "yes" or a "no, it narrowly focuses the discussion on the problem at hand.

Here are several other ways a limiting question might be posed:

"Is cost the particular reason you say that?" (the answer to which permits you to discuss your idea in terms of benefits of efficiency, economy, and so on).

"How many times would you say the problem has come up?" (which opens the door for you to talk about reliability, security, and the like).

"When do you expect the rental property to be available?" (the answer to which gives you a reason to bring in such benefits as timeliness, flexibility, and so forth).

HOW TO POSE AN OPEN-ENDED QUESTION

The second type of probe is one that gives the other person a chance to express his opinion. This is called an open-ended question and gives the other person considerable leeway in the choice of responses to be made.

"Can you tell me, please, what you had in mind?" is an example of an open-ended question. It encourages the other person to talk more or less freely.

Open ended questions, the sort that encourage the other person to expand their response, generally cannot be answered "yes" or "no."

Here are three ways they might be posed:

THREE WAYS TO RAISE OPEN-ENDED QUESTIONS

1. "Who is this (computer, automobile, program, etc.) for?" (the answer permits you to relate a benefit of your offering to the needs of the cnd-uscr).

2. "Can you tell me more about your (job, boss, problem, etc.)?" (the answer reveals issues of concern that can then be satisfied with a benefit of your proposition).

3. "What do you like best about your (house, apartment, club, relationship, etc.)?" (which gives you a chance to relate a benefit of your thinking to one or more of the customer's known interests).

WHICH QUESTIONS WHEN?

The type of question you choose to raise of course depends on how forthcoming the other person is.

Here are the specific guidelines I want you to follow:

▶ When they volunteer some information and appear willing to talk further, *use open-ended questions to bring hidden desires to the surface.*

▶ When they give you no information or insight into their needs, *use limiting questions to funnel the conversation toward benefits of your proposition.*

- -

Step Three: Support the Other Person

So far, you've learned how to make an IBS that wins immediate and favorable attention of the other person. You've also learned that careful use of limiting and open-ended questions not only brings hidden desires to the surface, it makes the other person feel you consider his opinions and feelings important.

The next step that shows you are truly interested in the other person is the skill of supporting: After probing, you listen for needs and when these arise, you acknowledge and support them. In a moment I'll show you how easy it is. But first, I want you to know why supporting the other person's point of view is ever so important. Basically, it shows the other person two things:

1. You understood what he said;

2. What he said is as important to you as it is to him.

SUPPORTING: A TWO-STEP PROCEDURE

This simple action—all it takes is a little human understanding and an honest interest in people—probably does more to move the conversation closer to agreement than anything else you can name.

Whenever the other person responds in a way that offers you an opportunity to introduce or reinforce a benefit of your thinking, follow this simple two-step procedure:

1. Agree with the remark, then,

2. Develop the thought. Build on what you know they know with a benefit that logically flows from the other person's statement.

Let's suppose you are out to sell grocer Esteban Warres a new brand of packaged chicken salad. You make your IBS and Warres responds,"What you say is interesting but, frankly, I am satisfied with the chicken salad I am carrying now."

So you probe with limiting question that will turn the conversation to a benefit you offer:

"Tell me, Mr. Warres, have you ever had complaints that the salad isn't as fresh as it might be?"

"Funny you should say that. Just this week a customer complained. She said it tasted funny—like it had been sitting around for days."

Your immediate response should agree with Mr. Warres so that he knows you understand his need and consider it important:

"I agree. Stale taste can be a problem . . . "

Then quickly follow your statement with a benefit.

"That's why we deliver fresh chicken salad every day. With us, you won't have any complaints about stale food."

Offering instant agreement serves two purposes. First, it encourages the other person to talk more about things that concern him. And second, by treating the other person's remark with respect, it makes him more receptive to the benefit you offer.

Bear in mind, however, whether you are talking business or a personal matter, you should agree with only the remarks that offer you a way to lead the other person closer to your position.

But suppose you aren't selling chicken salad. Suppose you are selling yourself, in a job interview, and you come up against the barrier of racism.

"I was applying for a management training position, and I opened by telling him that my creativity and a stick-to-it mentality could contribute to a company like his, a company on the move," reports African American businessman Steve Montague, 24, who hails from Romulus, Michigan. "The white interviewer tried to brush me off with a quick, 'Impossible! Come back in 10 years!!' So I thought for a moment. 'That's a great idea,' I said, striking immediate agreement with him. 'Would you prefer to meet in the morning or would the afternoon be better?' The interviewer became more constructive after that and, though he eventually offered me a job, I turned it down."

In Steve's case, things are pretty clear. Sometimes, though, people are not as direct as his interviewer. Their cues are often subtle and desires are hidden behind a lot of words. A true persuader watches for these cues and reads between the lines to understand what the other person really needs.

"So this guy tells me he drives a lot in the city and his monthly gasoline bill is beginning to look like a telephone number," reports Lee Ann Dixon, 38. She sells cars for a Port Arthur dealership. "What he is really saying is that he needs a car that will run more economically. That gives me a way to talk about our Swallow—it's got the best fuel economy on the American road."

Step Four: Ask for What You Want

Now that you've uncovered the other person's needs, told him all about the benefits, and supported his views, it is time to ask him to take action. Fail to ask for what you want and you'll never persuade anybody to do anything. Sales people call this step the "close."

WHEN TO ASK

When it comes to asking for what you want, timing is everything. Ask too soon and your idea is certain to be stillborn. Ask too late and you invite a memorial service. No matter what you want from whom, the time to ask for it is always the same: When the conditions are right.

The conditions I am talking about are these:

You and the other person agree that the benefits of your thinking will satisfy his needs.

TWO ELEMENTS MAKE FOR A SUCCESSFUL CLOSE

To close, you must assume the sale has been made by acting, speaking, and projecting mutual agreement. Then,

▶ Summarize the benefits that satisfy the other person's need in language that reflects the agreement. This prepares the other person to make a positive response to the request that immediately follows.

▶ Because uncertainty is the enemy of persuasion, you must ask for what you want in a positive way. Nothing should express doubt, hesitation, or uncertainty.

Let me give you an example of the points I am making here.

First, the positively charged benefit summary:

"Harmony, we've talked about superb data handling of the Presidio, especially for all of the number-crunching you do. I know you like the idea that no matter where you are transferred, even Alaska, we guarantee in-office service on a next-day basis . . .

Second, the confident request:

"I'll write up the order now if you'll just tell me which pointing device you prefer. Would you rather your Presidio came with a track-ball or is the mouse best for you?"

SIX WAYS TO OPEN A CLOSE

1. Well, Mr. Berken, when you own . . .

2. We'll have it at your place on Thursday.

3. Maybe you and your wife want to consider . . .

4. We've agreed that . . .

5. Would you like a few minutes to think it over?

6. Shall I order it in stainless steel or do you prefer white?

WHAT TO DO WHEN THEY SAY, "NO"

Earlier in this chapter, I told you about Lamar Thorpe, the Alabama recording contractor. He discovered people have two reasons for not going along with his ideas. The first reason is the one that sounds good, the other is the secret truth they try to keep to themselves.

Thorpe's approach is to uncover the hidden reason because, by leveraging it, he gets people to persuade themselves.

He found the best way to reveal the real reason for the other person's resistance is to restate the objection in question form and either

▶ Answer a misunderstanding directly, or

▶ Minimize the drawback by stressing another benefit.

"One of the major objections record producers usually talk about first is our location. But what they really lose sleep over is the cost. So I respond first by asking them, Do you know about our private jet service? Look, no matter where you decide to record, Mr. Producer—New York, LA, or Muscle Shoals—you're going to be flying people in. With our free private jet, it doesn't take longer to fly here than to fly anywhere. We pick you up at Atlanta and have you on the studio airfield in 44 minutes flat. You can't get from O'Hare to the Loop any faster than that. Then, when I ask them if there's anything else preventing them from using us, the issue of cost finally comes up. I turn it into a benefit by asking them something like, Are you willing to risk the success of a major album for a few pennies? I point out that by locating in southern Alabama, we can provide a fuller service at a cost that's still highly competitive. By the time you take into account the complaints you'll get from artists about commercial hotels, shabby dressing rooms, the lack of golf and tennis facilities, the time it takes to bring in special talent that's a regular part of our staff, you'll see I am offering you a superior service at a fair price. Of course, the final decision is yours, but I hope you realize that buying cheap to save a few pennies is like stopping a clock to save time."

You may not be a salesperson, but you can use Lamar's technique in almost any situation you can think of. All you have to do is to figure out how to turn an objection into a benefit and you'll get your way every time.

WHEN LOGIC DOESN'T WORK

But of course there are situations when logic and reason simply aren't enough to convince others to see things your way. In these cases, you must appeal to their emotions as well as their minds.

"I had my heart set on a beach vacation, but my husband, Dan, was talking about a trip to Disneyland," reports Dora Altman, 40, a Hartford instructional aide. "I argued cost, I argued travel time—nothing worked. Finally, I just looked at him and said how sad it was going to be not to see him in a bathing suit now that he had lost twelve pounds. Bingo! He got out the AAA Guide and called several resorts on the Connecticut shore."

Dora's appeal to Dan's pride may not have been enough on its own to get Dan to the beach but, coming as it did on top of cost and time advantages, it was the final straw.

A person doesn't have to be in a relationship to be affected by emotional appeals. Think back to your own life to see how powerfully persuasive emotions can be. For instance,

Was it logic and reason that led you to buy a red car . . . or was it the sense of fun a cherry-red rag-top conveys?

Did you buy your house solely because the plumbing is copper . . . or was it because, the moment you walked in, it smelled like grandma's when she was baking apple pie?

Buying clothes, changing jobs, relocating to a new city, getting married, raising funds for your church—selling others on decisions like these are situations in which emotions are certain to figure as much or more than economics.

So, if you want to persuade anybody to do anything, you must remember this: the best way to open purse strings is to pluck heartstrings. Yes, by all means appeal to logic and reason so that the other person can justify his or her decision to see things your way. But to really nail down the sale, make certain you've built-in an appeal to their emotional needs.

Do this, persuade the heart at the same time you persuade the mind, and whatever you want is sure to be yours.

A CLOSING PROCEDURE THAT WORKS LIKE MAGIC

Once you have overcome the other person's objectives, you must again attempt to clinch the sale with a close.

Here is a closing procedure guaranteed to work like magic. If paperwork is involved, have the contract ready. Be sure it is all filled in—the other person's name, address, amount to be paid, and so on. Every single item should be complete so all the other person has to do is sign on the dotted line.

If no contract is called for, write a memo or fact sheet that includes all of the pertinent information. Sign it yourself in the space you provide. Make two copies. Tuck them in your case. Make your verbal presentation to the other person. When you both agree your benefits satisfy his needs, pull out the memo and hand it to him by saying it is a memo of the understanding you have reached mutually. Just hand him your pen and show him where to sign.

This simple procedure concentrates the other person's mind on the idea of going along, not refusing. It crowds out any negative thoughts and leaves him with a positive action to bring the encounter to a meeting of the minds.

USING PERSUASION TO GET PEOPLE TO DO WHAT YOU WANT

What I have tried to show you in this all-important chapter are the principles of persuasion that will empower your life as they have the lives and careers of thousands of men and women all over the country.

The good news they bring is that success is a matter of mastering a very few skills. The bad news is that they do not make success automatic. They show you the best, most workable way to make your own success possible. Theorizing about persuasion is complex but easy. Doing something about improving your ability to persuade others is simple but hard.

Getting other people to want to do what you want requires painstaking effort. The tested techniques I've given you call for patience and practice. They may seem awkward at first but, believe me, they will bring you the results you want.

Before I conclude this chapter, I would like to summarize the sure-fire techniques you can use to persuade anybody to do anything.

1. To persuade, you must find out a person's wants and needs, and show him how your proposition satisfies them.

2. To get the results you want, use this six-step procedure:

   ▶ Introduce you or your idea with an Initial Benefit Statement that is logical from the other person's point of view. Begin with a general expression of benefit and conclude with a specific reference to your idea, product, or service.

   ▶ If you want to persuade your listener to give you his full and undivided favorable attention, probe the other person's mind with questions that elicit the information you want and only he can deliver.

   ▶ When he volunteers some information and appears willing to talk further, use open-ended questions to bring hidden desires to the surface; when he gives you no information or insight into his needs, use limiting questions to funnel the conversation toward the benefits of your proposition.

   ▶ When the other person reveals needs, you must acknowledge and support them. First, agree; then develop his thought by introducing a benefit that's appropriate to his frame of mind.

▶ To clinch the understanding, you must assume the other person has already been persuaded. Begin the close by summarizing the benefits you and the other person agree on. Then ask him to take the action you recommend.

▶ When objections arise, you must either answer a misunderstanding directly or minimize the drawback by stressing another benefit.

3. To guarantee your results, be sure to appeal to emotions as well as to logic.

I am going to close out this chapter by reminding you that gaining the cooperation of others is one of the keys to success in life no matter what you do for a living. Cooperating effectively in your business, family relationships, and church and social activities is a matter of delivering benefits others recognize and want.

There is usually a good reason to think facts are the ammunition of persuasion but, as I have been stressing in these pages, there's plenty of evidence that says facts are not enough.

It's what happens to facts, how we process them emotionally, often blowing them out of proportion, that counts.

When you turn the page, you'll see how one well known promoter of rock concerts defused emotions to get the performance of a lifetime from one of the best-known and craziest stars of the pop music world today.

EMOTIONS

Thirteen Workable Ways to Defuse the Emotions That Prevent You from Getting What You Want When You Want It

It was to be the final night of taping, and as far as music promoter Kenny Gordon was concerned, it couldn't come a moment too soon.

Gordon, who produced some of The Nashville Network's biggest and most popular specials, looked forward to wrapping his July Fourth show with a star-spangled finale—*America The Beautiful* performed by the hottest band on the country charts, backed with fireworks, lasers, a Mississippi paddle-wheeler, two university marching bands, Tuskeegee Tabernacle Choir, and Miss America.

Around noon, he took a call from the lead singer of the band, a man we'll call Delaney.

"Kenny," Delaney complained, "I am ragged out. My throat is killing me. I can't sing tonight and we leave for London in the morning."

Gordon, who had worked with Delaney before, had reason to suspect the singer wasn't really ill. Still, he rushed right over to the Spence Manor Hotel. There he found Delaney sipping iced tea laced with honey by the guitar-shaped swimming pool.

"What a bummer," Gordon said, dripping with sympathy. "Of course you can't go on. I'll cancel right now. It will only cost you 40 or 50 thousand dollars but that's diddly compared to your health."

"Well . . . " Delaney sighed, mentally calculating the money he'd lose, "before you do that maybe you ought to give me a call in the afternoon and let's see how I feel then."

P.S., the taping went off on schedule.

WHAT TO DO WHEN EMOTIONS DEMAND EXPRESSION

It didn't take an advanced degree in psychology to turn the tide as Gordon did.

Years of dealing with people taught him that emotions—anger, joy, guilt, shame, envy, fear—breed inner tension. And since tension is unpleasant, people do what they must to release the pressure.

For instance,

▶ Fear moves people to avoid or sidestep danger, whether real or imagined

▶ Anger pushes us to demolish the obstacles that we believe stand between us and what we want

▶ Joy insists on expression—we feel uncomfortable when we have to contain it

Since direct action as a means of expressing emotion is often unsuited to civilized society, conversation usually proves the most accepted way to bleed off emotional steam.

Here's the catch: What people in emotional situations choose to say can be more of a coverup than a clear reflection of their true feelings—and with good reason: The emotions that provoke their discomfort may be so deep even they are not aware of it.

Take our friend Delaney.

Gordon eventually learned Deleney had an irrational but paralyzing case of recurring stage fright, something even well-seasoned recording artists suffer from time-to-time. But he was unable to put his true feelings into words because he thought people would laugh at him. So he covered his secret fear with talk of illness.

Gordon didn't argue with Delaney, and he didn't try to convince him he wasn't clinically ill. He simply acknowledged what the singer said. This gave Delaney the psychological space he needed to recognize his emotional turmoil, freed him to reconsider the consequences, subtly encouraged him to change his mind.

WHY YOU MUST TALK THINGS OUT

Do not be too quick to put Delaney's behavior down. After all, it is not so strange.

A wall of resentment suddenly shuts you off from someone you love . . . you find yourself in a business argument in which neither party seems to hear the other . . . your daughter, overcome by anger, sheds crocodile tears . . . a friend who feels threatened shouts and blusters.

Defensiveness, aggressiveness, dependency—I want this chapter to show you how to use conversation to deal with these and other stressful, emotionally charged situations that are part of your daily life at home, on the job and out in the community.

Whether you are a supervisor or a manager, an engineer or a word processor, a mental health worker or a janitor, laborer, attorney, physician, clerk, garage mechanic, or minister I want you to have the practical skills that will help you to defuse emotions, resolve conflicts, and work out the problems that may otherwise prevent you from getting what you want when you want it.

HOW TO INSTANTLY UNLOCK THE LOVE AND RESPECT YOU CRAVE

To deal more effectively with the emotions that are so much a part of your daily business and personal life, I will give you 13 workable ways to control the attitudes and emotions of anybody—tested methods that guarantee the results you want from others.

If you are a parent or in a relationship, these principles and techniques cannot fail to unlock the family love you crave. An added plus, the very same methods are guaranteed to make you a better worker, a more considerate boss, a more respected leader in your business, professional, and civic activities.

Transform your life with my surefire techniques,

Three Never-Ending Benefits of Emotional Expertise Are Yours

The ability to resolve emotional difficulties will free you to create positive and meaningful work relationships at every level, and the ache of isolation will never again cast its dark, foreboding shadow on your career.

"They brought me in from the outside and put me in charge of senior people who had been working together for umpteen years, so trying to put in changes was like trying to rewrite the national anthem. I figured it was their problem but it turned out to be just as much mine," reports Halmar Ludvigson, 33, a Reno accounting specialist. "Finally, one guy told me that my suggestions about how to get better throughput came across as personal attacks that got people secretly mad. I am glad he gave me the heads-up. I made some adjustments and there seems to be less mistrust these days."

Whether you're operating out of the corner office or the corner store, your real job is dealing with people . . . which means, of course, dealing with people's emotions. Learn to defuse them and you'll be on the fast track to the career goals you have set for yourself.

By finding ways to communicate calmly in stressful, emotionally-charged situations, you will nourish the very lifeblood of the personal relationships you cherish most—the ones between mates, friends, parents, and children.

"I was torn between dreams, thirty-something and sure I wanted a baby but not as sure about giving up my career," reports Tomi Westham, who works for a public relations firm in Kohler, Wisconsin. "Thank God for Larry. One night, I was crying in his arms. He said when he didn't know what to do he tried not to do anything but wait until what he wants makes itself clear. That made me feel calmer."

It wasn't the facts of life that had Tomi in a tizzy, it was the conflict they generated. By responding to her feelings of confusion, Larry defused a potentially damaging emotional situation and strengthened the bond between them.

The lives of people with whom you interact are certain to be enriched by your ability to share and care. You'll be seen as a natural leader who makes people feel they belong, and others will more reliably support your views.

"Once upon a time, I thought my nursing education was all I needed to make a success of my career but now that I am night nursing supervisor of the coronary intensive care unit, I know better," reports Sheeannah Shabazz, 30, a Cincinnati RN. "Dealing with life and death demands coordinated action. It also makes for a lot of emotional tension that leads to burn out. By finding ways to help my nurses depressurize, I keep turnover down, and patients get the teamwork they need to recover."

If my techniques work for Sheeannah, who spends her every working hour solving critical issues of living and dying, they are certain to do as much for you.

By applying them diligently, you will deal with human emotions in a way that helps all concerned to see things in their proper perspective. This empowers you to solve problems cooperatively, and supports the best interests of everybody.

The skills of emotional mastery take practice but once they are acquired there is no limit to the success they can bring.

ARE YOU BLIND TO, OR BLINDED BY, EMOTIONS?

For practical people who would like to improve their ability to deal with and defuse the emotional reactions that come up everyday at work, with the family, or among friends and acquaintances, I suggest you take a look at the following exercise.

Below you will find ten situations. After reading each, you will be asked to make a choice. Just check the response that, in your judgment, is the better approach. There are no right and wrong answers, and there is no deadline. Just read the situations, think how you might feel if you were experiencing the emotions described, and make your selection.

1. Eleven year-old Randy comes home from school, visibly upset. He says one of the kids in his class has a pistol in his locker. What is a parent to do?

   ❏ A. Instruct the boy to stay away from the young hoodlum?

   ❏ B. Ask the child how it might feel to know a classmate had a weapon?

2. One of your employees, a woman with 15 years of unmatched experience and expertise, comes to you tense and fearful. She says all the news about layoffs has her so worried she's missing sleep. As her department head, you know for sure she is bulletproof. What's a boss to do?

   ❏ A. Patiently reassure her, explaining the reasons she has nothing to fear on the job front?

❏ B. Tell her that what she has told you sounds like it could make a person feel pretty uncomfortable?

3. You are facing unexpected surgery. In tears, you tell your husband that you really don't want to have it but the consequences of refusing it may be dire. What is your husband to do?

   ❏ A. Ask you to have the surgery?

   ❏ B. Ask if you could tell him more about how you came to see things the way you do?

4. You are having a bad-hair day—tension, hassle, pressure, anxiety—the whole nine yards. You have an appointment with your boss to go over your annual evaluation. You know in advance it will be an exercise in frustration. What's an employee to do?

   ❏ A. Get through the interview as best as you can?

   ❏ B. Reschedule the meeting until you've had a chance to gather yourself?

5. It is a very happy occasion, the bar-mitzvah of your dearest friends' son. Your son's was just a year ago. You approach the beaming parents. What's a friend to say?

   ❏ A. I know just how good you feel today?

   ❏ B. This sure is a day to remember?

6. It's supposed to be a dialog but it ends up a one-sided he-said-then-she-said-then-he-said sort of a conversation. It grows more difficult to follow by the minute. You lose track of who did what to whom, and when. Next thing you know, you are being asked if you agree with the speaker's outrage. What's a person to do?

   ❏ A. Offer an opinion?

   ❏ B. Say, I was with you until X. Tell me again, What happened next?

7. You are in a relationship with someone who is having a tough time but won't talk about it. You would do anything to help if only your significant other would let you. But every time a conversation gets down to the nitty-gritty, they clam up. What's a lover to do?

❏ A. Tell the other person it would be better if they shared their feelings more?

❏ B. Tell the other person you wish things were more open but you can accept that, for the moment, they are not?

8. One of your customers has a classy problem that's got him churning. Says he's gotten an offer from another company. Says he likes it where he is but that the new salary looks awfully good. He wants your opinion. How is a salesperson to respond?

❏ A. Well, let's add up the pluses and minuses and see where the balance falls?

❏ B. Let me see if I'm getting it: part of you wants to stay and part of you wants to go?

9. One of your friends has been laid off. He's taking it badly. He talks about feeling empty and blue. You want to help him through this crisis. What's a friend to say?

❏ A. Sounds to me like they had a heck of a nerve giving you the ax?

❏ B. Sounds to me like a sad situation?

10. You take one of your people aside to say that it might be a good idea if he took a course in statistics. He agrees but, as he speaks, yanks at the collar of his shirt. What's a supervisor to believe?

❏ A. The person is likely to do as you ask?

❏ B. The person probably will not comply easily with your request?

Now that you have completed the exercise, simply add up the number of "B" answers.

A score of ten or none means one of two things: either you are a master of emotions or you are kidding yourself into believing emotions play no part in the conversational failures you suffer. Either way, I strongly urge you to read this chapter with particular care. The time you spend on it will either polish your acknowledged expertise or help you start getting the kinds of positive results that now elude you.

A total of between one and nine "B" answers suggests you are sensitive to the emotional tensions underlying some conversations but certain factors may prevent you from tuning into the emotional content of others. Each "A" answer is an area you need to work on. If you will bear these in mind as you read on, you'll discover practical and specific techniques to overcome each and every one of your shortcomings.

How to Leverage Your Knowledge About Emotions

In a moment, I will give you 13 ways to deal with emotions that are guaranteed to produce the results you want immediately. Knowing these will make it extremely easy for you to leverage your knowledge of human behavior in ways that benefit both sides of the conversation.

But first, you need to know how emotions operate.

HOW EMOTIONS OPERATE

▶ Emotions have two sources

▶ You cannot predict the emotional responses of others

▶ Emotions are always proportionate to their real cause

▶ Some people use emotions as interchangeable parts

▶ Logic doesn't work to dispel emotions

WHERE EMOTIONS COME FROM

Emotional reactions have two sources. Some are generated by what goes on within an individual, some by external influences.

To illustrate the point, let me give you a couple of quick examples of how a potentially damaging emotional response—walking out—is generated first by an internal factor and, second, externally:

Paul wants to buy a car but cannot make up his mind. His friend, Ernie, has a two-year-old coupe he is willing to sell at a bargain. A brand new one costs about 30 to 35 percent more. Paul goes to Ernie for advice. Ernie's advice is to save the money. Paul wishes Ernie would have suggested a visit to a new-car dealer. Paul secretly feels anger toward Ernie. He expresses his feeling to himself by thinking that Ernie is selfish, doesn't really care about Paul but thinks only of himself. Paul leaves.

That's an example of an internal situation—Paul's brooding mind-set—producing a potentially damaging emotional response.

Now for the other side of the coin: Mary and Elizabeth, who are good friends, are competing with each other for a job. In conversation with an interviewer, Mary makes a remark that could be seen to put Elizabeth in a bad light. She becomes anxious that she has done something awful, more anxious than the harmless remark justifies. Secretly, you see, Mary wishes Elizabeth was out of the competition. It is this hidden feeling that drives Mary to cast verbal doubt on Elizabeth's credentials. She does not own up to this feeling because she is somehow unaware of it. But failing to see it affords her no protection: She doesn't know why but, in the midst of the interview, Mary feels ill, develops a sudden migraine, asks the interviewer to reschedule the appointment, and leaves.

That's a case of an external situation—competition for a job—kicking off an emotional response. My point in giving you these two examples is to get across the idea that emotional reactions depend not only on what is happening within the individual but also to him.

YOU CANNOT PREDICT EMOTIONAL RESPONSES

Emotional reactions of others are nearly impossible to predict. One person can be angry in the exact same situation that somebody else accepts with grace. And just because a person has acted one way in a situation offers no assurance he will act the same way later on. You cannot safely say a person will be angry because the circumstances call for anger. Nor can you say that he will be joyful because he is supposed to be.

Factors that stimulate an emotional reaction vary from individual to individual and from time-to-time in the same individual.

Just because it appears to you that a situation calls for a certain response doesn't mean someone else will do likewise for the same reasons . . . or even that they will do likewise at all.

"Sometimes I think the laundry is a place I send my shirts to get fresh wrinkles pressed in. I get mad as the Dickens but it doesn't seem to bother my bride," reports newlywed Herve DeVere, 29, who works for a bank in Montpelier, Vermont. "It's taking time for me to get used to the idea that what makes me angry doesn't seem to trouble her."

Herve, who ought to change laundries, is learning an important lesson in living we are well advised to heed: As long as we don't have X-ray vision on another person's inner world we can't be sure how that individual is going to react emotionally in any given situation.

EMOTIONS ARE ALWAYS PROPORTIONATE TO THEIR REAL CAUSE

Sit back for a moment and do us both a favor.

Think back to really long car drives, 40 minutes . . . an hour . . . maybe more. Drives when you were alone in the car. Tooling along, a radio station fades. Your mind wanders. Then something happens, exactly what you cannot say, but something. A thought crosses your mind, a memory and, Bingo! You suddenly find yourself brooding and there's no stopping it. Nothing you do turns off the tape that keeps on playing and playing and playing in your head. Imagine! . . . all this from a little pin-prick of annoying memory.

Or, maybe the feeling was giddy elation. Maybe the way it feels when you win the lottery. And you think, Ahhhhh, if this is the worst of life, it's okay by me. Imagine! . . . all this even though nothing wonderful is happening.

If the intensity of some of your most private emotional responses seem well out of proportion to the snippets of memory that trigger them, breathe easy: There is nothing wrong.

What may appear to be an overly strong emotional response to a trifle is really not overly strong at all. Not when you realize that the trifle isn't so very trifling.

You see, *emotional reactions are always proportionate to their real cause.*

The emotional memory is a reservoir. As you go through the normal events of daily life, things happen to provoke emotions. Rather than flow away freely in conversation, some of these emotions somehow get stored up. As the reservoir fills, the pressure of emotion steadily builds. Eventually, the buildup proves more than the reservoir can contain. The final drop of emotion—perhaps a fleeting recollection conjured up on a long, lonely drive—is the trigger:

It sets off an overflow of pent-up feeling. The stronger the reaction you are experiencing, the more emotions you've secretly stored up behind it. Like I said, emotional reactions are always proportionate to their real cause.

So, if you ever want to turn off the tapes that every once-in-a-while play on and on in your head, here's what you have to do:

Let's say you find yourself on a long drive and you begin a mental argument with someone who is not there. You can't dismiss it. It won't stop. And it feels like things are getting out of hand. Okay, the very first—and perhaps only—thing you need to do is this: Search your feelings. That's right, ask yourself, What *else* have I stored up to make me respond like this? Ask, and I guarantee you will immediately begin to see the situation in a new and truer light, a clear and shining light certain to burn through the shadows of self-doubt.

EMOTIONS ARE EASILY DISGUISED

When it comes to emotions, things are not always what they appear to be.

For instance,

- *Anger* smolders in argument, gossip, destructive criticism, teasing, or lack of cooperation.

- *Guilt* masquerades as self-criticism, confessions of real or imagined misdeeds, and acts of atonement.

- *Anxiety* surfaces in overcautious behavior, obsessive focus on a single point, secretiveness, withdrawal, avoidance of certain subjects or people.

The list goes on but I think you get what I am driving at. Psychologists call this displacement: One emotion displaces another.

People displace emotions—cover fear, for instance, with anger—to conceal something, divert attention—yours and theirs—away from what they are more truly experiencing but perhaps not feeling.

"It's like the magician who makes a diverting gesture to draw your attention away from what is really going on," reports social worker Shandy Claighborn, 34, who works in a hospice in St. Augustine, Florida. "You ask our clients to tell you how it feels to face the end of life and they start talking about what wonderful parents they were."

WHY LOGIC DOESN'T DEFUSE EMOTIONS

Since people often displace one emotion with another, logic can't dispel the underlying problem.

"My nephew, Kip, refused to go canoeing with me because he said he was afraid of catching a cold if the boat tipped. I tried to reassure him the water was warm—it was August—but it was no go," reports Kendra Harnes, 30, who operates a catering service in Flagstaff, Arizona. "When we got back to the house, my sister-in-law confided that Kip is afraid of drowning—he can't swim but he doesn't want to admit it."

No wonder Kendra's warm-water reassurance left Kip with cold feet: Her logic never addressed the real reason for his refusal. Here's a classic case in which making sense makes no sense at all. Kendra's logic only intensifies the underlying tension, makes Kip feel what he says to cover his secret fear is somehow irrational. This winds the emotional rubber band driving his tensions even tighter.

Next time you run into somebody who says they are afraid of dogs, cats, darkness, flying, catching a cold in warm water, or riding in elevators—anything—resist the temptation to apply logic.

Not only will it not work, chances are you will worsen the situation.

ELEVEN TESTED WAYS TO DEAL WITH EMOTIONS

Technique 1: Get and Keep the Other Person Talking

When you confront an emotional reaction, nothing does you more good in less time than giving the other person easy ways to conversationally release the inner tensions provoked by their emotions.

Let me draw you a picture: Imagine the other person as a house, his or her secret emotions as flames within it. Imagine yourself as a firefighter. What's the first thing you are going to do to prevent the structure from going up in smoke? Every trained firefighter, volunteer or paid, knows the one way to save it: Chop a hole in the roof to let the superheated air that's driving the fire escape harmlessly.

The same holds true for emotional fires smoldering deep within. The first, best thing is to help them burn off the emotional heat by encouraging open expression.

Technique 2: When Confronting Emotion, Less Said Is More Gained

To diminish tension, you must resist the temptation to speak, even if you are 100 percent sure you've got the answer to what appears to be bugging the other guy. I say this because no matter how sound your thinking, your answer is unlikely to address the real source of tension.

"I had one of the people who reports to me start a big brouhaha over the fact I assigned her weekend duty," reports Ray Casher, 36, a Covington, Kentucky plant safety supervisor. "There was nothing unfair about it. I explained my thinking. I assigned her to weekend duty because she was available, could handle the load, and she was part of the backup crew for the shift. That really got her mad. I later found out she was angry at herself about something at home and just used me as an excuse to blow up."

Casher's employee was tormented by angry emotions. These pressed for relief. Given what seemed like justification, she spouted off.

Like Ray, about the best you can hope to get out of trying to talk the other person out of an emotional bind is to make them stop talking—which amounts to guaranteeing a bad situation will become worse.

One of the earmarks of a person caught in the grip of emotion is difficulty paying attention to others. But let's just suppose you somehow force them to hear you out, then what? Just this: all the while you are talking and they are silent, tension keeps building. Your own experience with emotional reactions has probably shown you that there are times when less said is more gained. Heed the lesson and you'll come out a winner. I don't care what the emotional reaction you confront. It doesn't matter.

As soon as you sense it, stop talking. Let the other person take center stage.

THREE THINGS YOU MUST NEVER SAY TO SOMEONE IN THE GRIP OF EMOTION

1. Don't tell a female employee who's talking about her biological clock she's got plenty of time.

2. Don't tell a student with a straight A average he's got no reason to worry about an exam or paper.

3. Don't tell a subordinate who's feeling overworked that the facts argue otherwise.

Technique 3: Say the Five Words Guaranteed to Encourage Others to Express Emotion.

When you confront an emotional situation—anything from anger to joy—the five most powerful words in the English language, the handful guaranteed to get and keep the other person talking, are these:

"Tell me more about it."

For example,

▶ If someone says he's worried about an upcoming test for a malignancy, don't tell him not to fret. Instead, ask him to tell you more—the thinking that led up to the decision to undergo the test. Explaining will release his anxiety. After he's spoken for a while and the tension eases, you might share what you know from friends, that others were worried beforehand but things turned out better than they expected.

▶ If someone says she is worried that another person doesn't like her, don't rush to refute the premise. Instead, ask her to tell you more about her feelings, what leads her to feel the other person doesn't like her. Perhaps she is secretly angry with the other person and an imagined snub triggers it off. Talking eases the pressure. Eventually, when her mind is more open, you can move on to other things.

▶ If someone monopolizes the conversation with feelings of joy about something happy that has happened in his life, do not attempt to turn the conversation by changing the subject. Instead, ask him to tell you more about it. Only when he's talked the emotional pressure out will he be receptive to whatever may be on your mind.

There may be times you grow impatient with other people's feelings, moments when you are tempted to take over the conversation. Resist the temptation. If you will simply train yourself to say, "Tell me more about it," you cannot fail to defuse the emotional reactions that stand between you and what you want.

Technique 4: How to Stop Hearing and Start Listening

More than job skills, more than verbal skills, more than personality traits—more than anything else you can name, the ability to listen determines where you go in life and how fast you get there.

And no wonder. Science says we spend more waking time listening than on any other human activity.

Do it well, be the listener each situation requires, and you automatically make yourself more effective at work, at home, everywhere. This is especially true when you are dealing with emotional reactions. As we move ahead, I am going to give you several specific principles you can follow to become the listener emotional people want, need, and reward.

First, I want to point out what may seem obvious—the difference between hearing and listening. Hearing involves the head. Listening involves the head and the heart. Hearing is easy, listening is difficult.

Done right, listening liberates the speaker and leads to understanding, done poorly, it ratchets-up a tough situation to make it a potentially bad one.

WHEN *NOT* TO LISTEN

I can think of four things that are sure to lead to poor listening, and offer these to you as cautions.

When any of these is part of you, everybody's better off if you avoid even trying to defuse an emotional reaction.

1. When you are pressured.

2. When you are caught in a hassle.

3. When you are unaccepting.

4. When you are untrusting.

Technique 5: Never Fake Understanding

Have you ever gotten the feeling that the person who claims to understand you most probably understands you least?

"I could tell you about conversations—business and personal—where I've been okeydoked to death on every point and still leave feeling totally misunderstood," reports Port Deposit, Maryland shipping agent Sherry Dunne, 39. "You can see it with your own eyes, and when they pretend on the phone, it somehow sounds off key."

Maybe we pick up a glitch in body language, maybe there's some kind of hidden message in the words or the tone—it's difficult to say. One thing is for sure, though: Whatever it is, it triggers a warning, a heads-up that tells you you are dealing with less than the truth, the whole truth, and nothing but the truth.

Look, every once in a while even the best listener gets lost in another person's train of thought. That doesn't make the listener a phoney. It's what the person does next that lets you know whether what you've got is real turtle soup or merely mock.

When the phoney gets lost he pretends he understands perfectly.

When the genuine listener gets lost, he says,

▶ "I seem to have lost you."

▶ "Could you run that by me again?"

▶ "I was with you until X. Tell me again what happened next."

▶ "How about an instant replay on that last point?"

Want to defuse an emotional reaction that's getting in the way? Okay, it is a matter of dos and don'ts. Don't fake understanding. Do understand!

Technique 6: Never Say You Know How the Other Person Feels

"I was nursing but my baby fussed a lot and he was awfully slow to gain weight. When I told the doctor I was worried something was wrong with the milk I was producing he said he knew exactly how I felt. How could he possibly know how it feels to breastfeed a newborn? The next day I called one of the women I met in the hospital for the name of her doctor," reports Ethel Shirley, 24, a Laredo, Texas homemaker.

Ethel's former doctor is typical of untrained or insensitive listeners who, when finding themselves dealing with intensely emotional reactions, often feel compelled to say something like, "I know just how you feel."

No one can know fully what's going on inside anyone, not even a doctor or a psychiatrist. Reading another person's feelings is at best an approximation, at worst a fiction.

Either way, it raises doubts in the minds of the very people you are trying to help. They wonder just how much understanding you are bringing to the situation. Besides, it simply doesn't help an emotional situation to tell someone you understand their feelings. What is useful is to *demonstrate* some degree of acceptance for—not agreement with—what the other person is going through at the moment.

"I told the same things to my new doctor," continues Ethel, "and she said that the first weeks of nursing can be a challenge. Some mothers become anxious because their babies cry a lot or seem to reject the breast or lose too much weight. Some mothers' nipples get cracked or sore, and others find it harder than it has to be because the rest of the family doesn't provide the support structure a nursing mother needs to feel successful. I got the feeling she really sensed that a lot was going on and how upsetting all of this was for me."

There's a big lesson to be taken from Ethel Shirley's experience: Without ever saying, "I know just how you feel," her new doctor was able to get across the idea that she was really tuned into Phyllis's situation.

Do as much, *show rather than talk acceptance,* and people will instantly sense you are on their side.

Technique 7: Focus on Feelings

Every conversation is a blend of information and feeling.

In emotional situations, the words are usually far less important than the feelings that provoke their expression.

For instance, "We're all sitting around the lunch table the Sunday after Thanksgiving and my daughter, Mindy, starts crying all of a sudden," reports St. Louis broker Hugh Malten, 43. "She didn't want to go back to college, said she was afraid she'd flunk out. I said 'Mindy, the freshman year is always the toughest,' 'Mindy, you are smart,' 'Mindy, I know you've got what it takes to hang in.' Here I thought I was doing my daughter proud and don't you know it, she gets up and leaves the table, sobbing."

By responding 100 percent to the information Mindy delivered, Hugh ignored his daughter's feelings.

Tears should have clued him that there was more going on than her words suggested. Instead, he responded to her words with counter-arguments.

Sure these made sense. And look where sense got him—nowhere, fast.

Had he tuned in to Mindy's feelings, he might've simply asked her to tell him all about it. He may not have been able to assuage her underlying fear but, at the very least, she might feel less alone in her anxiety.

Technique 8: Remember That Agreement Is Less Important than Understanding and Acceptance

When you are confronted with an emotional reaction, be it at home, on the job, or out in the world, good listening is the best and only way to search out the meaning of what appears to be going on.

Question: What's a skilled listener to do when he or she makes such a discovery?

Answer: Be a mirror. Reflect the other person's content and feeling in ways that demonstrate understanding and acceptance.

"Being able to reflect the emotional reactions of the people who work for me has really kept things on a more even keel," reports section manager Jean Berhold, 37, who works for a Boston distributor. "I had to tell one woman, who was great at her job, that she wasn't going to get a promotion. Well, she broke down and cried and told me she was sure she'd be an assistant manager by now . . . one promotion after another going to other people. I realized she could be experiencing a lot of different feelings—anger, fear, frustration—so I simply said, 'It's really discouraging.' She must have sensed I was really trying to help her—we talked for nearly an hour."

Here's my take on Jean's story.

Mirroring feelings is like extracting the fuse out of an emotional time-bomb: You don't get rid of the dynamite, you just make it so it can't explode.

Technique 9: Paraphrase to Show Understanding

The technique of paraphrasing applies in situations where you sense the content of the other person's words is somehow more important than the unexpressed emotions that drive it.

A paraphrase is your take on what the other person is talking about, expressed in your own words.

Somebody says, "I don't know whether to take early retirement or not. I really like my work but there are a lot of days I'd rather go fishing."

You respond, "You enjoy your work but sometimes you feel a strong pull to say the hell with it."

Your response is a paraphrase. It signals you understand but neither agree nor disagree with what the other person is saying. When the paraphrase hits the bull's eye, the speaker almost always says "Yes," "Right," "Uh-huh!" and begins expressing more of the feelings that provoked the emotional tension in the first place.

Technique 10: Provide Emotional Feedback

Feedback is to feelings as paraphrase is to content. In other words, feedback is the technique you use to reflect the emotions you are picking up on.

"When my parishioners talk to me about a problem I try not to miss their personal reactions to the events they are describing—the joys, sorrows, fears, angers, griefs, and so on, they put into their words and gestures," reports Evanston, Illinois pastoral counselor Armando Faxas, 46. "I play these emotions back to them in my own words so as to encourage them to talk more about what is really troubling them."

The reflection of feelings is the same as paraphrasing except that it focuses on feelings expressed in words and gestures.

The more accurately you feedback your impressions of the feelings they are communicating, the more revealing the conversation will become.

Here is a list of words that convey specific feelings. Be especially alert to these in conversation:

FIFTY VERBAL SIGNS THAT DEMAND EMOTIONAL FEEDBACK

Words that signal feelings of *love* include affection, desirable, friend, like, devoted, cherish, adore, love.

Words that convey *joy* range from contented, satisfied, good, glad, turned on, happy, and cheerful to jubilant, ecstatic, and overjoyed.

Words than reveal *sadness* as the underlying emotional drive include under-par, glum, blue, sad, desolate, depressed.

Words that represent feelings of *anger* include annoyed, put out, mad, frustrated, furious, violent.

Words that suggest *fear* include worried, timid, on edge, frightened scared, terrified, desperate.

Words that signal *confusion* include undecided, vague, baffled, mixed up, foggy, lost, muddled.

Words that communicate feelings of *weakness* include feeble, weak, powerless, washed up, helpless, done for.

Technique 11: Look for Gestures and Postures That Confirm What's Being Said

Body language never lies. When the gestures fit the words you can safely arrive at a sense of what is going on in the other fellow. When there are inconsistencies between gestures and words, rely on body language to be the more accurate barometer of hidden emotion.

"I really liked this woman I met at a party but I wasn't sure if I should ask her out—she kept telling me how busy she was. I was about ready to fold my tent and move on," reports Russell Oster, twenty, a student at the University of North Carolina. "Then I noticed her feet—they were pointed directly at me as she spoke. I asked her for the next open evening she didn't have a appointment, and we agreed to meet at the library."

While you will easily find a complete discussion of the meaning of body language in Chapter 3, which begins on page 43, I want you to have a couple of the most common gestures and postures right now—the ones you are likely to run into on a daily basis.

In addition to the position of the feet, sexual interests are revealed through slow eye blinking, fussing with hair, a suddenly more-erect posture, dilated pupils.

A fear of vulnerability often shows up with arms clasping one another, especially when legs are also crossed at the knee.

Openness is usually transmitted by a smile, arms relaxed at the sides, and palms-up gestures.

Before this chapter ends, I want to be sure you understand the key points. Let me recap them for you as briefly as I can:

I. Emotional mastery will make your life better in three big ways:

▶ It frees you to create positive work relationships at every level.

▶ It nourishes the personal relationships you cherish most.

▶ It encourages others to see you as a natural leader.

II. Emotions operate in special ways.

▶ Emotional reactions depend on what is happening within the individual as well as what is happening to them.

▶ You cannot predict the emotional reactions of others.

▶ Emotional reactions are always in proportion to their real cause.

▶ Emotions can be—an often are—disguised.

▶ Logic will not dispel an emotional reaction.

III. Here are 13 workable ways to defuse emotions.

▶ Get and keep the other person talking.

▶ Remember, people in the grip of emotion don't listen.

▶ Be aware of the things you must never say to people in the grip of emotion: don't tell a female who is worried about her biological clock she's got plenty of time; don't tell an A student not to worry about an exam; don't argue facts with an employee who feels overworked.

▶ The five words guaranteed to encourage people to express their emotions are, Tell me more about it.

▶ Understand there is a difference between merely hearing another person's words and truly listening to what they have to say.

▶ Avoid situations in which listening is required when you are pressured, caught in a hassle, feel unaccepting, or untrusting.

▶ Never fake understanding.

▶ Don't tell anyone you know how they feel even if they say they are feeling good.

▶ Tune into the feelings the other person is expressing.

▶ When dealing with an emotional reaction, agreement is less important than understanding and acceptance.

▶ Paraphrase information to signal factual understanding.

▶ Feedback feelings to signal emotional understanding.

▶ Observe body language to confirm the emotions you sense.

TALK RELEASES TENSION

My 11 workable ways to defuse the emotional reactions that come up daily in family, social, and business situations are intended to help others bring their feelings out into the open.

When the people you work with, live with, interact with are in emotional states, getting them to talk out their feelings diminishes hidden tensions and makes a realistic appraisal of the underlying problem possible.

Rehearse my 11 techniques, apply them, live them, and you will never again have to raise your voice to get anybody to calm down.

Only after they've cooled their jets is the time right for negotiation —getting others to buy into your thoughts, plans, and views.

Watch, when you turn the page, as powerful TVangelists—men and women who have a shrewd understanding of the way the human mind works—leverage their negotiating skills to inspire and persuade others.

CHAPTER 8

NEGOTIATING

Twenty-Two Secrets of Professional Negotiators That Inform, Inspire, and Persuade Others

Every human contact involves a negotiation—for time, for space, for money, for something! That's because it is only human to always want something from others—anything from a raise in pay from your boss to a better reputation among your neighbors.

Love, sex, marriage, relationships, community life, buying and selling, business, power—no matter what the focus happens to be, our job is the same: To somehow convince others it is in their interest to allow us to have what we wish for and want from them:

- If you are single, it might be a first-date with someone special.

- If you are in the market for a car or a place to live, it might be the price you pay or the terms.

- If you are a party to divorce, it might be fair visitation rights.

- If you are in sales, it might be the business of your customers.

- If you are in management, it might be keeping your work group focused on your most immediate concerns.

- If you are in the clergy, it might be more parishioners.

Let me illustrate that last point since it sounds pretty extreme to think that negotiations are so much a part of our daily doings they figure even in our spiritual lives.

Have you ever watched a top-notch TV preacher work the audience?

To tell you the truth, I don't approve of their pleas for funds, but I have to admit they know a thing or two about how to manage successful negotiations.

Late one night, I got caught up in one ministry's program. A man and a woman were team preaching. Back and forth they took the sermon. First, him to her, quoting Gospel. Then, her to him, retelling parables.

As they developed long and vivid descriptions of the tortures of the unredeemed, I saw agony grow on the faces in the audience. It was suffering I imagined to come out of feeling like your legs straddle a spreading chasm: your back foot on the side marked yesterday, the front one on tomorrow.

The more the preachers talked, the more resolve I saw on the faces of those who seemed inclined to come forward.

In the end, hundreds of people, perhaps a thousand, rose in the audience and made their way to the stage!

THE MISUNDERSTOOD MAJORITY: WHY SEVEN OUT OF EVERY EIGHT PEOPLE CANNOT NEGOTIATE

Unlike the TVangelists who, broadcast after broadcast, successfully negotiate for souls, most folks don't always get what they want out of their business and personal negotiations. Obviously, the preachers know something about negotiating it might do the rest of us some good to learn.

The preachers know that failures of negotiation come not out of what we might want (after all, what could be more hopeless than a desire to save the unredeemable?) but about what we *do* about what we want. And what we do most of all is talk. Therein lies the problem. Let me explain.

According to a reliable national poll of Americans, roughly eighty percent of us think we belong in the top ten percent of how well we get along with others. Which means, of course, that seven out of every eight people who think they negotiate well with others, simply don't.

Are you among these? Well, if people stop listening before you stop talking, count yourself one of the misunderstood majority.

How to Make Your Dreams Come True

In this chapter, I want to show you the secrets of professional negotiators that turn indifference into attention, conflict into cooperation, rejection into acceptance, distance into warmth, dreams into reality.

Here you will find the proven methods that empower you to negotiate for anything and get it, and a step-by-step process to make it part of your life.

Using practical methods and surefire techniques, you will express yourself freely and fully, get results, and strengthen relationships—all at the same time—no matter what the issues, no matter what the circumstances, business, personal, or otherwise.

EIGHT WAYS NEGOTIATION MAKES EVERYONE A WINNER

Whatever your role in life, applying the skills of negotiating is a winning proposition all around. At the same time successful negotiations give you what you want, they

- Encourage the people who work for you to perform in the face of overwhelming odds.

- Inspire them to become more than they are.

- Correct them when they are in error.

- Stimulate them when action is called for.

- Give people in your personal life ideas they can build on.

- Direct them when they are confused.

- Enrich their lives.

- Help them sort out problems and find solutions.

With daily practice, the secrets of professional negotiators I am about to give you are certain to become part of your second nature in no time at all.

Whether you are a minister, marketer, or mason, a butcher, baker, or candlestick maker, a health worker, or homemaker, in commerce, private, or public life, they cannot fail to improve your business and personal relationships with people at every level. And when they do,

These Two Spectacular Benefits Are Yours for a Lifetime

For perhaps the first time in life you will experience rock-solid self-confidence and an automatic can-do response to the business challenges you face daily. Whether you are detached or emotionally involved, dealing with your CEO or your co-workers, prepared or ad lib, you make an on-the-spot difference. This is certain to give your career the growing influence and visibility higher-management recognizes.

"I got an e-mail note from the head honcho of the division the other day," reports Freddie Croft, 32, who works in pharmaceutical research in Triangle Park, North Carolina. "She asked me to tell her how we've been able to keep department payroll in line without losing key players. I said it took a whole lot of trust on everybody's part but we kept at it because we knew what we wanted, we knew what they wanted, and within our little group we worked out a fair shake all around."

Freddie's experience tells me plenty. Mainly, it says that negotiating to find common ground is a winning situation all around: Your career gets the attention it needs and deserves.

And, because you make others feel like they belong in your thinking, they give you the willing support and loyal cooperation that earns job security.

The agreements you foster in your social, personal, and private life have the power to last, and grow even stronger over time because you work to ensure that everybody's needs, including your own, are taken care of.

"I've been married 25 years and my colleagues kid around that if I had killed him the first time I felt like it, I'd be a free woman by now—the most I would have gotten would have been 10-to-15 years," reports Miami trial lawyer Isabel Bacardi, 54. "We were both adults when we married, we knew what we were up against, and give or take, we've made it last."

Here's the moral of Isabel's story: Each of us holds a permanent seat at the negotiating table we call life. The rules are simple. Perform skillfully and you get what you want, don't and you get dumped on.

ARE YOU ABLE TO NEGOTIATE WIN-WIN OUTCOMES?

To give you a personal portrait of your negotiating strengths and weaknesses, I've prepared several questions.

There are no right and wrong answers, nor is there any time limit.

After you read each question, simply choose the response that you feel is most appropriate most of the time.

1. Can you express in a sentence or two what you want out of this chapter?

   ❑ Yes

   ❑ No

2. When you negotiate, do you ask others what they want?

   ❑ Yes

   ❑ No

3. Some people discover what they want by putting their own interests first. Do you?

   ❑ Yes

   ❑ No

4. When you are dealing with what you want, are you one of those specificity nuts—people who dot all the "i's" and cross all the "t's"?

   ❑ Yes

   ❑ No

5. When you want to find out what others may think of as confidential information, do you begin with a general question? For instance, when you want to learn how much they make, do you begin, "Your field sounds like a rewarding one. Can you tell me something about it?"

❏ Yes

❏ No

6. If a person tells you what he or she wants, do you think it is a good idea to tell it right back to them?

   ❏ Yes

   ❏ No

7. Do you think a good understanding of where the other fellow is coming from is as important as a good understanding of what he wants?

   ❏ Yes

   ❏ No

8. Can you name the three powerful body signals that tell you a meeting of the minds is imminent?

   ❏ Yes

   ❏ No

9. In the heat of negotiations, when tempers are up, do you think it is a good idea to find something to admire about the other person's point of view?

   ❏ Yes

   ❏ No

10. When negotiations are showing signs of breaking down, do you think is better to hang in than to reschedule?

    ❏ Yes

    ❏ No

Now that you have completed the exercise, simply add up the number of "yes" answers.

Most people will score between four and seven "yes" answers.

Each question you answered with a "no" indicates an area of opportunity. As you read ahead, you will find practical, workable techniques to develop your skills in these areas.

HOW TO STOP AN ARGUMENT DEAD IN ITS TRACKS

In a moment, I am going to give you 22 secrets of professional negotiators. But first, to be certain we're on the same wavelength, let's agree that a negotiation is not an argument dressed in polite clothes.

An argument, you see, has two sides—yours and the other guy's—and it always ends winner take all.

A negotiation, meanwhile, has three—yours, theirs, and common ground—and the only limit on the number of winners is the number of participants.

To change an argument into a negotiation instantly, all you've got to change is the limits you place on winning. Simply by allowing more than one person to win, you cannot fail to come out with more than you had going in.

"They told us there had to be a temporary pay cut, so me and the wife tried to figure out what we needed rock-bottom to get by for a few months," reports Todd Mahlenberk, 36, a Torrington, Connecticut foundry manager. "Their offer wasn't enough. My first inclination was to walk, but I held on. I told them I wanted to stay, I knew jobs were scarce, but I had to take care of my family. I had to have more than they were offering. They said they wanted to keep me but money was tight. They offered to put me on nights until things turned around. That's keeping my check almost the same as regular. Under the circumstances, with three daughters in parochial school and tuition bills coming in monthly, well, I don't think I gave more than I got."

Todd walked into the situation with a mental demand—my way or the highway!

As the conversation developed, an alternative appeared. It was far from perfect . . . but just as far from awful. It was a trade off, middle ground, and it served Todd's family interests. It may not have given him all that he wanted but it delivered most of what he needed.

When the conversation was over both he and his boss could honestly say that they were better off agreeing than not.

THE SECRET WEAPON EVERY SUCCESSFUL NEGOTIATOR MUST POSSESS

For roughly 25 years, I've researched the topic of negotiations—hundreds of books and lectures by political, business, and labor leaders; thousands of articles by professors, lawyers, and other experts in the field; even personal interviews with hands-on practitioners.

I was looking for the secret every negotiator must possess to succeed. I was out to find the universal principle—that one that worked everywhere and all the time—the one that consistently brings about meetings of minds.

And what I found was this. Every negotiation that ends in success begins with three questions. Negotiations in which at least one side raises and answers these three questions invariably produce the best possible compromises. Absent these, there is bound to be dissatisfaction between the parties.

It is these three questions that I want you to have straight away since these are the basis for the techniques I will be giving you as we move forward through this chapter.

THREE QUESTIONS GUARANTEED TO GET YOU WHAT YOU WANT EVERY TIME

The following questions are based first on knowing your needs, second on understanding theirs, and third on identifying the opportunity in between.

- What do I want?
- What does the other side want?
- Where is the common ground between us?

- -

How to Determine What You Want

Secret 1: Put Your Own Interests First

"I used to get the short end of the stick coming to agreement with others because, being a trained sales person, the first thing they teach you is to look at the world through the customer's eyes," reports Cassandra Herman, 30, a Tulsa manufacturers' representative. "I got much better negotiating results, and so did they, when I started putting my own interests first."

By putting her interests first, it sounds like Cassandra is being selfish, doesn't it? Well, she's not. She's not basing her actions solely on what she wants, she's just following the advice of history—know thyself.

By determining in advance what she really wants out of the negotiation—not what she hopes or wishes or dreams about but, in concrete terms, what she is prepared to agree to—she establishes a solid foundation for further discussion.

This gives Cassandra several advantages: First, there's the comfort factor. Knowing exactly what she wants immediately scotches the possibility of confusion and self-doubt. She knows in advance what she will agree to and what she will not. This makes her feel more comfortable and relaxed, less likely to feel threatened and combative—even in the face of strong opposition.

Second, there's the control factor. She knows that by establishing her bottom line before negotiations begin rather than after, she can't be debated, detoured, or derailed by side issues. An amount of money, a pledge of respect, a clause in a contract, a job offer—whatever she is after, she occupies a more powerful position by defining it than by not.

And third, there's the no-hassle factor. By keeping the focus on issues instead of the buildup of emotions that raises barriers to agreement, she doesn't get trapped in the dead end of who is right, or why me, or how do I feel about this? Instead, she asks the one question that empowers her to negotiate effectively—What do I want?

Secret 2: To Decide What You Want, Examine Your Options

If you have trouble deciding what you want in a particular situation, it is probably because you have too many general ideas competing for attention and not enough specific ones upon which to focus.

The way to beat it is this: Simply write down some possibilities of what you want.

Make them as specific as you can—not "earn more money" but, rather, "make a six-figure income before I am 45."

Alongside each of these, note an alternative. List it even if the alternative seems outrageous and off the mark—"Earn $XX,000 next year."

Obviously, some of what you write down will not represent things you can act on, but they nevertheless serve a purpose.

What listing these options does for you is this: It jumpstarts your thinking, gets your mind working, prompts other approaches and ways of looking at things.

Eventually, you will run out of options and alternatives, and your list will narrow down to just a few specific points. These, you can be sure, are things of greatest importance to you under the circumstances.

All that remains is for you to decide which of these deserve priority. With sufficient practice, this process of noting possibilities and alternatives will become a mental rather than a written technique, an automatic part of your personality.

Unlike most of the options we can exercise, the ones associated with what we want don't cost anything to access . . . and plenty if you fail to.

Secret 3: Be Specific About Your Wants

"Once upon a time when the world was a little younger, I made disagreement rougher than it had to be, a battle of egos," reports Jeeter Byrd, seventy, a retired Washington, D.C. government worker. "Now I tell myself, well, this or that is exactly what I want. It looks like this, it weighs probably about this much, it's painted that color—you get my drift? The more I focus on the details of what I want, the less this becomes an ego issue for me. The other person might want something else, I know that. And that's okay too. That still doesn't give us the battle of the egos, it just gives us different points of view looking to somehow get together."

By focusing on specific details Jeeter takes the emotional conflict out of reaching agreement with other people.

When it comes to determining what you want, being specific saves time and eliminates the possibility of misunderstanding. Even if you are the only person dotting the "i's" and crossing the "t's," it's effects are sure to be felt.

The more specific you are about your wants, the less room you leave for emotional tensions to affect coming to terms.

Secret 4: Accept the Strengths and Weaknesses That Make You You

Deciding what you want in a negotiating situation is a whole lot less uncertain when you can speak from the honest conviction of your beliefs, values, and commitments.

There's just one source of these—yourself. Who you are, your strengths and your weaknesses. What you stand for. What's really important.

"It's a day-to-day thing, keeping in touch with myself," reports Atlanta bookseller Leigh Edin, 31. "Five years ago the most important thing in my life was to be a mother. Today, I still want to be a mother but the other biggest thing in my life right now is getting my own business up and running. Things don't change but the emphasis you put on them does. You've got to stay in touch with those changes or, the first thing you know, you are living in yesterday instead of today."

When I talk about knowing what you want, I mean it in the sense Leigh alludes to—knowing what you want *now*, not yesterday and not tomorrow but at this very moment.

Here are a couple of easy ways to start the process. Get out a piece of paper and rule it into three columns. Headline the first column, "What," the second column, "Who," and the third column, "Targets."

In the first column, list the 10 most important things in your life.

Under the second headline, note down the ten most important people in your life. On the right, list your ten most important goals in life. When you've completed this exercise, I'd like to give you just one more.

Please rule a second sheet of paper into two columns. Label the left one "+" and the right one "-." Under the plus sign, list your five best personal strengths. Under the minus, list your five greatest weaknesses.

Once you have completed these exercises, you'll have a fair picture of who you are—your values, commitments, strengths, weaknesses, goals.

The rest is a piece of cake: next time you find it hard to decide what you want, think about the choices in terms of your profile—the real you.

Abracadabra!

You'll be amazed at how easily you come to a fitting conclusion about what you want.

Remember, the fastest and best way to figure out what you truly want is to figure out who you truly are.

How to Determine What Other People Want

Once you know what you want, the next thing to learn is what the others hope to get out of the negotiation.

Sometimes their expectations are unreasonable. And sometimes, people don't themselves honestly know what they want. Either way, you've got to get their position out on the table so you can deal with it. The best way, of course, is to ask.

"Most people are so flabbergasted when I ask them what they want, it takes them a minute or so to catch on that I really do want to know," reports Chattanooga credit agency worker Lisle Krigel, 30. "A family owes a nursing home some money, says they are going to file a counter-claim for wrongful death if we go for a judgment against them. I ask them what they want. They're speechless. Then I say I can't promise to make it all happen but if I know their thinking, well, who knows? Maybe some of it can be worked out."

Lisle's message is as old as the Bible: It is a lesson every professional negotiator knows and never forgets. "Ask and ye shall receive."

Secret 5: Make the First Questions Broad

The broader your first couple of questions, the more information you are likely to get.

Sure, at first you'll get back answers that are as general as your questions . . . but that's okay: you can get to specifics as the conversation develops.

"Job training candidates come to me looking for help getting into a new field," reports private education counselor Don Attwood, 36, who consults in the Silicon Valley. "The first thing I ask is what they're looking for out of life, where they see themselves 10 years from now. As we talk, I get a better idea of who they are and the way they see things. That gives me leads to more specific questions."

▶ What would you like out of this conversation? . . .

▶ Please tell me what you have in mind? . . .

▶ Can you tell me more about X? . . .

▶ How do you feel about X? . . .

There's no limit to the general questions you can invent to encourage people to start talking about what they want.

Secret 6: At First, Open-Ended Questions Are Best

In the early stages of negotiation, when you are exploring what others want, try to avoid queries that choke-off expanded talk, questions that can be answered either yes, no, or with a fact.

Instead, begin with open-ended questions, ones that require the other person to explain and talk more than a minimum. Encouraging them to go past what is absolutely necessary, combined with careful listening, gives you a better handle on the things that are important to them.

"I thought the first few minutes of our planning meeting was a disaster—interruptions, raised voices, ugh!," reports sanitary engineer Oliver Pellington, 36, out of Charlottesville, Virginia. "The first thing I wanted to say was, hey, look, we're not getting anywhere, do you want to call this off? I thought it would be better to put a little nicer spin on things so I said seeing as how we couldn't get off the dime, what direction do you think we ought to take on this? That got us on a better track."

From the sound of things, I'd say that if Oliver followed his first impulse, asked them if they wanted to quit, there'd be as many yes as no answers. That would leave him in the dark about their wants, and them still fighting.

Instead, his open-ended question covered the same ground but invited them to talk about how they saw things, what they wanted.

Secret 7: Consent to Advice

Often, the best time to seek advice is when you need it least . . . and by this I mean at any point in the negotiations after you have determined what you want.

Asking for advice can be a subtle way of asking people to tell you what they want most. Rarely will you run into an individual whose advice is truly impartial. Nine times out of ten it's a reflection of what they'd like for themselves, what they want.

Asking them to share it with you shows a lot of respect. Whether you take it or leave it is another question.

"I bought these vitamins, and the gelatin gave me a rash. I brought them back to the health food store. The lady there started yelling—no cash refund!," reports Shari Zein, 19, a New Hampshire college student. "All I wanted was a credit for the pills that were left. I asked her advice, how she'd like to handle it. She was so relieved I wasn't going to make a fuss I ended up with a free package of the hypo-allergenic kind."

There is ample evidence to think that free advice is worth precisely its cost. However, what is true of life is not quite as true of the hide-and-seek of negotiations. Here, even the worst counsel can be a valuable insight.

Secret 8: Playback Your Understanding of the Other Person's Desires

It is never enough merely to listen to someone. You must listen in ways that tell them you are listening. One of these ways is playback. The idea is simple. They say something. You listen. Then playback—using your own words, tell them your understanding of what they want.

It goes like this.

He says, "I want to retire at age 55."

She says, "Let's see if I understand what you are saying. You'd like us to have your finances in such good shape by the time you reach 55 you never have to work again, right?"

He says, "Not quite. I'd like to leave the field I am in and start a little bed-and-breakfast up near Tahoe."

Playback confirms and clarifies your understanding at the same time it tells them they are being heard.

The process encourages them to share and develop their ideas. This works in your favor because the more you know, the easier it will be to establish a meeting of the minds.

Secret 9: When All Else Fails, Be Direct

Let's face it: there are people who will do everything *but* name what they want.

"Couple times a day single women come up to the pharmacy counter and sort of don't want to talk about what they need," reports Pierre, North Dakota dispensary worker Karl Hess, 26. "I can't be a mind reader here and shilly-shally around—there are other customers. Would you like to speak with a woman pharmacist?, I ask."

When people are embarrassed to ask for what they want, or fearful they will be rejected, don't hesitate to use direct questions. These are your only hope of determining their stake in the outcome.

When all else fails, say as kindly as you can, words to the effect of:

"I've told you what I need. I'd like to work things out. But I can't if I don't know what you want. Please tell me."

Secret 10: Assume Nothing

Words mean different things to different sorts of people . . . even to the same sorts of people at different moments . . . and even to the same sorts of people in different places.

"It was quite a surprise to learn that my eight means somebody else's eight-thirty," reports Samantha Couerdelene, 24, who works in the banking business in New Orleans. "I invited people for drinks at seven-thirty and dinner at eight, but the couple from Buenos Aires didn't arrive until half past. They were surprised we had begun without them. I took the lateness as an insult. A friend told me later that, in Argentina, half an hour late is expected."

The trouble arises when we assume that everybody understands what we say in the way we want to be understood.

English comedian Benny Hill used to write **ASS - U - ME**, on a chalk board.

"When you assume," he'd say, "you make an *ass* out of *you* and *me*.

Don't assume what they mean is what you might mean if you spoke their words. Forget your assumptions. Check it out. Play it back.

"Do you mean that what you want is X?"

Secret 11: Keep Hopes and Fears Out of Listening

When you are trying to find out what people want, it's important to make direct listening contact with what they are saying—not what you want them to say or are afraid they will say.

That means you must not filter their words through your hopes, fears, and anxieties.

THREE WAYS TO LISTEN BETTER

▶ *It is counterproductive to listen for words that tweak your worst fears.* What you fear the most from the other person is very unlikely to happen.

▶ *Stop looking for hints that suggest you are less powerful than the other person.* You have more power than you are willing to allow. However, to experience its fullness, you must exercise it.

▶ *You mustn't lock-on phrases that lead you to hope everybody wants the same thing.* They never do.

Secret 12: Be a Stranger to Your Friends

Because we tend to be too wary of strangers, we sometimes come across as skeptical. That gets in the way of coming to agreement.

On the other hand, we are often oh-so-casual about accepting what friends say; we usually don't bother to check it out. That gets in the way of a share-and-share-alike outcome.

"I sort of took it for granted my department head knew what I wanted. Jeez, we knew each other a long time, we even play poker a couple of nights a month. He kept telling me I'd get what I want at my annual review," reports Duane Leary, 27, who works in manufacturing in Winnetka, Illinois. "What I wanted was line responsibility. What I got was to stay in the same old staff job with a fairly nice raise. I know it sounds crabby to poo-poo a salary bump like that but, well, I thought he understood."

Here's a trade secret of professional negotiators that cannot fail to payoff:

Next time you find yourself trying to determine what people want—for themselves or for you!—treat friends like strangers and strangers like friends.

Secret 13: Empathize, empathize, empathize!

Got a coin handy? A quarter? Better yet, a silver dollar? I want you to close one eye. Then, hold the coin very close to the open one. What do you see? The coin, of course. Now open both eyes and hold the coin out at arm's length.

Tell me what you see.

Sure, you are still looking at the coin but now your view also includes your hand, the wall and floor in the distance, and so on.

My point is this: What you see depends on the breadth of your perspective. The same thing holds for any situation in which you are trying to discover what other people want.

Persist in seeing things from your own narrow point of view and you'll never get a complete picture of how your desires affect the other parties, cause them to do and say the things they do.

On the other hand, take a look at your ideas from their perspective, and you open a direct route to the part of them that understands and can connect with your thinking.

"We've had a very good little hair-care business with a special line for African Americans. When the time came to get out, I was surprised and disappointed, too. My son-in-law, Anfernee, who had worked with me for 12 years, didn't want any part of it. Said he did it for the family's sake but never liked it," reports Chicago entrepreneur Mason

Wattley, 63. "If I'd've bothered to go over things from his point of view, I might've made changes along the way, gradual, and kept the company in the family—for my grandchildren."

Mason's family interests are admirable in any circumstance but insofar as his son-in-law, they weren't sufficiently compelling to keep him in the business.

The business didn't excite him in the way he wanted to be excited, didn't offer him a way to get what he really wanted out of life.

Seeing people as they see themselves, viewing life from their vantage point, forces you to align your thoughts in terms of their views.

There's a word for the ability to see things their way without necessarily agreeing with them. The word is empathy.

HOW TO DEVELOP EMPATHY

To be empathetic is to be aware of what makes the other fellow the other fellow.

It's not difficult to do.

Just ask yourself some questions, among them:

What drives their engine?

- Are they more concerned with show than with substance? Do they look up to anybody special?

- Do they enjoy life or do they seem to be having a hard time?

- What do they like and what do they hate?

How does what they are affect what I want?

- Will they see potential pressure points in your thinking, and what can you do to work around them?

By mentally rasing these questions, you heighten the empathy in each of your encounters. This automatically aligns your thinking more with theirs—no matter who they are, no matter where you encounter them.

Secret 14: Read Body Language

Here's my 10-second theory about the way impressions are formed.

Everything you need to know about a person you pick up in the first ten seconds of contact.

All the rest—hours, days, months, even years!—is a matter of confirming your gut-level impressions.

What I am saying here is that, in no time flat, nonverbal signals tell you all you ever have to know.

They either confirm or condemn the words people speak. Read properly, nonverbals are the litmus test of truth.

Gestures, postures, and actions tell you if a party to the negotiations is credible, aggressive, confident, easy to be with. Even the way they walk into a room can speak volumes.

"So the thing I hate about working with women is how much time it takes them to get down to business," reports N.C. Kiefer, 40, who is in the entertainment field, in Tampa. "She comes in . . . she takes off her coat . . . she fluffs her hair . . . she puts down her handbag, her attache case, and her computer . . . she arranges things at her place at the table . . . she fidgets with the waist of her skirt . . . she looks for a pen in her handbag . . . she removes a calculator from her briefcase . . . she checks her watch and asks if she can make a call—all this before she even sits down. I'll tell you, I'm going to be very skeptical about anything she says that includes the words 'businesslike' or 'efficiency'."

Psycholinguists say that we extract about three times more meaning out of nonverbal signals than we do out of verbal ones. No wonder N.C. nets out where he does.

People pass important information via body language, especially in negotiations.

Tone of voice is an almost perfect barometer of their personal confidence level. The higher their tone, the less self-assured they are about their wants.

The faster their words pour out, the less comfortable they are about yours. *The attitude, posture, and movement of the body is an instant rating system: it tells you in a flash how they feel about what you are saying.*

The more they fidget, the more you can be sure that something about your thinking provokes emotional tension.

The more their feet turn away from you, the more certain you can be they'd rather not be in a give-and-take with you.

In general, you are most likely to find common ground with people who appear comfortable in their posture whether seated or standing, who ever-so-slightly lean towards you when you speak, and who don't jiggle their fingers a lot.

Because, to the careful observer, eyes cannot lie, in them you can often read a person's truest feelings.

The secret is to go beyond the conscious gestures made with the eye—attempts, for instance, to alarm, bedevil, bemuse, comfort, and seduce. Instead, focus on the eye's *unconscious* eye movements . . . the ones that come up when a person isn't trying. Notice the pupils, if you can. When they seem to grow wider, something you said either surprised or pleased.

Observe the blink rate. If they blink much faster than six times a minute when they are speaking, the things they say they want may not be the things they *really* want. To play it safe, check out your specific understanding every step of the way.

If, on the other hand, they blink rapidly while you are speaking, it signals their immediate discomfort with the last thing you said. Unless you get the discomfort factor resolved—finesse it or overcome it—your chances of reaching agreement are compromised.

For a fuller discussion of nonverbal communications, you may wish to refer to Chapter 3, which begins on page 43.

- -
How to Find Common Ground

Earlier in this chapter, I told you there were three basic questions that determine the success of all negotiations.

The first concerned how to determine what you really want before negotiations begin.

The second was devoted to determining the desires of others.

Knowing clearly what's wanted on both sides sets the stage for the third and final question, Where's the common ground—the point of comfort at which give precisely and invariably equals take?

Common ground comes in every form you can imagine and several that might surprise. In a moment I will give you a number of ways to identify it in its various forms.

But first, a point needs to be made. They say the foundation of negotiating success is preparation. That the realization of it is courage. The limit on it is imagination. But what they don't say is what drives it. I say the engine is attitude. I'm talking about the attitudes of good will and spiritual generosity we bring to the table:

The goodwill that enables us to see things not as better or worse but as choices, to respect difference without feeling the need to agree with it, to be able to disagree without disengaging; the spiritual generosity that commits us to expect others will do the very best they can under the circumstances.

"If there was goodwill on either side they wouldn't need me," reports Russell Kirk, 40, who does conflict resolution for the American Arbitration Association on Michigan's upper peninsula. "Let's face it: good attitudes make good deals."

According to basketball coach Pat Riley, "Attitude is altitude." The same holds true of negotiating. Good attitudes make the best deals.

Secret 15: Put Their Case First

When you put forward your own needs first, only you are interested in what is being said. On the other hand, when you put their needs first, both sides are immediately drawn together on common ground: a shared interest in their desires.

Imagine, simply by speaking to their case first, you give them a personal reason to listen to, respect, and remember you.

So it stands to reason that when you begin talking about satisfying wants, you are best off identifying and speaking to theirs before you address your own.

"Now look, I know these folks before me aren't all sprouting wings and halos, but that's no reason to make things rougher than they have to be," reports Denver parking violations bureau officer David Laryton, 37. "I always talk about what they want first to reassure them that I am going to listen to what they have to say and take their story into account. That usually gets the tension down a smidgen."

Speaking to the needs of others before you talk about your own is a simple and powerful approach. It costs nothing, takes no time at all, and makes positive results more likely.

Secret 16: Build Two Bridges

Once you've got their wants out on the table, the next step is to relate them to yours.

Imagine, if you will, a picture of the negotiating situation as two banks of a river. Between them lies an island.

Your task is to build two bridges, one between your side and the island, and a second between the island and their side.

"They wanted me to transfer to Dallas but with a computer and a modem, I knew I could handle 90 percent of the load from Des Moines, with a couple of short trips a month," reports Barbara Liskin, 31, a package designer. "When I met with my boss I began by talking about the objections he had. Then I showed him how I could establish a presence in the Dallas market while operating out of the Iowa office, and save money while I was doing it. We set up a test for six months. That was a year-and-a-half ago."

Barbara first spoke to her boss's concerns about her ability to work out of the Des Moines office. Then she identified common ground—the need for more business out of the Dallas market. Finally, she went into how she could be as effective from Iowa and save money to boot.

Use the bridge building technique to span the gap between your interest, their interest, and common ground. It's quick. It's sensible. And nine times out of ten, it is going to work.

Secret 17: Offer a Choice

When you talk somebody into something with a take-it-or-leave proposition, chances are any agreement you reach will not last.

That is because when people are forced to assent they end up feeling they never had a strong a say in outcome.

The way to get around it is simple:

Give people two choices, either one of which suits your interests.

By freely selecting an option, they stake a claim to the results and are more likely to see things through.

"I always give my children a choice when it comes to yard chores," reports Howard Sochurek, 38, a Wilmington, Delaware administrator. "They can rake the lawn on Friday afternoon and have the weekend free, or they can get it done by Sunday evening. Either way is fine by me."

Even if the choice you offer is not precisely what others want, the opportunity to choose—or suggest yet another alternative—commits them to active participation in the outcome, hence to its success.

Secret 18: Give to Get

Offering something without being asked for it sets up a situation that leads others to feel obliged to do as much for you—even if it is only to listen.

"We offer everybody who comes into the gallery a cup of tea or coffee or bottled water," reports Berkley, California oriental rug dealer John Whelan, 36. "If the person eventually shows real interest in a particular piece, I might concede a point of negotiation unilaterally—for instance, right up front I might offer to pay for an independent appraisal, or offer free shipping."

By giving people something they do not expect, you make them feel special. This leads them to be more reasonable and encourages their active participation.

Secret 19: Defuse Conflict

There are two ways to look at disagreement.

You can see it as the beginning of the end, in which case all is lost. Or you can see it as the end of the beginning, in which case you are almost certain to bring negotiations to a successful conclusion by overcoming the objection.

The best way to defuse conflict and move toward success is simply to air it openly. After all, you can't resolve differences you can't talk about.

"The morning before the sale of my house was supposed to close, my lawyer got a call from the buyer saying the deal looked like it was off," reports Ida Foukarini, 34, a Seattle department store assistant manager. "I called them and said that whatever might be in the way of a closing I would do my best to clear up. It turns out they wanted one of the skylights replaced. I told them I would have my lawyer put it into the contract immediately."

Unacknowledged differences rarely go away by themselves. Worse, they drive people apart. Working things out brings people together. The process begins when you air things openly.

Secret 20: Find Something to Admire

The tougher it becomes to find common ground, the more important it is to find something about the other side's position to admire.

Your interest in their best qualities encourages them to be cooperative.

"To tell you the truth I hate dealing with the know-it-alls fresh out of business school," reports Digby Kates, 47, who is comptroller of a Fortune 500 company headquartered in Oklahoma. "Short-term thinking, immediate payoffs—they drive me nuts. But in the end, I try to find something to admire—maybe they're newly married and want to make a quick reputation so they can provide for their families. It's not much but without it, things might break apart."

When the going gets toughest, when you least feel like doing so, find something to admire about the other fellow. It may prove the key to bringing your negotiation to a successful conclusion.

Secret 21: Don't Make Quitting an Option

When you've reached the end of your string, don't offer others the option of quitting.

Instead, ask them to identify the benefits of continuing.

"Quitting in the middle may look like the easy way out but it is really the road to nowhere," reports Rhode Island marriage counselor Crystal Ellis, 44. "I try to turn the conversation around by comparing the benefits of going on versus the certain disaster of throwing it all over. If you go on, I say, the worst that will happen is that you will get some of the changes you want. But if you quit, things will never be any better and you will have wasted a lot of time and money."

Another way to get people back into the game is to review the progress that's been made so far.

"It was late, they were frazzled, and things were getting ugly," reports lawyer Jack Kaptur, 37, house attorney for a shopping center developer on New York's Long Island. "Look, I said, we've gotten past the biggest hurdle by selecting the site. All that's left is to work out the details and we can all go home knowing we've got an agreement both our companies will be proud of."

It is almost always better to continue than to quit.

When you feel the urge to take your bat and ball and go home, do not make quitting an option. Instead, treat the very idea of the impasse as an issue of the negotiation.

Indicate your interest in continuing. Ask them for their views.

In the end, you may have to give a little but that is far better than complete failure.

Secret 22: Stake Their Claim Every Step of the Way

When the going gets tough, staying power is tested.

According to one arbitration organization's guidelines, the biggest reason people quit is that they lose sight of the benefits that will come to them through agreement.

To keep them involved and interested every step of the way, make sure they know what's in it for them—either personally or for the organization they represent.

"The danger in getting a youthful offender to agree to a visitation schedule is they begin to think it is jail without the bars. Some of them get the idea it might be better to be inside," reports Chicago probation officer Tammy Tatreau, 29. "When it looks like they are going to walk I tell them that the court allows some flexibility and that I will do my best to be sure some of what they want happens, but first I've got to have their input."

Making certain others are aware of their stake in negotiations increases your chances of coming out with satisfying results for all concerned.

Before we leave the subject of negotiation, let me give you a quick recap of the major points we've been working with in this chapter.

1. When you develop negotiating skills, two benefits are yours for a lifetime

   ▶ You give your career the growing influence and visibility higher-management recognizes.

   ▶ Your personal agreements will stick and your relationships will grow stronger.

2. Successful negotiators always ask three questions

   ▶ What do I want?

   ▶ What do they want?

   ▶ Where is the common ground between us?

3. Four techniques to determine what you want

   ▶ Put your own interests first.

   ▶ Examine your options.

   ▶ Be specific.

   ▶ Accept the strengths and weaknesses that make you you.

4. Ten techniques to determine what other people want.

   ▶ Make the first questions broad.

   ▶ Ask open-ended questions.

   ▶ Consent to advice.

▶ Playback what you hear.

▶ When all else fails, be direct.

▶ Assume nothing.

▶ Keep your hopes and fears out of listening.

▶ Be a stranger to your friends.

▶ Empathize, empathize, empathize.

▶ Read body language.

5. Eight techniques to find common ground

▶ Put their case first.

▶ Build two bridges.

▶ Offer a choice.

▶ Give to get.

▶ Defuse conflict.

▶ Find something to admire.

▶ Don't make quitting an option.

▶ Stake their claim every step of the way.

HOW TO BE CRITICAL . . . AND GET YOUR FRIENDS TO LOVE YOU FOR IT

Negotiating skills help you cut through tension to find practical, workable solutions to the business, social, and family situations you encounter daily.

But what happens when you honestly believe things are beyond negotiation?

For instance, suppose you've got a friend, and suppose your friend kept on ticking you off—What in the world are you supposed to say that allows you to speak fully, freely, and leaves your relationship as strong as it ever was?

If that's a question that tweaks your interest, I think you'll want to turn to the next chapter.

It is all about handling criticism—the giving and the getting there-of—a subject every communicator needs to master.

CORRECTING OTHERS

Thirteen Workable Ways to Change What People Do . . . Without Arousing Resentment

"I tried to keep my cool but I blew it," reports working mother Chu Lee, 29, corporate travel manager for a Honolulu research center.

She and husband Sam, 33, took the children to visit his parents over a weekend.

"From the minute we unloaded the station wagon and William had an accident in his pants trying to find the bathroom, they started in. When they said it was thoughtless not stop on the road to give the kids a chance to go to the potty, I just smiled. When they wondered why I hadn't cut down on their beverages in the car, I still didn't say anything. But what made me mad was when they said that if I spent more time with the kids they wouldn't behave this way. It started an argument that went on for 30 minutes. They had no right to say what they said."

A great many of our business and personal conversations focus on correcting the mistakes others make. In these situations, many feel they must be critical or others will never improve.

- Parents think they need to criticize their children or they will never grow up to be responsible adults

- Bosses think they need to criticize workers or production will slip

175

▶ Teachers think they need to criticize students or they will never learn

Chu Lee's experience with her in-laws illustrates the problem: sooner or later, criticism always backfires.

Nevertheless, for some people it seems much easier to criticize and condemn than to try to understand, more natural to find fault than to praise, more useful to talk about what they want rather than what others need.

Why Criticism Is Like Acid Rain

There is a very big difference between correcting what you believe to be someone's mistakes, and criticizing them.

It is an acknowledged fact of human psychology: You cannot use criticism of a person to produce useful, positive change. You see, positive change is really a process of building up. Criticism does not work because it tears down.

Because it compromises their ability to solve problems, isolates them, increases emotional distance; and because it destroys love and marriage, erodes a person's self-esteem, ruins friendships, and creates enemies, criticism makes it more difficult—not easier!—for people to solve their personal and business problems.

So if you really have a decent respect for others, if you want to help them change for the better, never, ever criticize them.

Like acid rain, everything criticism touches—every person, every relationship—dies a little.

▶ In 8 out of 10 divorces, one or both parties say critical censure destroys love.

▶ More than half the first-line managers who quit one Fortune 500 company say a climate of destructive criticism was one main reason.

▶ Seven out of ten dysfunctional families report constant parental criticism leaves everybody feeling like a loser.

CRITICIZING OTHERS UNDERMINES MOTIVATION TO CHANGE

Now look, don't get me wrong. I am not saying that there is not a legitimate need to correct the mistakes others make in personal and business situations. Far from it. After all, things are rarely perfect for very long—at home or on the job. When something goes wrong and it needs to be changed—for instance, handling a child, winning your spouse to your way of thinking, or satisfying an irritating customer—thoughtful and empowering words can work wonders.

What I am saying is this: Criticism isn't an option. It attacks others, undermines their motivation, triggers anger, makes them more resistant, rebellious, and argumentative. There is no place for it when it comes to correcting the mistakes made by your family, friends, co-workers, and customers.

The Dirty Dozen of Personal Criticism

Mean? Vengeful? Spiteful? Nasty?

Here are 12 ways we censure others when we try to correct their mistakes with criticism.

Form of censure	Example
Negative evaluation	"You've got nobody else to blame."
Name calling	"What a dope!"
Diagnosing	"You are doing this to irritate me!"
Ordering	"Do it now!"
Moralizing	"You ought to say you are sorry!"
Interrogating	"Why didn't you . . . ?"
Diverting	"You think you've got it bad?"
Logic	"If you didn't buy the car, then . . . "
Faint praise	"I think you are smarter than that . . ."
Phoney compassion	"I know you mean well, but . . . "
Needling	"I suppose you think it's clever."
Threatening	"Do it or else . . . !"

I want to use this chapter to give you 13 workable ways to correct the mistakes people make without criticizing them personally for having made them.

Here, you will find rock-solid, time-tested methods and principles that make correcting others a positive experience for both you and the other person—a win-win proposition that works for and not against your mutual interests.

When you apply these principles at every opportunity . . .

When you use them to help you solve your daily problems . . .

When you operate on the belief that the best way to correct the mistakes of others is to get them to want to make the corrections themselves . . . you start a chain reaction in your life:

By mastering the techniques of good human relations you will find in this chapter you will give others a feeling of importance, a sense of personal worth, and a true feeling they belong.

Together, these add up to emotional security.

Emotional security makes your friends and family, your peers, superiors, and subordinates—everyone—*want* to do their very best for you.

"What's in it for me?" I can hear you say. "Sure, they get the warm fuzzies, but how about me? Where's my edge?"

When you can correct a person's mistake without criticizing them for having made it, the dividends you receive are tremendous.

The Two Enormous Benefits You Gain When You Change What They Do Instead of Attacking Who They Are

Performance, production, and profit will all improve because your subordinates will never again make the same business mistake twice in a row. Their growing respect for your judgment will lead them to accept your leadership, and your organization will always achieve the challenges issued by upper management.

"When you notice there's a pattern to the mistakes employees make, what you are seeing is not bad employees causing bad results so much as it is bad managers," reports Washington, D.C. organizational consultant Harold Ivans, 47. "A good manager shows the worker he's got a stake in instantly changing the way he does something, so mistakes in a well-managed environment are one-time events. When managers fail to correct their people on a timely basis, they get people into a bad rut—which is nothing more than a grave open at both ends."

Remember, abilities wither under criticism but blossom with encouragement. Correcting the mistakes of others in ways they can accept and act on immediately motivates people around you to perform not merely up to your expectations but up to their full business potential.

The emotional security you project by understanding that mistakes are really learning opportunities will make your family and social relationships ever so much stronger. The people you cherish most will give you their willing cooperation and loyal support, and you will know in a new way what it feels like to belong.

"If you are not making mistakes, you are not alive, is what I tell my kids," reports New Brunswick, N.J. mother Zina Janssen, 34. "Life's not about mistakes. It's all about what you do about mistakes. You get a choice: use them to help you get smart or allow yourself to be their victim. Learning becomes a lot less painful and it makes kids more willing to try new things."

Simply by helping her children discover new and wonderful ways of looking at how they do the things they do, Zina more than corrects their mistakes: she encourages their active participation in family life.

ARE YOU A HALL OF FAME CORRECTOR?

To help you improve your ability to correct others at home and on the job, the first thing we need is an honest assessment of your strengths and weaknesses.

Below you will find 10 brief statements. After reading each, you will be asked to make a choice. Just check the response that, in your judgment, is the better approach.

1. The one thing that, more than anything else, determines success in correcting others is:

   ❏ A. How carefully you choose the words you speak and how well you speak them.

   ❏ B. The importance to you of your relationship with the person being corrected.

2. When you discover a mistake, the best thing to ask is,

   ❏ A. Who did it?

   ❏ B. What happened?

3. The best time to correct 99 out of 100 mistakes is

   ❏ A. When they happen.

   ❏ B. When you are ready to make the corrections.

4. You are feeling some anger about the person you are correcting—someone in your business or personal life. The rule you must follow when this happens is:

   ❑ A. Express your anger in the kindest way you can, but express it.

   ❑ B. Cool your jets.

5. In business as well as at home, it is a good idea to get the person you are correcting to relax. People who are relaxed are always more receptive. In trying to relax others, the best thing to do is:

   ❑ A. Talk about how well they look or how much they have achieved.

   ❑ B. Talk about things like religion and sports.

6. Sessions in which you correct others need to be controlled, that is for sure. The best way to keep control is to speak in which order?

   ❑ A. You speak first?

   ❑ B. You let him take the lead?

7. The way you serve up a correction has a lot to do with its acceptance. Is it better, do you think, to:

   ❑ A. Tell the other person, in an unemotional yet thoughtful way, what is plainly wrong?

   ❑ B. Tell the other person what is right twice as much as you tell them what is wrong?

8. Many people don't know what to do to overcome a mistake. For their sakes and yours, it is always better to

   ❑ A. Lead them step-by-step to exactly what you want.

   ❑ B. Give them two alternatives.

9. Body language is an important part of the correction process. So is tone of voice. When you are correcting someone, it helps if the pace at which you speak is

❏ A. Normal?

❏ B. Slower?

10. To close out the correction, it's wise to:

❏ A. Reaffirm the message has been received and understood

❏ B. End on a positive note?

Now that you have completed the exercise, simply add up the number of "B" answers.

A score of 10 or none means you are either a Hall of Fame corrector or your ability to bring about useful change without rousing resentment is nil. Either way, I strongly urge you to read on. These pages, with their 13 workable ways to change what people do without attacking them for having done it, will either polish your skills further or lead you out of your slump.

A total of between one and nine "B" answers suggests you are sensitive to some of the issues of correcting others but not to all of them. Each "A" answer is an area you need to work on. If you will bear these in mind as you read on, you'll discover practical and specific techniques to overcome each and every one of your weaknesses.

THIRTEEN WORKABLE WAYS TO CHANGE WHAT PEOPLE DO . . . WITHOUT AROUSING RESENTMENT

Technique 1: How to Tell When to Correct Others

Your first goal is to determine if a correction is in order. The cardinal rule you must follow, almost without exception, is this: Unless there is a bond of relationship between you and the person making the mistake—slight or tight, business or personal—you might as well save your breath.

If you do not wish to relate to the person (even if only in a remote way), you can bet the person will not be interested in relating to the changes you want.

I know there are times when you see something wrong, when you see a mistake being made, and the consequences of allowing the mistake to continue are serious. The best thing to do in that situation—the only intelligent thing to do—is step in with a question, "What's up?"

But aside from urgent situations that require you to get to the bottom of things in a hurry, there's always time to consider whether it's useful to seek change.

Let me illustrate the point with a quick example.

"For years I tried to figure out if it was better to get him to change the things he did, or to just walk away. In the end, I gave up," reports recently divorced Chicago commodities broker Jenny-Lou Pullem, 38. "I got so tired of being patient I just wore out all the interest in him I ever had. When there was nothing more I wanted from him, the relationship was over. What's the sense of asking for something you don't care about anymore?"

The point I am making here is as simple (and as complicated) as this:

Before you can bring about change you've got to want to use it to strengthen the relationship—no matter if the relationship is with someone you love or someone you lead.

Remember, if the person doesn't matter neither will a change. Find a way to make the person matter.

Technique 2: How to Tell the Difference Between a Mistake and a Condition

Mistakes and conditions require different responses. I learned a long time ago to tell the difference between a mistake and a condition. My teacher was a grizzled old coot named Ed Barthelmere. He was copy editor on the daily that gave me my first newspaper job at the *Geneva Daily Times*.

It was my first day, and I was on rewrite.

Ringling Brothers was in town. A tragic and devastating fire struck the big top. Hundreds were injured. Several people were killed. Some circus animals had to be destroyed. My copy was as uncertain as the breaking story lines—full of "believed to be's."

I had no more gotten the lead into the copy editor's slot when Barthelmere was a looming presence at my desk, my marked-up lead in hand.

"Son, when you misspell "believe" once, that's a mistake. When you do it twice, well I'd say that it's getting to be a habit. But when you misspell it three different ways in four lines, what we've got here isn't a mistake or even a habit, it's a condition. Now I don't know there's a market for any working reporters with conditions, so maybe you'd prefer to take care of it from now on before it gets to me!"

Handing back my lead, he left me with a clear and abiding awareness of the difference between a mistake and a condition. A mistake is a one-time event. It happens. It can be corrected. A condition is a mistake with a broken chromosome. It happens. And it happens. And it keeps on happening—a growing cancer!

When you confront a condition, it is well to remember that nothing—but nothing—happens for nothing.

People repeat their mistakes not just because it's by rote but because they get something out of it . . . perhaps something as simple (and spitefully self-defeating) as showing that the people in charge don't know it all.

It's up to you to figure out what they get out of doing what doesn't work. Once you do, the rest is a piece of cake. All you have to do is to relate the changes you want to their stake in the situation.

Technique 3: Look to Create Solutions, Not Victims

The key is to mentally separate people from their behavior, to accept the person but reject what he or she has done. The only possible way to do this is to focus on events instead of personalities. For instance, when you confront a mistake, never ask who did what. The minute you do, you tell people you intend to identify a mistake with a person. Because that makes it risky for people to be open with you, the possibility of change is instantly choked off. The whole idea is make the mistake go away. The trick is to take personalities out of the equation, to defuse the situation, to show everyone your focus is entirely on the mistake itself. How do you do that? With the simplest, most obvious questions: What's up?, or, What happened?

"The crew on this beach believes in professionalism," reports Los Angeles lifeguard Kevin Brokin, 23. "If we're called to a situation, you can bet somebody's made a mistake. We don't care who did it; we need to know, Hey, what's going on?"

Kevin is in the business of correcting life-threatening mistakes. When he is on the job, he's more concerned with events than with personalities. His experience confirms what I have been saying all along—what you want are facts, not scapegoats.

Technique 4: Go Slow to Hurry Up

Unless an urgent situation requires on-the-spot correction—for instance, your toddler is about to follow an errant basketball rolling down your driveway towards traffic, or QC alerts you: A batch of bad product is about to go out the door—do not be too quick to seek change.

Let me give you a couple of illustrations to nail down the point.

"Jumping right in on the case when speed is uncalled for is like crying wolf—people figure when everything is made to seem urgent nothing really is," reports Louisiana small businessman Ben Arlen, 44. "Upshot? You lose credible authority among the very people you are supposed to be leading."

Ben's point is one reason why it is a good idea to go fast by going slow.

THREE TIMES YOU MUST NEVER CORRECT OTHERS

1. When you are angry at the person for having made the mistake, angry over the consequences of the mistake, or just plain angry

2. When you've got a lot on your mind and correcting someone is going to require more time than you think you can easily afford

3. When you feel pressure from others that has nothing to do with the mistakes you wish to deal with now

---

Here's another example.

"We often feel let down—you could even say, betrayed—by some of the mistakes other people make." reports Kansas industrial psychologist Julie Browerstein, 30. "These inner feelings produce mental tensions we may not even be aware we have. Even if you control the tensions, you can't make them go away. They linger and fade. It takes a little time."

How much time?

That of course depends on the situation: you want to make your corrections on a timely basis rather than on a hurried one. Generally, the more important the correction, the more time you must give yourself.

"I've developed a little rating scale from 1 to 10 to tell me how much time I can allow to pass before correcting a mistakes," reports Sid Van Umberg, 34, a high school athletic coach in Detroit. "A student drops a pass—that's a 1, and I give myself an hour. When a kid has a bad attitude it is a 10—and I wait overnight to be sure I don't over- or under-react."

What Van Umberg is saying is this. You come up with better solutions—changes others will more readily buy into—when you arrive at them feeling comfortable than when you're feeling under pressure.

Now I know you are going to say you've been taught that the best time to correct a mistake is the moment it happens. To tell you the truth, that kind of thinking works fine when you are dealing with the limited intelligence of dogs and the artificial intelligence of robots.

Barring an emergency, humans—folks like you and me, with active imaginations and the ability to recall events—need some time to let emotions quiet themselves down.

That's why I want you to allow yourself plenty of time to come to a clear idea of exactly what you want changed, the results you expect *before you speak with the person who made the mistake.*

Take as much time as you can reasonably afford. Going slow will get you where you want to go in a hurry.

Technique 5: Cool Your Jets

Some recovery gurus are fond of saying that, for the sake of honesty, the only way to deal with anger is to get it off your chest, let the other person know. I say these gurus are wrong, and here is why. Anger will push you to say things that cross the line between being honest, which is good, and being brutal—which is not.

Brutal confrontation invariably begets anger. Instead of working to correct someone's mistakes, your anger is certain to provoke argument. Instead of reasonable people trying to come to a meeting of the minds, what you are left with is two tempers far too hot to arrive at anything constructive.

"My ex-boss lost his temper and chewed me out when I didn't have it coming," reports Phoenix production manager Herb Williford, 29. "He did that to a lot of people. I never forgave him. From the way things sorted out, he must have made a lot more enemies than friends."

When you are helping someone correct a weakness or overcome a problem, the ironclad rule you must always follow, without exception, is this: You must never, ever lose your temper.

I'm not saying it is against the law to think angry thoughts—after all, it is only human.

I am saying that just because you feel something doesn't mean you have to express it. Let's put it this way: Cool out to get more of what you want in the way of change.

Technique 6: Put Yourself on the Same Team

When you and the person you are correcting share some of the same business or personal values, everybody's more relaxed, trusting, and open to change.

What you want is cooperation, not revolution. When you appeal to shared values, you put yourself on their team, change the mentality of the conversation from "us-against-them" to "us."

Shared business values might include:

▶ Loyalty

▶ The bottom line

▶ Empowered employees

▶ Initiative

Shared personal values might include:

▶ Philosophy of life

▶ Religion

▶ Leisure interests

▶ Family

"My teenage son really cares about the family so when he missed a week's contribution to our family's Caribbean camping-trip fund, I didn't want to sound like a bill collector," reports Arne Bildersson, 39, from Edmonton, Alberta. "I had a way for him to make it up but I wanted it to come out like his idea. I said we were working for the same thing, snorkeling and diving the reef off Grand Cayman. He came up with a couple of good ideas and everything worked out hunky dory."

Arne aligned with his son's values before anything else was said. He put himself and his son on the same team. This made it easier for his son to overcome his mistake, to work out a change for the better.

Technique 7: Let Them Speak First

The reason you correct a situation is so it will not happen again. Sometimes, you can get that by simply allowing the other person to speak first.

"Thank God it wasn't worse—my daughter was drying her hair at pool side and she got an electrical shock. I came running," reports Santa Barbara civil engineer Lorna Ward, 37. "I didn't have to say anything because, as I walked up to give her a hug, she said, 'Oh, Mommy, I forgot to put my sandals on and I got zapped. I'll never forget again, I promise.'"

Even if the person you wish to correct is not as forthcoming as Lorna's daughter, it is still a very good idea to get him to speak first—to ventilate the tension he is feeling.

Most people are anxious to unload—to tell you what happened and why. They want you to understand and will talk readily when you give them the chance.

If a person seems reluctant to speak first, you may have to draw him out. Here, questions are the answer. Your questions should convey a sense of appreciation for the information the other person makes available to you. Even though you may be impatient to get to the heart of things, give the other person's response the time and attention it deserves.

Here are some guidelines to follow when asking questions:

▸ Make your questions easy to understand.

▸ Phrase them in language everybody understands.

▸ Use them to cover one point at a time.

▸ Start with questions that are easy to answer.

Everybody enjoys giving answers they know are right. That's why your first question must be one you are confident he can answer effortlessly, e.g., "What's up?"

Follow with questions that cannot be answered with a fact.

Once answers are flowing easily, frame your succeeding questions to get the other person to talk at length about the topic at hand rather than provide a simple "yes" or "no".

For instance, "Why do you suppose the automatic collator hung up? Got any ideas on how to get it up and running?"

As the conversation develops, feedback to the other person your understanding of what he is saying. Structure the feedback in question form. For example, "Am I right in saying that you think the root cause was a broken timing motor?" If he agrees, move on to the next topic. If he disagrees, allow and encourage him to give you more information by prefacing his key thought with the words, "What about," as in "What about the basic input/output drive?"

When you ask questions, you give the person a chance to unload, and it is likely they will reveal the real reason for the mistake. This gives you the chance to take the corrective steps that will prevent it from recurring.

Technique 8: Build a Sandwich

The psychology of correcting others in ways that are useful and positive is this: It is always easier to listen to unpleasant things after we hear some praise.

The key is to praise the person at the same time you are pointing out a mistake that needs to be corrected.

"I call it my sandwich technique," reports Dobbs Arlington, 42, a software programmer, from Indianapolis. "My sandwich is a slab of criticism between two slices of praise. It begins when I tell the person how good she is, how pleased I am with her work—except for this small point. But then I quickly add that, when this gets fixed up, I know she will do even better."

Praising first before you correct the mistake and again afterwards, too, makes the process of correction foolproof.

FOUR WAYS TO PUT THE SANDWICH TECHNIQUE TO WORK AT HOME AND ON THE JOB

- ▶ "Rosemarie, your report card is so much better than last term, I am really proud of your progress. The only grade that's still off is advanced algebra, but, seeing all the progress you've been making, I know you can bring that one into line . . . "

- ▶ "Arnold, I know you've been working on ways to improve order entry, and I am grateful for the results we've been getting. I'd like to suggest one thing that will improve things even more."

▶ "Mary, your desktop publishing is better than we've ever had around here before. The work is neat, your proofreading is excellent, but I did find three small errors in the last brochure. I know you'd like to see your work free of defects, so I wondered if you had considered . . . "

▶ John, I know in my heart you love me and that makes me very happy. But there's something I'd like you to consider that I know will make our relationship an even stronger one . . . "

When you sandwich a slice of correction between two slices of praise, unpleasantries are made to appear minimal and the good things people do will be reinforced while the poorer shrivel up from lack of attention.

The key is balance: make your praise as pertinent as the faults you are out to correct.

Technique 9: Correct One Mistake at a Time

If you overload people with corrections, you either make it impossible for them to change, or you earn a reputation as a nag.

"I always stick to one mistake at a time," reports Greenville, South Carolina's Jean DiBlassi, who works in product development. "Next week, next month, next year—there's plenty of time to get to the rest. And by then, who knows? Things might take care of themselves."

Jean's lesson is mighty important if you want to get people to change.

It suggests several useful guidelines:

▶ Don't bring up mistakes from the past that have already been corrected.

▶ Pick the most important current mistake and work on that.

▶ After the person has made the necessary corrections, call another session to deal with the next most important thing.

Technique 10: When People Get Stuck, Offer a Choice

There are moments when, despite your best efforts, the conversation stalls because the other person cannot figure out what to do to correct his or her mistake.

To get the momentum going again, offer the person a choice of two alternatives—either one of which gets you what you want.

For instance:

▶ "Would you rather get the changes made by Friday and have the weekend free, or wait until Monday morning?

▶ "Would you prefer to let the customer know, or do you think it might be better to let the person whose account it is get in touch?

"Even if neither alternative is exactly what they want, they feel better when they can make the choice," reports market researcher Harold Steinberg, 44, who works in Fairfield, Connecticut. "They may not be able to choose what gets done but they get a strong say in how, and that makes people more comfortable about making the changes I want."

When you give them a choice between two alternatives, either of which works for you, people are more likely to change their ways.

Technique 11: Talk Body Language

When you are correcting someone, the way you move, gesture, sit, smile, and look at others can make a very big difference.

Here are several guidelines:

▶ Keep your hands still.

▶ Make every movement count.

▶ Keep the pitch and pace of your voice down by speaking at a slightly-slower-than-normal conversational rate—about 100 words a minute instead of the usual 125 to 150.

▶ Face the person squarely, lean forward slightly.

▶ Make eye contact about 60 to 70 percent of the time, focusing on a point between their brows and slightly above the bridge of the nose.

▶ Smile to establish and maintain a friendly connection.

It is a scientific fact that what your body says is at least as important as your words. Controlling your gestures, movement, and posture helps give others the confirmation they need to be certain the changes you are talking about are the ones you really want.

Technique 12: Close on a Positive Note

You always want to close out a correcting session by leaving the person with the idea that he has been helped and not hurt by your efforts.

"I make a point of closing with a verbal pat on the back," reports high school principal Arlen Hatcher, 39, of Grand Junction, Colorado. "I want the student's last memory of the session to be positive so that he will seek to better himself from here on out."

The whole idea is to find something the person did or does that deserves an accolade. Among the things you might close on:

▶ The overall value of his or her contribution to the organization

▶ A specific act that merits a good word

▶ A generally praiseworthy pattern of performance

▶ An appeal to the person's demonstrated strength

Never let a correcting session end on a sour note.

Technique 13: Praise, Praise, Praise

If you will train yourself to be more eager to praise than to find fault, people will always perform to the full extent of their talents and abilities.

"I praise the slightest improvement and I praise every improvement," reports Holly Krausher, 29, who works with educationally handicapped men and women in the Baltimore area. "It's like candy—they always want more and will do everything in their power to get it. The more they get, the fewer the mistakes I am called on to correct."

Before we close out the topic of getting others to change without arousing their resentment, let me quickly give you a recap of the 13 techniques I've just discussed.

1. However slight, unless there is a bond of relationship between you and the person you are correcting, you might as well save your breath.

2. If you come up against a habit of mistakes, it is up to you to figure out what they get out of doing over and over what doesn't work. Then, you must relate the changes you want to their stake in the situation.

3. You must always look to create solutions, not victims.

4. Except in emergencies which require immediate action, do not be too quick to seek change.

5. When correcting someone, the ironbound rule you must follow without exception is, never lose your temper.

6. When you and the person you are correcting share personal or business values, changes come about more easily.

7. Give them the opportunity to speak first.

8. Use the sandwich technique to praise twice as much as find fault.

9. Correct one mistake at a time.

10. Offer people a choice of two alternatives—either of which work for you.

11. Use body language to help get your message across.

12. Close the correcting session on a positive note.

13. If you train yourself to praise at the slightest improvement and to praise every improvement, you will be called on to correct fewer mistakes.

How to Work Miracles

The art of leadership is to bring out the best in others.

Helping people overcome their mistakes helps them grow to the outer limits of their talents and abilities. It requires patience and determination, but most of all, praise.

Praise inspires others to realize their latent strengths, encourages them to blossom under encouragement.

In this chapter, we've taken up the techniques that will get people to want to change their ways. Next, we'll focus on words and phrases that work miracles. Watch, when you turn the page, as a butcher's boy gives you a magic phrase guaranteed to satisfy your customers and put money in the till.

CHAPTER 10

WORD POWER

Fourteen Workable Ways to Crumble Barriers, Turn Disappointment to Success, and Convert Impossible Dreams to Realities

"Two pounds of flank steak, please."

Between college semesters and over summers, I worked in my father's butcher shop. I quickly discovered that cuts of meat rarely fell into pound or half-pound measures. Yet customers always asked for specific weights.

I'd read the scale and say, "That's two-pounds, seven-ounces—is that alright?"

"No, I want two pounds."

I'd have to trim here and there until I got the order to weigh out exactly. My father was patient. He asked me to watch him work. The next customer asked for four pounds of lamb for stew.

He made the cut, put it on the scale. It weighed four-pounds, three-ounces. He didn't say that to the customer, though.

"That comes to $5.48. What else can I get you?"

"Perfect," replied the customer.

I never mentioned weight after that, just the amount and the words, "What else can I get you?"

- -
Big Words Are Less Important than Effective Ones

The first person in my family ever to have gone to college, and I was top in my class. But when it came to six everyday words that worked magic on Pop's customers, I was too educated to be smart.

Take it from someone who has been there: you really don't need to sound like a walking dictionary to get what you want from other people.

And here's conclusive proof: Most conversation is built on ordinary words you've heard before. According to linguists, less than 200 words make up about 95 percent of everything we say in the course of a day.

So, it figures: To communicate better you don't need Sunday words. You just need to learn to use the everyday ones better.

"Avoid the elaborate, the pretentious, the coy, and the cute," one Pulitzer Prize author advises. "Do not be tempted by a $20 word when there is a 10-center handy, ready, and able."

The goal of communications is clarity. We speak to make ourselves understood. A good vocabulary is one that helps you get your point across in ways other people can understand instantly.

EVEN COMPLEX IDEAS NEED SIMPLE WORDS

Although Baseball Hall of Famer Yogi Berra quit school at the age of 16, several books of notable quotes recognize the powerful expression of his World Series management style in simple, one- and two-syllable words:

▶ "It ain't over 'til it's over."

▶ "You can observe a lot just by watching."

▶ "Baseball is 90 percent hard work and the other half ain't easy."

THREE REASONS TO DEVELOP WORD POWER

If you intend to be as successful in your conversations with people at home and on the job as Yogi, my father, and millions of others, you must be able to use words that let others know you are smart, persuasive, and informed.

Knowing which words to use and how to use them are the keys to getting the most out of your intelligence.

I can think of three compelling reasons to develop your word power:

▶ *You want a better job.* Most employers are looking for people with strong word skills.

▶ *You want to make a better social impression.* Nobody wants friends who don't know what they are saying.

▶ *You want your opinion to count in family and community matters.* Knowing which words to use makes you more influential, gives you a greater say in the way things are done.

WORD POWER = WINNING

When you are the master of your words, people listen.

That's because they judge you—your background and your future—by what you say. To them, your words are you! Say memorable words . . . and you rivet and hold attention. Say persuasive words . . . and you sell opinions, ideas, products. Any way you say it, say it clearly, vividly . . . and your words sell you.

Whatever your field, whatever your goals in life and career, word power is synonymous with winning. That is why I want this chapter to show you several things.

First, I want to give you 191 words guaranteed to move minds your way, to get others to do what you want when you want it.

Then, along with your library of words that work, I want you to have the fastest, easiest, and by far the best way to steadily build it up in the most natural way possible—with no special research or extra effort on your part whatsoever.

And third, I want to show you how to leverage word power to crumble barriers, turn disappointments to success, convert impossible dreams into hard realities, and develop the inner confidence it takes to guide and control each and every one of your conversations—be they business or social.

- -
Two Extraordinary Benefits Are Yours for a Lifetime When You Make Word Power Your Personal Calling Card

No matter what line of work you are in or where you earn your daily bread, once you know how to use words to serve your thoughts and ideas, your earnings will increase tremendously, you'll get the respect and recognition of your colleagues and customers, and promotions will come your way faster and faster.

"I was still in the tool-and-die shop, going to school nights, but I had my eye on a management job," reports Ugo Chiulli, 36, who now runs a machine-tool company in Cincinnati, Ohio. "I wasn't the only one. Other people had credentials as good—maybe even a little better than mine. It all came down to how I came across."

Employers are always looking for signs of leadership potential. They want people who are strong, determined, persuasive—people who get what they want. Your words tell the boss, This person is going places. Because an effective vocabulary gets noticed, all other things being equal, promotions always go to the standouts who have a way with words.

As you translate your ideas, thoughts, and plans into words and phrases that are clear, vivid, and instantly understood, your family, your friends—even your most casual acquaintances—will pay closer attention to what you say, interrupt less, and cooperate always. By placing your verbal skills at the service of family values and friendship, there is absolutely no limit on how strong your relationships can become.

"My pastor was making a sermon and quoted Matthew—the part that goes, 'Thy speech betrayeth thee.' As I walked out of church with the family, I kept thinking about the love I felt for the children and my husband, and that biblical quote," reports Houston's Doreen McAllister, 39, a nurse-practitioner. "It made me see that I've got to put more effort into being as clear as I can—not to confuse my family with my words."

Doreen's point is this: When you are unclear about telling others what you want and expect —when your words fail to make your needs and desires clearly heard and respected—you betray your relationships with the most important people in your life.

It's a lose-lose proposition: You lessen your chances for the sharing and caring that nourish love; they are robbed of the chance to be full partners in your dreams and hopes. That's what makes word power so very important in your personal life.

It gives you the means to express yourself fully and freely, get your intentions across, and produce the results you want—all at the same time you maintain and nourish strong personal connections.

TEST YOUR WORD POWER

If you don't have the words, how much good can your ideas deliver?

Knowing which words to use, and how and when to use them, is the key to getting the most out of your own mind.

Improve your ability to translate your thoughts into words and you automatically increase your chances of getting what you want at home and on the job.

To give you an idea of your word power, I've prepared an exercise.

Below, in the column on the left, you will find twelve fairly common words. Match each word in the first column with its definition in the second column.

1.	abash	_____	a.	libel or slander
2.	banal	_____	b.	unoriginal
3.	capitulate	_____	c.	unjustified
4.	defame	_____	d.	even-handed
5.	ebullient	_____	e.	place side-by-side
6.	frugal	_____	f.	lively, active
7.	gratuitous	_____	g.	bequest
8.	hiatus	_____	h.	interruption
9.	impartial	_____	i.	penny pinching
10.	juxtapose	_____	j.	embarrass
11.	kinetic	_____	k.	bubbling with excitement
12.	legacy	_____	l.	surrender

Now that you have completed the exercise, simply compare your answers with this list:

Answers: 1. j, 2. b, 3. l, 4. a, 5. k, 6. i, 7. c, 8. h, 9. d 10. e, 11. f, 12. g

Three or more errors indicates a strong and immediate need to develop your word power.

Please don't try to read this chapter in a single sitting. You'll learn more in less time if you tackle it one technique at a time. Please pay special attention to techniques one through four. These will give you the basic, everyday words you need to revolutionize your vocabulary. But don't consider these lists final or all-inclusive. Use them instead as a foundation for the more advanced techniques you will find further on.

Fewer than three errors indicates fairly good vocabulary skills, but with room for development. If you are reading this chapter to polish a good vocabulary, you are certain to find my more advanced techniques, dealing with extending your word power, of special interest.

One Hundred and Ninety-One Power Words That Work

Technique 1: Activate Your Verbs

People with word power speak with active verbs—words that directly express action. What's the difference between an active and a passive verb?

Active is, "Sales *increased* 16 percent last quarter."

Passive is, "Sales were *increased* 16 percent last quarter."

Thoughts expressed in active verbs sound better, hence are easier to grasp. And because they are inherently more energetic, they add lift to your thought.

To animate your conversation, I've prepared a list of simple verbs you can use to describe anything. These must be in your everyday vocabulary—you must know what these mean and be able to use them freely.

ONE HUNDRED AND SEVEN POWER VERBS

Ache	Break	Close	Hate
Act	Bring	Come	Have
Add	Buy	Cover	Hear
Aim	Call	Crawl	Help
Ask	Can	Cut	Hide
Bear	Carry	Go	Hold
Begin	Catch	Happen	Hunt
Bind	Check	Handle	Hurt
Blow	Claim	Hang	Keep

Kick	Pitch	Shut	Test
Know	Plan	Sit	Think
Lay	Play	Skip	Throb
Lean	Poke	Slip	Throw
Leave	Press	Smell	Tie
Let	Pull	Split	Touch
Lie	Push	Stab	Try
Like	Put	Stand	Turn
Look	Raise	Start	Twist
Lose	Reach	Stay	Upset
Make	Run	Stick	Use
Mark	Say	Stir	Walk
Mean	See	Stop	Want
Mind	Sell	Strike	Watch
Move	Seem	Take	Wear
Owe	Set	Talk	Whirl
Pick	Shake	Tear	Work
Pin	Show	Tell	

When you use these simple verbs, everything you say will take on greater force. Like it or don't, they force you to be direct, concrete, and specific.

Once you've mastered this basic list, it is a good idea to breathe even more life into what you say. I'll give you a plan to do just that later in this chapter. But first, let me start you off with,

SEVEN MORE ACTIVE VERBS

Adulterate: *to make something impure,* e.g., Water adulterates gasoline.

Connive: *to plot against,* e.g., When industry and government regulators connive, laws are sure to be broken.

Discern: *to see,* e.g., Art critics can discern the quality of a painting.

Extrapolate: *to forecast by using past experience,* e.g., Meteorologists extrapolate expected weather patterns from field data.

Improvise: *to create ad lib,* e.g., When a set play is blown, basketball players need to improvise.

Peruse: *to study carefully,* e.g., Lawyers peruse contracts.

Spurn: *to reject with contempt or to refuse,* e.g., She spurned his advances.

Technique 2: Make Your Nouns Vivid and Specific

The secret of good communication is this: The more vivid the word picture you paint in your listener's mind, the more likely he is to accept and act on your thinking. Vividness is achieved by choosing nouns that are direct, concrete and descriptive. For instance, take the noun that describes where you live.

House creates a general picture; *shack, mansion, colonial*—these generate more definite images.

When your listeners can focus on a definite picture of what you have in mind, you capture their interest, and the likelihood of getting your idea across increases.

There are thousands of nouns in the English language if you don't count personal names, more if you do. Which ones are right for you depend on your lifestyle, the kind of work you do, the sorts of people you come into contact with, and so on.

It will be up to you to build your own personal library of vivid nouns—and further along in this chapter I'll give you a foolproof, three-step plan. First, I wanted you to have six of my favorites.

SIX VIVID NOUNS

Amenity: *an attractive or comfortable feature,* e.g., The amenities at my exercise gym include a steam bath and a swimming pool.

Attrition: *decrease in number or size,* e.g., Attrition is what happens when a company does not replace workers who quit, transfer, or die.

Bigot: *narrow-minded, opinionated person,* e.g., Religious bigots often advocate anti-Semitism.

Duplicity: *deception to hide the truth,* e.g., Abraham Lincoln, not known for his looks, stood accused of political duplicity. To his attackers he said, "If you were as two-faced as you say of me, tell me now, honestly, Would you present this one?"

Logistics: *managing the details of supplying anything to anybody,* e.g., The logistics of Operation Desert Storm were staggering.

Rage: *a form of anger that has a beginning and a middle but
                    never an end*, e.g., The smoldering rage of black America
                    counts more victims than victories.

Technique 3: Add a Splash of Color

What's the difference between "reject" and "blackball?"

No one can say for sure. There is nothing wrong, really, with any
word—all are good. But, in certain situations, some are better than
others. Everybody knows blackball adds oomph to what reject says,
makes it memorable. What nobody seems to be able to explain is,
why?

All the neuro-scientists can tell us is words linked to colors seem
easier to picture. Here are 12 ways words can be linked to color. As you
read the list, imagine how color might enter your vocabulary.

A RAINBOW OF TWELVE WORDS THAT WORK

black hole	grey matter
black magic	greenbelt
blackmail	greenhorn
blue blood	redneck
blue chip	red tape
golden rule	whitewash

Technique 4: Use Words to Create Pictures

Words that conjure up definite, concrete pictures, whether verbs or
nouns, do more to get your message across than words that merely
describe something.

For instance, if you talk about a person who never lends money to
anyone, the first word to come to mind might be cheap. Others might
include stingy, tight, frugal, penurious, and so on—all of which are
legitimate. The trouble is, none of them really captures and conveys a
true picture of the person.

So what's the right word?

"My last fare squeezed nickels so hard the buffalo gave milk,"
reports Duane Helmas, 29, a professional musician who drives a New
York taxicab to make ends meet. "That's five times worse than a
penny-pincher."

Like Duane, you must choose your words carefully to capture and convey the essence of your thought. Here is a list of 25 of my favorite picture words. Later in this chapter, you'll learn how to add to it in ways that require almost no effort at all.

TWENTY-FIVE WORDS TO CREATE INSTANT MENTAL PICTURES

axe	hush
backbite	icy
commotion	jitterbug
dawn	keen
eclipse	lullaby
false alarm	murmuring
gobble	numb
oaf	unlock
partition	verve
quiver	waver
racket	yawn
spasm	zest
tranquil	

Technique 5: Ten Vocabulary Errors You Must Avoid at All Costs

Most vocabulary errors involve everyday words so familiar hardly anyone thinks of looking them up.

Here, as reported by the Educational Testing Company, the people who prepare and administer the Scholastic Aptitude Test, are 10 of the most common usage errors.

Among/Between: *Among is used with three or more, between is used with two,* e.g., Among the nine senators . . . Between you and me.

Anxious/Eager: *Anxious means fearful or filled with anxiety, eager means urgent interest,* e.g., I was anxious about my medical exam but eager to attend the party.

Can/May: *Can means you are able, may means you are allowed,* e.g., You can do it if you are able but unless you have permission, you may not.

**Compare To/
Compare With:**   *Compare to suggests likeness, compare with suggests difference,* e.g., My voice compares to Jeff's, but compares with Frank Sinatra's.

**Different From/
Different Than:**   *Different from is correct,* e.g., My house is different from yours.

**Each Other/
One Another:**   *Each other is used with two, one another to distinguish three or more,* e.g., Twins should love each other but teams need to get along with one another.

Farther/Further: *Farther refers to distance that can be measured, further refers to distance that cannot be measured,* e.g., I live farther than the town limits, I've taken the relationship further than a movie date.

Fewer/Less: *Fewer refers to numbers, less refers to quantity,* e.g., I use fewer lumps because I own less sugar.

Former/Latter: *Former refers to the first of two or more, latter to the second,* e.g., Of the two ideas, I agree with the former but disagree with the latter.

Lay/Lie: *To lay is to place or set, to lie refers to resting in a horizontal position,* e.g., Now I lay me down to sleep, but my golf ball lies in the rough.

Technique 6: Thirteen Computer Words and Phrases You Must Know to Survive

ASCII: (Pronounced, asky) *A code system to transfer data that most computers can read and write to.*

Boot: *To start a computer.*

Bug: *An error in a program.*

Chip: *A series of microscopic, linked switches embedded in silicon wafer, the heart of a computer.*

DOS: (Pronounced dahs) *Disk Operating System,* the basic software that sets up the computer to run word processing, spreadsheets, and other programs.

Hard Disk: (Also called **Hard Drive**) *An internal means to store the data your computer is intended to massage.*

Hardware: *Chips, drives, keyboards, modems, monitors, mouses, printers, scanners and other fixed parts of a computer.*

I/O: *Input/Output* Input is what you say to the computer, output is what it says back.

Laser Printer: *Prints documents using an internal laser similar to the ones used in photocopiers.*

Modem: *Connects computers by telephone line.*

RAM: *Random Access Memory,* the memory you can access.

ROM: *Read Only Memory,* the memory containing instructions and data that cannot be accessed or changed.

Software: *Computer programs* including, but not limited to, data base management, spreadsheets, word processing, utilities, and more.

Technique 7: Eleven Business Words and Phrases You Must Know to Survive

APR: *Annual Percentage Rate,* the true interest rate of a loan when all costs are taken into account

Asset: *Something with positive value,* as opposed to a liability, which is something you owe

Bankruptcy: *A legal means of discharging debt which requires deeply indebted people or companies give up assets*

Capital: *Money used to found a business or make an investment*

Capital Gain: *The difference between the amount of capital invested and the amount of profit realized*

**Compound
Interest:**   *Interest paid on interest previously paid*

Dividend:	*The distribution of profit*
Mortgage:	*A loan secured by real property*
Mutual Fund:	*An investment pool to permit relatively small investors to invest in various geographic and business areas of the world economy*
Price/Earnings Ratio:	*The relationship between what a stock sells for and what it earns per share*
Prime Rate:	*The rate banks charge their most creditworthy customers*
Yield:	*The amount of profit expressed as a percent of cost of an investment*

THREE STEPS TO WORD POWER: AS EASY AS GROWING UP

The simplest, best, and fastest way to learn new words is to do what children do.

For the first few days after a child hears a new word that captures his interest, he doesn't look it up, he doesn't ask a grown-up to define it, he doesn't study its origins, he doesn't make flash cards, he doesn't even try to memorize it. He simply repeats it—at the dinner table, with friends, at school.

Eventually, he comes to understand the meaning of the word by paying attention to how it is used. Adults who want to develop word power must do the same. Here is a three-step plan that is as natural as growing up:

Technique 8: Pay Attention to Context

Each and every time you encounter an unfamiliar word—it could be when you are reading a newspaper or a book, or talking with someone, or listening to a broadcast—the ironbound rule is this:

Put your mind to figuring out its meaning by thinking about the context in which the word is used.

The context includes other words in the same sentence as well as the words in the sentences that may precede or follow its use. These point toward probable meaning.

"I never heard the word "lucrative" before my friend Harriet told me her new job was so lucrative she could afford a three-week vacation," reports Eileen Cowper, 26, an office worker in Orlando, Florida. "From what she said I figured it meant well-paying."

Follow Eileen's example and you will learn new words in the natural way children do. Simply by putting your mind to work on words that attract your attention, you develop a powerful and highly effective vocabulary that correlates with success.

Technique 9: Use It or Lose It

You hear a lot of talk about how to memorize words. The one thing all these theories have in common is that they are all a pain in the keister and a waste of time. You can write it down and you can look it up but you will never remember it if you do not put a new word to immediate use. The whole idea is, once you've figured out the meaning from context, add it to your vocabulary as quickly as you can, and use it every chance you get.

"My travel agent talked about the markets in Mexico City where everybody haggles over price," reports Dick Bresciatto, 37, a dry cleaner in Simi Valley, California. "I really never heard the word haggle before, and at first it stumped me. So I mentally substituted the word bargain and it seemed to fit. Then I tried it out on a customer who complained about cost. Our prices are fixed, I said, we don't haggle."

Use new words over and over—at work, at home, out in the community. You will be amazed at how quickly they become part of you.

Technique 10: Look It Up

If you are serious about developing word power, you must eventually use the dictionary. Any dictionary will do—for most people a small paperback edition is perfect. You see, sometimes context isn't enough. Most words have several meanings or shades of meaning. It's a good idea to be familiar with all of them.

Take the word *formidable.* If the context in which you learn it refers solely to *awe-inspiring,* your understanding of the word is incomplete because it also means *frightening.*

"I didn't get mad when she called me crass because from the sense of it, I figured she meant I had bad table manners," reports Paul Knopf, 20, a Chicago transportation worker. "Later, when I found out what it really meant—gross, unfeeling, and stupid—I got pissed."

The point is, you can't understand a word unless you know its full meaning. To know it is to make a word your own.

HOW TO SUCCEED WITH WORDS

Remember Hogan's Law? I think Hogan was an optimist. I say, Anything that can be misunderstood is! That's why striving to be understood is not enough. You must be sure you are not misunderstood.

Whether you are a salesperson, manager, executive, supervisor, parent, doctor, lover, friend, or legislator, when you put your ideas into words that are unmistakably clear, you create the instant understanding that gets you what you want. That's why I want you to have three additional ways to succeed with words.

Technique 11: Speak to Express, Not Impress

Calling attention to yourself with pompous, overblown language works against you. The big idea behind human communication is to be understood, not to show a captive audience how smart you are.

Using $20 words to deliver 10¢ ideas is generally difficult to digest and sometimes downright nauseating.

"I was sort of interested in her. She asked about the 200-year-old barn I was restoring. She told me it sounded like a grimthorpe. I asked her, What's a grimthorpe? She told me to look it up," reports Harvey Ujifusa, 38, a stockbroker in Keene, New Hampshire. "It means badly remodelled. I can just imagine a relationship with her—lying in bed . . . she pops a multisyllable zinger across the pillow . . . I get up to check the dictionary. No way, Jose—what kind of a love life is that?"

If you use simple, everyday words—words everybody understands in the time it takes to speak them—people will always know what you mean right off the bat.

Look, I'm not saying there's absolutely no reason to be familiar with some pompous words. There is one, and only one: The singular reason you need to be familiar with pompous words is to understand what people are saying when they use them on you.

Speak to express, not impress, and the impress part of the conversation will always take care of itself.

Technique 12: Do Not Overstate

It is important to choose words that convey precisely the shade of meaning you intend. When you overstate things—for example, use words like *always* and *never to* describe someone else's behavior—it puts the other person on guard, makes what you say suspect in his mind. It sometimes leads to a vote of no-confidence.

"People in a crunch blow things out of proportion," reports Cleveland 911 operator Lois Meredith, 47. "I've got to feel confident that what they are saying is what is really going down before I dispatch."

Lois is not saying that it's a mistake to overstate things when a crunch comes down. She's implying it is a mistake, period!

Most words have many different meanings and, within those meanings, shades of nuance. Sometimes the difference between words is meaningless, but often it is not.

The more words you know, and the more you know about the words you know, the more choice you have in any given situation. The more choice, the less chance you will turn others off with overstatement.

Technique 13: How to Select the Perfect Word

To decide which is the right word, you need to think about three things:

▶ the idea you want to get across

▶ the intensity of it

▶ the ability of the listener to comprehend

For instance, suppose you want to describe someone who willingly gives away the shirt off his back to please others. The first word that comes to mind is *generous*—it's the general idea you want to get across. Looking up *generous* tells you that you have a choice of words:

These suggest *fertile, large, tolerant, plentiful, indulgent, liberal, hospitable, magnanimous.*

Hospitable seems to be the right general direction, so you look a little further. You find that words that convey the idea of hospitality include *receptive, welcoming, cordial, amiable, gracious, friendly, neighborly, openhearted.*

Receptive is the right word if you want the image to be passive.

Welcoming is the right word if you want the image to be of a homebody.

Cordial is the right word if you mean to suggest warmth.

Amiable is the right word if friendliness is the image you wish to capture.

Gracious is the right word if your aim is convey a sense of politeness.

Friendly seems far too-overused to be the right word.

Neighborly is the right word if what you wish to convey is a willingness to help out in tough times.

Openhearted is the right word if you mean to suggest generous in a kind way.

The word fits the situation, you will recall, when three conditions are met: When it says the right thing, with the right intensity, in a way others understand instantly.

That makes *openhearted* the word of choice.

Technique 14: Feel Words Work Harder than Think Words

There are basically two kinds of words: the kind that get people to reason something out and the ones that give people an emotional stake in the outcome. Emotional words are invariably the ones that get people to act or think or do whatever it is you wish. That's because people are ruled more by their emotions than by their logic. Because they act on their feelings, the idea is to choose words that tweak their emotions, too.

To nail down the point, let's take a look at the strong differences between the words themselves—the gap between *think* and *feel*.

Think. It's what IBM used to do. It's cold and its distant and of course, smart. It appeals right away to your head. It does what it says— it makes you think.

Ask somebody, "What do you think?" and you are sure to get logic—which is a polite way people distance themselves emotionally from what is going on in the conversation.

Ask, on the other hand, "How do you feel about X?" and you get instant head and heart.

"What do you do when your kids are 0–10 and the next game's against the best team in the division?," reports Carbondale, Illinois college soccer coach Ray Titmuss, 32. "Well, if you tell 'em to think about winning, a lot of them will also think about the odds of not winning.

That'll make things even harder. No, you gotta find a way to give them the feeling of what it might be like to win."

There is a lesson in Ray's experience for all of us—athletes and couch potatoes: what the heart can't hear, the head can't do.

Before we leave the topic of word power, I want to give you a rundown of the key points in this chapter:

1. If you use simple everyday words instead of long and complicated ones, people will be sure to understand you.

2. The best way to develop word power is not to learn a lot of Sunday words. It is to learn to use everyday words better.

3. Activate your verbs.

4. The more vivid your nouns the more likely people are to understand and act on them.

5. Words that are linked to color are easy to understand and capture the listener's instant attention.

6. It is not enough to make yourself understood. You must choose words that eliminate the possibility of misunderstanding by avoiding, at all costs, the 10 most common usage errors.

7. The three rules for learning new words are:

   ▶ Pay attention to the context in which unfamiliar words are used.

   ▶ Put new words to immediate use.

   ▶ Look up words you add to your vocabulary to be sure you understand all of their meanings and nuances.

8. Speak to express, not impress.

9. Do not overstate.

10. To decide which word is right in any given situation, think about three things:

   ▶ the idea you want to get across

   ▶ the intensity of it

   ▶ the ability of the listener to understand

11. When you have a choice of words, always go for the ones that convey emotion.

The techniques of word power, discussed with considerable detail in this chapter, are the fast route to business and personal success. They represent one of the best ways to put yourself across with people who count.

In the next chapter, I want you to see how easy it is to make your vocabulary work on paper in strong, clear, and concise letters, memoranda, and reports. The idea is to make yourself understood in writing so that you can increase your chances of becoming successful and getting ahead.

CHAPTER 11

PUTTING IT ON PAPER

Eleven Workable Ways to Write as Easily as You Talk

"Have you ever gotten the feeling your world is shrinking to the narrow confines of a rigid job description?"

Danny Lanier's note didn't look special. No fancy paper. No gimmicky letterhead. Just words . . . and not very many of them at that. But boy oh boy, what words.

Lanier's very first line evoked memories. It reminded me of the main reason I left a vice presidency in corporate America to go out on my own.

His simple, everyday language tweaked my empathy, focused my thoughts, made me want to go out of my way to help.

Lanier, 29, a Norfolk, Virginia manager, was in a dead end job. He had more brains and ability than his boss knew what to do with. He was looking to make a new connection.

The whole letter wasn't more than two or three paragraphs. It covered a one-page resume. I sent these on to my friends at Pepsi-Cola®. Within a month, they hired him. Imagine, all that from less than 100 words.

GOOD WRITING IS GOOD CONVERSATION IN PRINT

The point I make here, the meaning of Lanier's experience, is this: The written word opens doors!

Teacher, preacher, lawyer, or lawn doctor—it doesn't matter who you are, what you do, or what you want. One of the best ways to make your dreams come true is to put yourself across with clear and concise writing that is easy to understand. I am talking about writing that earns you attention, respect, prestige, influence, and yes, love.

But the prospect of writing scares a lot of people half to death. The threat of facing a blank page or computer screen raises more questions than answers:

How should I open the letter or memo?

What should I say next?

Just what information do I need to include?

How do I know what to leave out?

What closing will bring the action I want?

They know that the written word is either your best friend or your worst enemy.

It can bring you attention, promotion, admiration for your point of view . . . or the complete opposite. If putting it down on paper is a problem for you as it is for so very many others, then please be reassured: If you can speak with confidence, by the time you finish this chapter you will write with confidence . . . guaranteed! You see, I think good writing is nothing more than good conversation in print.

Read on, and you'll quickly see what I mean.

ONE SET OF SKILLS FOR ALL YOUR COMMUNICATION NEEDS

In our social lives, all of us need to put things in writing from time to time—a condolence note, a complaint about a bill, even a letter to the editor or your representative in Congress.

On the job, of course, there are all kinds of letters and memos.

The very first thing I want this chapter to show you is that good personal writing and good business writing both spring from one source—a single set of basic skills.

Because these are truly universal, you have only to learn them once. Then, no matter what form your writing takes—everything from a love letter to a logistics report—you are in complete control of the situation.

After you've mastered the basics, I want to use part of this chapter to give you still more ways, five more, to improve your business letters and memos.

And finally, I want you to have a portfolio of 17 model letters and memos you can follow and be guided by. These cover a variety of situations—a powerful sales letter, a note to express your condolences, a memo to call a meeting, and more. Many of these may require very little in the way of rewriting to make them appropriate to your situation. Others may benefit from additional editing. Either way, I want you to feel free to create your own documents by combining paragraphs from different models.

Two Phenomenal Benefits Are Yours When People Can Enjoy, Understand, Believe, and Act on Your Writing

When you handle yourself well on paper, your work will shine with all of the clarity and compelling power it takes to get others to cooperate as you wish. This is certain to enhance everyone's performance, win the favorable attention of upper management, and better your chances for getting ahead in your career.

"I recall one time many years ago when a young man relatively new with Procter & Gamble wrote a two-page memorandum proposing that our company develop and market our first liquid household cleaner," reports Edwin Artzt, P&G's CEO. "I've never forgotten that illustration of the power of good communication in the management process. With the power of two pages, he convinced the company to take a major initiative in a new business when it already controlled the market. We all felt like winners that day, believe me."

The organization you work for can be as big as P&G or as small as Mom and Pop but one thing is for sure: if it is successful, one of the hallmarks of its leadership is clear, concise business writing.

Whether it is a note for the door of your fridge or a news article for a local weekly, when your personal writing comes as easily as your conversation, your family, friends, and community will see you in a new and powerful way. They will think of you as more than just a good communicator. They will see you as a better human being, too. This is sure to strengthen the bonds between you and those to whom you are closest in life.

"I used to go away on business for a few days, and she asks if I missed her, and if I don't answer in just the right way because, hey, maybe I'm worried about something, she reacts with a quick maybe-you-don't-want-to-be-with-me-anymore," reports Hubert Burgher, 38, who works for the State of Oklahoma, out of Oklahoma City. "I finally got smart and sent her a fax my first day on the road. Can't wait to see you, I wrote. Sure made things a lot nicer to come home to. Now I make a point of faxing her a different little message every trip. It's fun thinking them up, and it gets my mind off work for a few minutes."

Isn't it amazing the power simple words take on when they are set to paper! By taking the time to put down what he'd say if he were there to say it, Hubert's humanity shines through. And that—his humanity—gets him the happy and welcoming home life he wants.

DO YOU KNOW HOW TO WRITE AS EASILY AS YOU SPEAK?

With letters and memos you can come across any way you wish—super salesperson, clever manager, charming friend, or lifetime partner.

Indeed, for many people personal and business letters, and memos, are the key to turning a career foothold into a stronghold, establishing a happy social life, securing a new job—even conducting a romance.

To determine where you stand when it comes to putting your thoughts on paper, I think it is definitely in your interest to take a look at the following exercise.

Below you will find 10 brief statements.

After reading each, you will be asked to make a choice. Just check the response that, in your judgment, is the better approach.

1. Someone on your staff violates strict policy. It's a major league offense—may even call for termination. What do you do?

   ❏ A. Get out an immediate memo to establish, for the record, the transgression.

   ❏ B. Hold off on the memo, call the person in for a counseling session?

2. Everybody knows love letters should be sincere and unselfish. But should they also be spontaneous? Or, is it a better idea to think about what your heart dictates before pouring it out?

❑ A. Good idea to think first?

❑ B. Best to be perfectly spontaneous?

3. The best way to get what you want out of writing is to:

❑ A. Mentally picture the results you want before you begin?

❑ B. Mentally picture the person you are writing to before you begin?

❑ C. Both of the above.

4. The opening sentence has two purposes. The first is to grab reader attention. The second is to set readers up to expect a benefit from reading what you have to say.

❑ A. True.

❑ B. False.

5. The very best way to make sure what you write is easy to read is:

❑ A. Say it aloud before you write it, then edit it for grammar and vocabulary?

❑ B. Say it aloud before you write it, then put it down just the way you said it?

6. The best way to check your writing is to look for which of the following:

❑ A. Check the way ideas flow, make sure they are easy to read?

❑ B. Cross out words, sentences, even paragraphs if they don't add to meaning?

❑ C. All of the above.

❑ D. None of the above.

7. The very best way to show your interest in the person who will be reading your writing is to:

   ❑ A. Be respectful and polite in your choice of words?

   ❑ B. Use the person's name and make your points from their perspective?

8. Many people don't catch on when you tell them what is not. They feel the word "not" is evasive, a coverup. People are much more receptive to the positive approach. They want you to tell them what is!

   ❑ A. Agree.

   ❑ B. Disagree.

9. Nothing improves your letters and memos better or faster than cutting out the deadweight. Most of this will be found among:

   ❑ A. The nouns and verbs of your sentences?

   ❑ B. The adjectives and adverbs of your sentences?

10. The best read part of every letter and memo is usually the last paragraph. The simplest and best way to go out with a bang is to:

   ❑ A. Recap all your key points?

   ❑ B. Offer the reader a benefit?

   Now that you have completed the exercise, simply compare your answers with this list:

   Answers: 1. B, 2. A, 3. C, 4. A, 5. B, 6. C, 7. B, 8. A, 9. B, 10. B

   A score of five or fewer correct answers suggests an urgent need to improve your ability to put your thoughts down on paper. As you read on, you are certain to benefit from techniques 1 – 6—the basic skill package. Later, when you have mastered these, move on at your own pace. Of course, do not fail to take advantage of the portfolio of model letters and memos in the pages ahead.

A score of six or more correct answers suggests you are already benefitting from writing ability but not to the full extent you are capable of. For you, a quick review of the first six techniques is probably all you need. Then take a harder look at my six more ways to boost the octane rating of your letters and memos in a hurry. They'll show you the practical fast way to take what is good and make it even better.

Good Writing Is Easier than You Think

There are basically two ways to learn to write. The hard and impractical way is one. It is all formulas, rules, thou-shalt-nots, grammar, homework, and God only knows what else.

The easy way is the other. Imagine, nothing to memorize, no rules to follow, no grammar, no highfalutin vocabulary—just practical skills, proven techniques, and common sense that work wherever and whenever you do.

I vote for the easy way. It begins with a belief. `The key to improving your ability to get things down on paper is to believe that good writing is good conversation in print—and act accordingly.

Like conversation, there are several things you must know in advance if you expect to get the most out of each writing experience.

First, you must develop some ideas about the plans, points of view, or propositions you intend to write about. Second, you have to weave these ideas together in a message that makes sense to the person who will read your work. And third, you've got to find a way to make your reader care about what you have to say.

Good writing is not easy. But it's probably not as difficult as you might think.

SIX WORKABLE WAYS TO WRITE AS EASILY AS YOU SPEAK

Technique 1: Think Before You Write

It is a mistake to use the process of writing to find out what you want to say. I am not telling you that groping for ideas with pencil in hand isn't useful now and then. But the process is always time consuming and usually involves rewrite after rewrite.

You make far more efficient use of your time—the one resource you can never replace or replenish—when you know what you want to say before ink meets paper. It's all part of learning to put it down on paper as easily as you talk.

Before you sit down to write, take the time to think about what you might want to say if you and your reader spoke one-on-one.

If you are like most people, a number of thoughts will come to mind. The first thing to do is to say each of them out loud. That's right, just as though you were talking with the person, in just the way you would be likely to say it. Then write down exactly what you said.

Please notice I did not say to just write it down. I said, "write down exactly what you said." Don't change the vocabulary. Don't correct the grammar. Move a word here or there? Oh, please! Just write it down word-for-word.

Do the same for each of your thoughts—say them aloud and note exactly what you say.

Eventually, you will run out of ideas. That's the time to cull your notes. The idea is to get rid of the deadhead ideas, the duds that might've sounded good but somehow die on the written page.

You want to reduce your ideas to the three or four best ones, then mentally boil these down until you can get the whole idea across in just one sentence.

"I am an ex-bush pilot, not a writer. But when you run an executive charter flying service and it needs a brochure, you learn fast. We had several ideas worth talking about—on-board secretarial service, in-flight computer and fax services, radio-telephone scramblers. My people wanted me to wrap them all up in one package, one sentence," reports Ernest Van Gundy, 40, whose service flies out of Alaska's North Slope. "I said, When you fly with us, we take you seriously."

Van Gundy's one sentence became the theme of his brochure—the central idea of it.

You can do as much with any subject: just think it through, say your ideas aloud, get rid of the duds. The one sentence you are finally left with is the theme—the invisible hand that guides, shapes, and ties together what you write and how you write it.

Technique 2: Organize Your Thoughts

The thoughts that led you to your theme automatically give you an outline to write against.

Take Van Gundy's project. Here is his bare bones outline:

I. Every competitor meets FAA standards. We go further.

II. In addition to a captain and first officer, trained executive assistant on every flight.

III. Not only state-of-the-art avionics but powerful in-flight business electronics—a mini computer network with three workstations, satellite link, videophone, radio-telephone scramblers, and more.

IV. When you fly with us, we take you seriously.

Technique 3: Fill in the Outline

Now, you want to develop your outline.

The simplest, fastest, and by far the most practical way to do it is to think up a little story not so much to explain each feature of the service as to illustrate the benefit of it.

On that point about FAA standards—if you want to underline the idea of reliability in a positive way, you might come up with a little story about being Pratt & Whitney's only certified repair center in the region.

And about the trained administrative assistant, you could think up something that might let prospects know that you deliver the kind of service the upscale market demands by researching your customers' needs.

Eventually, your outline might look like this:

I. Every competitor meets FAA standards. We go further.

   ▶ *Why Pratt & Whitney chose us as its' only certified repair center in the region*

II. In addition to a captain and first officer, an executive assistant.

   ▶ *Our regular customer polls revealed the need for in-flight administrative support*

III. Not only state-of-the-art avionics but powerful business electronics—a mini computer network with three workstations, satellite telephone, and more.

   ▶ *Quote from one CEO who said. "It is like having an office in Washington only better—you stay in complete touch with no interruptions, no media."*

IV.   *It all adds up to this: When you fly with us, we take you seriously.*

Technique 4: Draw the Reader in

Now that you have the ideas mentally laid out, you need to develop a way to grab the reader's attention and hold it. The best way to do
it is with a strong opener. Say it in a sentence. Say it in a paragraph or
with a headline. Whatever you say to grab attention, write it the way
you would say it in person. The strategy is to set the hook as fast as you
can.

For instance, here is Van Gundy's first sentence.

"We treat every charter like our livelihood depends on it . . . and
it does."

It was created to appeal to his customer base—corner-office-types
in the international oil business. These guys don't mind spending
$10,000 a flying hour. Its just that they like to feel they're getting
$15,000 worth of value for it.

No matter what sort of grabber you use, it should set readers up to
expect to benefit from reading what you have to say.

Technique 5: Write the Way You Talk

It is always better to have readers understand what you say than
to have them admire the way you say it but fail to get the point.

The very best way to make sure what you write is easy to read is
this: *Say* what you mean to get across. That's right, just say it to yourself. Put the idea you want to get across in words you can easily imagine yourself saying out loud. Then, just write those words down.

"People tell me reading one of my letters is just like talking to me
in person," reports Debra Shankel, 27, a Dallas marketing manager.
"My grammar is not always perfect, I don't pepper my letters with
words I'd have to look up before using, but still, my point gets across in
a conversational way others can understand and relate to."

The reason Debra doesn't worry more over the grammar of her
writing is that she doesn't have to worry at all about the grammar she
speaks. You see, grammar is really a set of rules to help make things
clear. If you are clear when you speak, don't give grammar a second
thought when you write. Automatically, you'll make the same grammar choices you make when you speak.

Technique 6: Be Your Own Toughest Editor

Once you've written your document, go back over it. Read it as if you did not write it. Look for and correct every flaw you can find.

▶ Check the way the ideas flow, make sure they are easy to read.

▶ Cross out words, sentences, or even whole paragraphs if they don't add meaning.

▶ Break any sentence that contains more than 20 words into two shorter sentences.

When you have done all of this, read what you have written aloud. If it sounds right, go with it. If it doesn't sound urgent enough, or persuasive enough, or clear enough, keep revising until it does.

Unless you've got a knack I'd be willing to pay good money to learn, the chances are you won't have a finished piece of writing ready to go on the first attempt. No professional writer is immune to the need for revisions. Neither are you. There is no offense in having to rewrite. The only crime is failing to do so. The only victim, yourself.

FIVE MORE WORKABLE WAYS TO IMPROVE YOUR LETTERS AND MEMOS

If you are in a job where you write and receive lots of letters and memos, learning to do it better could be a big plus for you.

But good letters and memos don't just happen: they're planned.

▶ You must decide what you want and be able to express it in one sentence.

▶ You need to consider all the points you wish to make, organize them in a logical sequence, and think up a way to illustrate each one.

Technique 7: Personalize It

Write as if the recipient was sitting across the table. Use the person's name, and make your points from his or her perspective.

"We raised the rent, so I wrote a letter to each tenant," reports Trenton, New Jersey managing agent Lyle Burton, 36. "I said I can understand why you think a 7 percent rent increase is high, Ms. Jones, but let me explain it in terms of the services the building has provided, free, and the skyrocketing costs management can no longer afford to absorb. Last year, the local surcharge for your store's fire and police services rose 17 percent. Not a cent of this was passed on to you—the landlord absorbed it fully . . . "

The whole idea is to get up close and personal. Write it to Ms. Jones. Give her a stake in what you have to say.

Technique 8: State Things Positively

Readers don't catch on when they are told what is not. Most people feel the negative shot is evasive, a coverup. They want to know what is. That's why your letters and memos must make definite assertions wherever possible. The key is to express even negative statements in positive ways. For instance, you can take the negative approach and say, "He did not think it was the best use of his time." This speaks with forked tongue: What does he think? How does he use his time?

Or, you can create instant understanding by taking the positive approach: "He thought it was a waste of his time."

"I try to say what is right or how to make it better," reports Dunstan Heard, 30, a Chicago political fund raiser. "When you dwell on what is not, people just don't contribute as much as when you tell them, this is what is."

The villain in all of this is the word *not*.

Get it out of your writing and you'll always state things in the most positive terms possible. This alone will make people want to read the letters and memos you write.

Technique 9: Smile

Try to write with a smile on your face. Let's say you are really ticked off. You are in serious correspondence with the wonderful folks at your credit reporting agency. They keep on telling you they'll correct the records but you must notify them in writing. So you write. And somehow the records never seem to get fixed. Even under circumstances as trying as these you must not let negativity show.

"Saying things in a pleasant way is especially important if you turn out to be wrong," reports Heidi Ziegler, 30, a consumer affairs specialist for a Denver manufacturing business. "It's easier to have to eat nice words."

The point I draw from Heidi's experience is this:

It pays to be positive. People are much more receptive when you are.

Technique 10: Cut Words

It is an acknowledged scientific fact: The fewer the number of words in a letter, the more the letter will be understood. Do not be content with two words where one word will do—especially if the second word is an adjective or adverb.

If a noun or a verb cannot stand on its own, propping it up with a crutch—*grateful* thanks, *true* facts, *usual* habits, *unexpected* surprises—doesn't make it any stronger.

In fact, it weakens it. I can think of nothing to improve your letter and memo writing more, in less time, than cutting out the deadweight. How do you know when you need to cut? Any memo longer than a single-spaced page is two memos. Any letter longer than two single-spaced pages is at least two letters.

Technique 11: Close with a Bang!

Readership studies at several universities confirm the fact that the best-read part of any letter or memo is the ending. The last words create a moment of truth, the point where the recipient decides to go along or disagree. That's why you must make the ending the strongest part of your correspondence. The simplest way to do that is to offer the reader a benefit in the last paragraph—some idea that makes it easy to go along with your thinking.

"Accounting sends me a memo about my expenses and I am ready to put it in my brief case and work on it on the train," reports White Plains, New York commuter Jean Sporitter, 39. "Then I catch the last paragraph. It says that as soon as I initial the forms, they'll process my check. I signed it then and there."

Go out with a bang and you'll get a lot more action out of every letter and memo you write.

- -

A Portfolio: Twelve Model Letters and Five Model Memos You Can Follow and Be Guided By

A LIBRARY OF PARAGRAPHS FOR A LIFETIME OF SUCCESS

Are you one of the people who will do almost anything to avoid writing letters . . . even when it means losing sales, losing promotions, or losing love? Is the thought so overwhelming that no letters get sent?

Or, do the ones that go out work against your interests instead of for them?

In the pages ahead I want to give you your very own file of concise, crisp letters covering a dozen business and personal situations. Of course, life is too complicated to think a dozen of anything will suffice. So I want you to think of these 12 letters as a library of paragraphs. Use them as is, modify them, or mix and match the ones that work for your situation.

Love Letter

Dear Lois,

As an engineering type, I can talk technical jargon with the best of them, but when it comes to the beautiful and poetic language of love, it is as though I cannot speak at all.

What I want you to know, really, and it comes from my heart, is, I love you.

Lois, I've loved you since the first afternoon we spent together, when I lost a contact lens and you found it for me—in the cuff of my trousers. That experience, your patience, told me everything I needed to know about your sweet, sweet attitude toward life, and it has been confirmed time and again over these last few months.

Do you remember that incredible roller-coaster ride, or the day our picnic got rained out, or the homecoming game? There were moments I wanted to tell you but never seemed to be able to get up the courage speak. But our talk last night makes me believe you care for me as deeply as I care for you, and I wanted to say so.

I don't know if I am speaking out of turn here, but I know my happiness will never be complete without you.

I think of you always.

Letter of Resignation

Dear Charlie,

When I was a kid fresh out of school, you gave me more than just a job—you gave me a chance to prove myself.

These 10 years with the firm have been among the best and most satisfying of my life. Whatever I achieve in my career, I will always be grateful for the leg up you and Harry and Ken and Smitty gave me.

But now the time has come to move on.

Penta Systems has offered me an opportunity I cannot in good conscience turn down. I'll be running a division of my own from a base in Shreveport, and with almost no travel, I'll at last have the chance to be with my family for more than one or two weekends a month.

Considering all you have done to make my success possible, thanks seems like an awfully small word to convey the genuine sense of gratitude I will always feel toward you and the company. But small words—at least these small words—mean an awful lot to me:

Thank you.

Letter to Cover a Resume

Dear Mr. Shelley,

Have you ever gotten the feeing your world is shrinking to the rigid confines of a narrow job description?

I have . . . and it is beginning to feel like my career track at Xanadu Properties is a highway of tears that ends up at the grave-yard of hope. That's why I am making discreet inquiries about opportunities in the industry.

My credentials speak for themselves.

What I am asking for is this: Give me five minutes of your time and not a second more. If I can't prove that my talent and abilities will definitely contribute to the progress of Tenakill Land Holdings, I'll be on my way.

I'll look forward to those five minutes.

Condolence Letter

Dear Rigby,

It is always a sad thing to have to write a letter like this, but the death of your son, Ellis, makes it even more difficult to find words.

I know that nothing I can write will dull your pain and sense of loss since only time can do that—and it will, Rigby, I know it will.

Please let me know if there is anything I can do to help.

Sales Letter

Dear Mr. Kearny,

I have good news and I have even better news.

The good news first: According to our records, your customers have made you one of the nation's ten leading retailers of our Sutton line.

Here's the better news: We have just added a new collection that is likely to double your profit since it appeals to customers with a similar eye for current trends.

The enclosed brochure with color photographs of each of the 10 numbers in the new line gives you complete measurements and prices.

I'd like to ship an introductory assortment of 100 pieces but your sales representative, Verna Dahlberg, thinks you will be out of stock in two weeks. What she suggests is this: once you've had a chance to look over the enclosed, we'll give you a call to put together an opening order that gives you the mix and amounts just right for your business.

When you hear from us, we'll also tell you about an attractive promotional offer that makes even more sense.

Until then,

Thanks for Hospitality

Dear Harry and Allan,

After just two days in Manhattan, it is a pretty amazing thing to feel like I got to visit the New York tourists never see. But thanks to you, I really had a chance to discover what makes New York the belly button of our industry.

I hope you will give me a chance to do as much for both of you when the convention is here in Oakland next spring.

Thanks for a the chance to explore a fabulous city with people who really know what makes New York New York.

Former Customer Follow Up

Dear Dr. Greenberry,

I wonder if you've had a problem with Techo-Medical Services, Inc. because, if you did, I'd like to set things right.

You see, Dr. Greenberry, I've noticed that your name has not been on our list of service contract customers for about two years.

We're under brand new management here, and we've improved and expanded our 24-hour service fleet to the point where I can offer you an ironbound guarantee:

Either we are at your office servicing your blood analyzer within an hour of your call—day or night—or we'll refund the entire cost of your service contract.

I'll telephone in a week to welcome you back to our satisfied customer family with a special, money-saving offer. Meanwhile, I am enclosing a copy of our current service agreement so you can see for yourself the improvements we have been making.

Complaint Letter

Dear Ms. Pagoda,

I've been a frequent guest at Arizona Biltmore for about six years and until last Friday I was ready to recommend it to friends without any hesitation.

I returned to my room to find that the maid had discarded a sheaf of papers I had placed on the bureau next to my bed. What makes it so devastating is that the papers are the originals of my daughter's adoption. We had planned to review them with our tax attorney.

I spoke with the front desk and I know they made an effort to recover my documents but it was no-go. The dumpster had already carted them off.

The assistant manager at the desk that morning kindly tore up my bill. Nevertheless, I want to be sure this painful episode is never repeated. Please note in your records that on subsequent stays—and I hope there will be many of them—my room is to be cleaned but nothing is to be thrown out—not even the contents of the wastebasket—until I check it out.

Letter to the Editor

Dear Mr. Browning,

I am sorry to have to bring this matter to your attention but one of your reporters, Tracey Kitts, seems unable or unwilling to return even one of my six telephone calls.

The article she wrote about our church's role in AIDS prevention gave an inaccurate account of our needle swapping program for substance abusers in the downtown community. Specifically, it is not true that we are using United Way funds to pay for the program. As you can see from the attached annual report, we draw on a special endowment provided by several supporters within the merchant's association, who prefer to remain anonymous.

I do not know who Ms. Kitts relied on for her information, but she got it wrong, and the number of angry phone calls we have had since her article appeared has caused our parishioners great worry. That's why we would be grateful if you would print this letter or a correction in the next edition.

I can understand why some people wouldn't wish to personally support the needle replacement portion of our program, but we do not think it is fair to have the rest of our work damaged by an inaccurate impression.

Letter to a Public Official

Dear Senator Simpson,

I think it contributes to the wrong impression of Congress among the American people when a man as respected as you characterizes sexual harassment in the workplace as, "What is this harassment crap?"

It was the sort of remark one would expect from Saddam Hussein, not from a man who represents Montana's citizens—a state whose traditions of fairness and equity are what America's western legends are made of.

I do not argue with your stand on the confirmation of Mr. Thomas. It is the way you expressed your views that causes harm. To the degree you diminished Anita Hill in the Thomas hearings, you diminished yourself, every fair-minded American, and the Senate in which you serve.

Your behavior in the hearing room saddens me, and I hope you will take steps to right the wrong you have committed by issuing a public apology not to Ms. Hill but to the nation.

Letter to Handle a Customer Complaint

Dear Mr. Incastro,

Thanks for your call.

I can't take back what happened to you and your family at our restaurant last night but I can assure I have taken steps to see that it never happens again . . . not to you, not to anybody.

As you know, we pride ourselves on good food and good service. With that kind of outlook, I frankly cannot see any reason for you to have been treated as you were.

To show you how much we value your business, Mr. Incastro, I'd be grateful if you and your family would join me for dinner, on the house, at your convenience. Please call me and I will be glad to make the arrangements.

Thanks again for giving us the opportunity to set things right.

Letter When Other Letters and Calls Don't Work

Dear Mr. Horowitz,

Considering that I have sent you three letters and left four unreturned telephone messages, I am beginning to get the idea I have somehow offended you.

If that is the case, please accept my apology. I did not mean to cause you any problem.

More important, I hope you will give me the chance to set things right between us.

I look forward to hearing from you.

FORMAT, BUSINESS LETTER

Letterhead
1 to 12 blank lines
(the shorter the letter the more blanks)

Date

1 to 12 blank lines

Person's name
Title
Company name
Street address
City, State, Zip

double space

Dear (salutation):

double space

First paragraph.
Body of letter is single spaced. Paragraphs flush left, or five-space indent.

double space

Succeeding paragraphs

double space

Sincerely yours,

quadruple space

Typed name
Title

Why You Must Use Memos to Sell Yourself

Every memo you write is a sales tool for you!

When you conduct business through writing—even about such simple things as meeting agendas, due dates, and the like—part of your message is unwritten. It tells your boss, your subordinates, and your colleagues about your professionalism, your interest in business matters, the way you do the work you do.

Crisp, concise, and clear memo writing sends a message that you are capable, professional, and exercise good business judgment.

Here is a brief portfolio of model memos covering five of the most routine situations—the ones that most often seem to call for putting it down on paper.

Each is designed to provide a template: Use it as is or customize it to meet any special requirements you might encounter.

Memo to Remind Others About Deadlines

To meet the schedule we agreed on this morning, several things need to be accomplished without fail this week. Bids are required in hand by noon Tuesday. Accounting will analyze bids and prepare a recommendation by the close of business Thursday.

The committee will meet to review bids Friday at 9:00 A.M. in the main conference room.

Please confirm your understanding of this.

Memo, Approve/Disapprove

This recommends purchase of a StaxMax Data Compression software for our PCs.

The reasons for the recommendation are:

1. StaxMax priced is 16 to 19 percent below competition and offers features other packages cannot match. These include a proprietary technology to give us 60 percent more data per unit of storage.

2. Because it backs up on floppy diskettes, or tape, or both, it meets the mixed requirements of our installed base.

3. Training requirements are minimal—a single 30-minute class per location.

Approve_____Date_____

Disapprove_____Date_____

Memo to Recommend a Candidate

You asked me to recommend a candidate for the staff opening we discussed last week.

After making several inquiries and considering them all, I am delighted to be able to recommend Betty Laudon as best-qualified.

Betty has been with us for eight years and has gone from a campus representative to her present responsibility. Her growth record is one of imagination, enthusiasm, and a high level of energy. Each of her performance reviews place her in the top ten percent on measures of skill and adaptability. She is known and well-liked by the staff. Harry Leland, her assistant, is ready to move into Betty's slot when she moves up.

Memo to Set an Agenda

A meeting will be held in the main conference room between 1:00 and 2:00 P.M. tomorrow, July 17. The purpose is to set objectives and discuss approaches. Below is a suggested agenda. If you wish to make additions, please get back to me before the end of the day today.

Subject	Purpose	Time	Presenter
Competition	Background	5 min.	J.R.
Staff Feedback	Criteria	10 min.	D.C.
Cost factors	Criteria	10 min.	B.D.
Solutions	Brainstorm	35 min.	All

Memo to Follow Up Assignments

As of this morning, these are the assignments and due dates:

Action	Responsibility	Due Date
Develop demand pattern	G.K.	September 18

Chart: Best, worst, most
likely demand V.L. September 26
Cost estimate, basic and complete N.H. October 14

FORMAT, MEMO

Letterhead

triple space

Date:

double space

To:

double space

Copies to:

double space

Subject:

triple space

First paragraph, single spaced, flush left

double space

Succeeding paragraphs

double space between paragraphs

Last paragraph

double space

Writer's initials, centered

Since writing can be one of the most important things you do, I am going to summarize the main ideas of the chapter in three big points:

1. The secret of writing as easily as you talk is to believe that good writing is good conversation in print.

2. The six workable ways to do it are these:

- Think before you write.
- Organize your thoughts.
- Fill in the outline.
- Draw the reader in.
- Write the way you talk.
- Be your own toughest editor.

3. Here are five workable ways to improve your letters and memos

- Personalize it.
- State things positively.
- Smile.
- Cut words.
- Close with a bang!

IF YOU CAN WRITE AS EASILY AS YOU SPEAK, YOU CAN SPEAK PUBLICLY AS EASILY AS YOU WRITE

What I most want this chapter to leave you with is a feeling—the feeling that good writing is a powerful weapon in the game of life. If you can't put yourself across on paper, chances are you aren't getting yourself across, period.

I can think of only one other thing that will do as much to make your life better than writing as easily as you speak, and that is to speak as easily as you write.

If you think that's turnabout, wait until you read the way my friend, the late Ben Dugas, achieved exactly that.

Ben—personal platform trainer to dozens of national politicians and Fortune 50 CEOs—takes an approach that is absolutely bassack-wards.

Here's the funny thing. It works.

PUBLIC SPEAKING

Fourteen Workable Ways to Be as Effective on Your Feet as You Are in Private

"The most important thing I can tell you is not how to open a speech or the words to choose. What I am going to tell you is how to hold on to an audience."

I was a young and rising manager at Pepsi-Cola Company when I first heard training consultant Ben Dugas talk about the ins and outs of public speaking. My boss, who was big on the ability of his people to get up on their feet and speak, sent me to a course Dugas ran. It was called, *Secrets of Platform Professionals.*

The idea was to prepare me to talk up the work of our department at every opportunity—inside the company mostly, and outside too.

IT'S AS EASY AS ONE-TWO-THREE

"It may sound like putting the cart before the horse but believe me, it makes a lot of sense, " Ben announced.

Dugas, whose clients included well-known national politicians, Fortune 50 CEOs, and corner-office wannabes like me, was about to reveal the most important trade secret of all.

"The key is to plan the end of the talk first.

"You see, the finish is the part of the speech the audience takes home. That's why the best speakers write the end of the speech first then go back to create the start and middle.

"Next time you are on the spot to speak, don't even think for a second about what you are going to say to open your remarks.

"Instead, devote all the time you've got to how you are going to close.

"And what you should think about is one, two, three.

"What you must remember, you tell the folks, is,

"One—go jump in the lake . . .

"Two—swim out . . .

"And three—hang yourself out to dry.

"Now sit down and you will find you have made a memorable impression.

"Your organized ending will make them think you are one smart person. Believe me, this platform professional secret will work for you every time, and here's the best part: Remembering it is as easy as one, two, three."

YOU CAN NEVER CROSS OUT WHAT YOU JUST SAID

I've never forgotten the usefulness of Ben's thinking. His words have served me well over the years.

You can safely bet the farm they will do as much for you whether you are reading this chapter because you're going to make a talk and need some instant guidance, or because you want to get ahead of the curve on public speaking.

Either way, the ability to talk on your feet is a mighty handy business and community skill.

You never know when you might be called on to persuade bankers to go for a deal, motivate employees to go the extra mile, or simply inform others in your church or civic organization.

There's no end of opportunities to stand up and speak.

Whatever the occasion—anything from a Sunday school class to a service club meeting—one thing is dead certain:

If you are at all normal, the first few times you speak in public are certain to mark good news/bad news milestones in your life.

The good news is that nothing raises your stock out in the community or on the job faster than making an effective speech or presentation (which is nothing more than a speech dressed up in work clothes). When you get your ideas and plans across with confidence and clarity, you can literally talk your way to anything you want—business, social, you name it.

The not-so-good news is that nothing raises personal anxieties faster than having to make one. Dry throat, sweaty palms, chest a size too small for your pounding heart—speaking in public strikes terror in nearly everyone at first.

And here is why: The science of psycho-linguistics tells us that audiences identify people with the messages they deliver. They think of people who say smart things as intelligent, and those who say silly things as mental klutzes.

Here's where the problem comes in: It often turns out that the dumbest thing you say ends up the most memorable.

Since you can never cross out the words you just spoke, it is no wonder people get more heebie-jeebies about speaking in front of strangers than about writing to them or talking with them one-on-one.

When you put your conversational foot in your mouth, it's tough enough dealing privately with your diminished self esteem. Who needs to convince a room full of strangers that if your IQ drops any lower you'll need to be watered twice a day?

LEVERAGE YOUR NERVOUSNESS TO BOLSTER YOUR CONFIDENCE

That is why I feel it is so very urgent to tell you right off that I intend to use this chapter to show you two important things:

First, I want you to have scientifically tested and practical ways to leverage your nervousness—use it to build and develop personal confidence.

And second, I want to give you the skills to create and deliver talks that will get people to pay attention to you . . . encourage them to do or think or believe something you want—all without looking like a dunce or dying of cardiac arrest.

Believe you me, whether it is an impromptu talk you are called upon to make with no preparation, a speech you have carefully prepared and wish to give as if it is being thought up as you talk, or a serious address in which you write out and read every word, my practical, tested techniques have never failed any of the thousands of people who invest the hour or two it takes to learn them.

TEN QUESTIONS EVERY SPEAKER MUST ANSWER

Your skills as a speaker are guaranteed to improve greatly simply by raising and answering ten questions:

▶ Why am I speaking to this audience?

▶ What am I speaking about?

▶ How can I make it interesting?

▶ What is the best way to organize my material?

▶ What is the best way to present it?

▶ What must I do to overcome stage fright?

▶ How do I get the audience to connect with my thinking?

▶ What can I say to overcome disinterest?

▶ What kinds of visual support will make my words more convincing?

▶ What else can I do to be sure I am getting my message across?

TWO UNBEATABLE BENEFITS ARE YOURS WHEN YOU EASILY COMMAND THE POWERS OF PLATFORM PROFESSIONALS

When you communicate as well on your feet as you do from behind a desk, you win the confidence of your customers and colleagues. As they come to admire your ability to think and perform under pressure, they will accept your point of view and consider you a source of sound thinking. This is certain to give your career just the boost it needs.

"The day before I made my first talk at a regional meeting of one of our biggest customers, I panicked. The only way to calm my nerves was to promise myself three things. Come what may, I was going to make myself stand up to be seen, speak up to be heard, and make my points as brief as possible so that I could shut up to be appreciated," reports recently promoted Thistle Glenburnie, 33, who now manages a marketing group at AT&Ts New Jersey headquarters. "Afterwards, one of their senior people invited me to make the same talk at their annual management retreat. Since then, our business with them nearly doubled."

The idea of standing up in front of 300 or so people made Thistle nervous. But it was only by making herself the center of attention that she could get her company's plans across.

Speaking out was a winning strategy all around: The customer got the attention it wanted. AT&T got the business it needed. Thistle got the promotion she deserved.

As you rise to speak out about things that matter to you within the community, others will identify you as a winner with an outgoing personality, and you cannot fail to be invited to positions of growing leadership.

"Racism is like acid rain. Everything it touches dies a little. Whether I was based in Georgia or Ohio or California, I spoke against it at Rotary, Lion's Club, church suppers—all the local organizations that would have me," reports Lloyd Ward, 47, president of Frito-Lay's central division. "That got me invitations to speak at regional minority conferences. From there I talked at colleges. Within a couple of years I was speaking pretty regularly all over the country, and I sit on the board of several national organizations."

Take it from a winner—one of the best ways to become prominent and well known in your circles and beyond is to speak on something you believe in every chance you get.

TEST YOUR ABILITY TO SPEAK IN PUBLIC IN THE PRIVACY OF YOUR HOME

If your work or interests keep you in front of an audience, improving your ability to speak in public can be very important. But even if not, public speaking is a skill that is sure to come in handy just when you need it most.

To determine where you stand when it comes to putting your thoughts across in public, I want you to take a look at the following exercise.

Below you will find 10 brief statements. After reading each, you will be asked to make a choice. Just check the response that your judgment calls for.

1. The audience will accept my leadership when I earn it with what I have to say and the way I say it.

❏ A. True

❏ B. False

2. I should speak only about something that is of vital interest to me, something I care about passionately.

❏ A. True

❏ B. False

3. To make the speech enjoyable to others, I must tell a joke or a funny story.

❏ A. True

❏ B. False

4. To organize my speech, I need to list every point about my topic and write at least a sentence on each.

❏ A. True

❏ B. False

5. It is a good idea to memorize my talk. That way I can deliver as if I am thinking it up as I go along.

❏ A. True

❏ B. False

6. The best way to overcome stage fright is to prepare and rehearse my talk until I am comfortable with what I have to say and how I will say it.

❏ A. True

❏ B. False

7. To connect with the audience as I speak, I will get as physically close to the audience as possible

❏ A. True

❏ B. False

8. Among the things I can do to overcome disinterest are 1) make sure I know my audience's needs, 2) keep my talk narrowly focused on them, and 3) offer them not the proposition that is best for me but one that is best for me and them.

   ❏ A. True

   ❏ B. False

9. Visual aids have a place in every speech.

   ❏ A. True

   ❏ B. False?

10. The part of the speech my audience will take home is the ending. The simplest and best way to go out with a bang is recap the key points of my talk.

   ❏ A.True

   ❏ B. False

   Now that you have completed the exercise, simply compare your answers with this list.

   Answers: 1. A, 2. B, 3. B, 4. B, 5. B, 6. A, 7. B, 8. A, 9. B, 10. A

   A score of five or fewer correct answers suggests an urgent need to improve your ability to develop the skills of public speaking. If you will learn and practice my 14 workable ways to be as effective on your feet as you are in private, you cannot fail to thrill to the greatest satisfaction a speaker can have.

   A score of six or more correct answers suggests you are already benefitting from the ability to plan and deliver an effective speech but not to the full extent you are capable of. For you, a quick review of the 14 techniques is probably a good idea. They will not only show the way things should be done from scratch, they'll give you practical tips on how to take what is good and make it even better.

When you know how to speak on your feet you develop a sense of personal mastery and fulfillment unlike anything you ever felt before.

To help you experience the tremendous rush of accomplishment that nothing else matches, I want you to have,

-- --

Fourteen Workable Ways to Be as Effective on Your Feet as You Are in Private

FOUR WORKABLE WAYS TO BREAK THE STRANGLEHOLD OF STAGE FRIGHT

Technique 1: Get Tense

Remember the old saying, Knowledge is power?

When you know why public speaking kicks off tension, you've got a chance to handle it in a way that helps rather than hinders you—focuses your thoughts.

The point I mean to make is that tension can be your best friend or your worst enemy—the choice is yours.

Let me give you a quick example.

When I was writing scripts for documentaries, my favorite director, Randy Paulson, had a pretty novel way of getting the best out of his crew and cast. He almost never needed more than two or three takes—and often just one—to put a shot in the can.

Sure, he'd do all the conventional things in conventional ways—block out the action, check cues, adjust lighting. The unusual part came in the hushed quiet a heartbeat before tape rolled. Sounding more like a television golf announcer than a teledoc director, he'd stage whisper to cast and crew, "Okay people, let's get tense!"

Randy uses tension to get everybody focused to create a better product in less time. What works on the set works just as well at the podium. Stage fright is shorthand for the pulse and the pace of things that your body does to get you ready to make a better speech.

For instance, your quickened heartbeat makes you more alert. In the minds of the audience, alert people who stand tall are more believable than the ones whose bodies sag. And then there's your pounding chest—nature's way of delivering the extra oxygen you need to make yourself heard.

I could go on with examples but why bother? You get the picture, I am sure.

Stage fright is more than normal and natural—it's necessary. That extra shot of adrenaline is nature's way of helping you think faster, talk more easily, get your ideas across with emphasis and intensity.

Stage fright strikes indiscriminately: It happens to expert and novice alike. Here is the only difference: The expert uses tension to make a better speech while the novice often allows it to wither his. A certain amount of nervousness is useful. Don't let it alarm you. Just use it to make a better talk.

Technique 2: Steadily Build Confidence

"If anxiety's the poison, just doing it is the antidote," reports June Taylor-Dancer, 36, who produces news shows for one of the cable services in Atlanta. "If you are afraid of it but do it anyway, it loses its power over you and you can go on to be all that you want."

June's right—just do it. But do it sensibly. First time out, pick a situation that's safe, say a local PTA meeting. There, you can gain some confidence in yourself and your abilities.

When you rise, no doubt you'll feel a jitter or two.

Try to remember that you are the only one aware you're nervous. If you don't make a big deal about it, hardly anybody will even notice.

Just concentrate on what you are doing and saying, not on how scared you are. Stand tall. Breathe deeply. Use the surge of energy that's coursing through your body to connect with the audience—people you know and trust.

When you've got that one talk under your belt, go on to a bigger group if you can. And an even bigger one after that. There's just one way to become a good speaker and that is to speak.

There is no faster or better way to dispel fear than to steadily develop confidence in your proven ability to overcome it.

Technique 3: Prepare to Win

The better prepared you make yourself, the more confidence you'll have as the moment to speak draws near.

For one thing, you've got to get comfortable with the material of your talk. The ideas and their implications—you must have them down cold.

And for another, you've got to practice your delivery until it looks and feels like you are totally comfortable with everything you are saying and the way you are saying it.

"I practice in the downstairs bathroom—the one with a full-length mirror," reports Harvel Brzynski, 41, who represents a New York television station in the Chicago market. "It usually takes three or four tries before my voice mellows and the words flow naturally."

You can dream all day long about what a great success you are as a speaker, but until you develop the confidence it takes to truly wow the audience with your words—confidence born out of practice—you will never gain the power to do it.

Practice, practice, practice. And when you've done that, practice some more!

Technique 4: Rehearse, Don't Memorize

Let me share with you another of Ben Dugas's practical and powerful prescriptions for public speaking. I offer it to you now because it has proved effective time and again—not just for Ben and me but for everybody who heeds the point.

It concerns the problems that arise when you memorize a talk.

Ben, a native of New Orleans, was the valedictorian of his high school. His graduation speech was on the spirit of patriotism that emerged in the pirate Jean Laffite just prior to the battle of New Orleans. It was then Laffite joined forces with General Andrew Jackson. Together they demolished the British assault force and saved America from almost certain defeat in the War of 1812.

Ben memorized each and every one of the three thousand words of his long and inspiring talk. Then came the moment of truth, the moment in which he was to deliver his address. He rose, cleared his throat, and began . . .

"Jean Laffite is dead but his spirit lives on . . . "

That was as far as Ben got.

His mind went totally blank.

He could not remember another word of his 15-minute address.

An embarrassed silence came over the crowd as he struggled to recall the brilliant speech he had so diligently memorized.

It was to no avail. So Ben did the only thing he could. He sat down.

"Ben," said his principal, rising to continue the program. "You bring us sad news."

The point I make with Ben's experience is this:

There is nothing wrong with memorizing certain key phrases of your talk. But to memorize it entirely invites disaster: If for any reason you forget where you are for one split second, like Ben Dugas, you are dead!

On the other hand, if the sense of your talk comes out of a natural flow of ideas, there is no need to memorize.

Instead, you can move smoothly and logically from one idea to the next using a written script or note cards.

All you need to do is arrange your ideas so they flow in a logical sequence before you start.

SIX WORKABLE WAYS TO PLAN AND ORGANIZE YOUR SPEECH

Technique 5: Put Last Things First

The best place to begin working on a speech is with the results you want, not with the issues you plan to discuss.

"The audience expects me to know my topic cold, but they don't really want me to mention every little detail. They expect me to filter it down to what is relevant to them," reports Ivan Chessley, 44, a Detroit management executive. "So I list the three most important points—the ones I want the audience to know, understand, and connect with. These become my objectives—the basis for everything else."

Ivan's point is well taken. Deciding what you want to end up with gives you a rough shape on which to focus all your efforts. Notice that Ivan selects three points, not two or four or any other number. Let me tell you why.

It is an undisputed scientific finding that the ability of an audience to absorb information is inversely proportional to the amount of information presented. The more you present, the less they take home. Researchers say three points seems to be the ideal number. Fewer and your speech will appear to lack substance. Any more and you might as well talk to the wall for all they will be able to absorb.

Once you've identified and pinpointed your three main ideas, write each one on an index card. Try to express each thought in one concise sentence that clearly reveals exactly what you are getting at.

Let's say you are going to talk about the glass ceiling that hangs over corporate America, the one that blocks women from the higher echelons. Your three points might be stated as follows:

Card # 1:   We treat women like second-class citizens.

Card # 2:   This is self defeating because when it comes to sound business leadership, sex doesn't count.

Card # 3:   Competition will produce change, the glass ceiling will eventually shatter, because no business can afford to neglect one out of two of its most precious human resources.

I'll tell you what to do with these cards in just a moment. But first, I want to make a point about timing.

Technique 6: Meet Time Constraints

CBS newscaster Charles Osgood, instructing listeners on how to make a speech, reminded them that the standard length of a vaudeville act was 12 minutes. "If all those troupers singing and dancing their hearts out couldn't go on for more than 12 minutes without boring the customers, what makes you think you can?"

Part of the skill of pleasing an audience lies in filling allotted time without exceeding the limits imposed by a meeting agenda.

"When you speak before 100 people and go just 60 seconds over your allotted time, you do not spend an extra minute," reports speech writer Harriet Dean, 45, whose office is in Washington, D.C. "You squander an hour and forty minutes of time that never belonged to you in the first place. Believe me, audiences resent it."

In ordinary conversation, thoughts are exchanged at a rate of roughly 125 to 150 words per minute. A somewhat slower rate—100 words a minute—is preferred for public speaking. This translates to roughly two minutes per double-spaced typewritten page.

Presuming your speech aims to make three major points and your allotted time is 10 minutes, you can safely explain each of these thoughts in about two minutes using one page per point; devote an additional two minutes to thank your host and make some opening remarks; and a final two minutes to conclude.

Let me wrap up the point I am making about time constraints with a quick Mark Twain story.

Seems the author was in church for a sermon.

After the preacher had spoken five minutes, Twain said he was ready to put $20 in the collection plate.

Five minutes later it was down to a dollar.

Five minutes after that, Twain said the preacher owed him $10!

Technique 7: Flesh Out Your Ideas

Now I want you to see how easy it is to develop your three main points into a powerful outline.

Several paragraphs back, I asked you to put aside your three index cards—the ones which reduce to a single sentence apiece the three ideas you want the audience to take home.

Now I want you to consider each idea. Then, just write three or four sentences that add depth to each of the three points you wish to make.

Flesh out each idea with explanation, supporting examples, techniques, case histories, names, and so on.

Let me show you what I mean.

OUTLINE FOR A TEN-MINUTE TALK

	Subject	Time	Pages
I.	Opening remarks	1	1/2
II.	We still treat women like second class citizens		
	▶ If we continue to make artificial distinctions between goals of women and goals of business, everyone is short-changed	3	11/2
III.	This is self-defeating because, when it comes to sound business, sex doesn't count		
	▶ Three examples:	3	11/2
IV.	These exceptional women dramatize the point: in business, women are an under-developed asset	1	1/2
V.	Competition will produce change, the glass ceiling will eventually shatter because no business can afford to neglect one of its two most precious resources	1	1/2

VI. Close	1	1/2
Total	10	5

Technique 8: Open with a Grabber

It is always best to use a grabber to gain the immediate attention of the audience because the opening of your talk sets the theme.

If you don't catch them with the first few sentences the rest amounts to shouting down the wrong end of the megaphone.

But unless you are a professional comic, it is never a good idea to make your grabber a joke. First of all, your name is probably not Eddie Murphy, which means you do not have Murphy's talent, skill, and experience. And second, how do you get an audience to believe in you *after* the joke lays an egg?

Instead, find a story that illustrates the point of your talk.

Here are three tested and proved speech openers you can use as is or modify to meet any special requirements you may have.

1.

One very dark night, a Navy captain was on the bridge of his ship. Suddenly, coming over the horizon, he spots the lights of another boat, and it's headed directly at him. So he tells his signalman to blink the other guy:

"Change your course 10 degrees south."

Back comes a reply:

"No. Change *your course* 10 degrees north."

The captain replies: "I am a captain. Change *your* course south."

The reply comes back: "I am a seaman first class. Change yours *north*."

This makes the captain mad. "Dammit, I say, change your course south. I'm on a *battleship*."

To which the other man replies: "And I say steer north. I'm in a *lighthouse*."

I think that is a wonderful example of human empowerment, which is the subject I want to discuss with you today . . .

2.

I intended to make this the shortest speech on record. Then I did some R & D. I discovered the shortest speech on record was delivered by Dr. Alfred Kinsey, the noted sex researcher. He was asked to make an after-dinner speech on his life's work, sex.

He did it in exactly 10 words.

This is what he said:

"Ladies and gentlemen, it is indeed a pleasure. Thank you."

Well, my friends, the pleasure in being with you today is all mine . . .

3.

At a press conference, Ross Perot was asked,

"Just how much money is enough?"

While he mulled that one over, visions of millions—even billions!—danced in reporters' heads. And why not? Here was one of the richest men on Earth!

But Perot, true-to-form, surprised with his reply.

He measured off about an inch between his thumb and forefinger and spoke just four words.

"A little bit more," he said.

Which brings me to the point I want to make with you, and that is, how we are going to get a little bit more of the business we want and need in this difficult economic climate . . .

Technique 9: Make It Worthwhile for Them to Listen

Good speeches, like good conversation, are based on the needs-benefits approach.

Your audience has certain unmet needs. When you position your ideas to satisfy these, their attention is yours.

The whole idea is to make choices about what to say and how to say it in ways that are faithful to your goals *and* the needs of your listeners.

"I am in complete control of the audience when what I say gets them to feel I am talking about my subject the same way they might if we changed places and I sat in the audience," reports Neville Stratton, 37, who runs a market research business in Seattle.

Neville's point is useful.

It suggests the best speaking outcomes occur when you make an effort to understand the needs of the audience and slant your ideas accordingly. Simply say the things you would want to hear if you were seated on the other side of the podium.

This gives people the idea you are on their side—that they are serving their own interests by listening to what you have to say.

Present the proposition you'd want to be offered—not necessarily the one that's best for you but the one that is best for both you *and* the audience—and they will listen to your every word.

Technique 10: Close with a Recap

The end of the speech, as I have been stressing, is the part the audience takes home. Because it is your last chance to register your thoughts, the moment of truth when they must think for themselves, your conclusion must be compelling and strong.

The way to power your closing is by reprising the main ideas. Tell the audience, in a fresh and memorable way, the main points of what it is you wish them to do or think or believe.

Here's a quick example:

"So let me wrap up by saying that our studies show we need to do three things to improve our management information systems.

"One, we've got to simplify the organization. Two, we need to install state-of-the-art hardware. And three, we must revamp the reporting relationships. "

"Making these improvements may not result in more decisions. But one thing's for sure:

"It is guaranteed to help us arrive at better ones."

FOUR WORKABLE WAYS TO SPEAK LIKE A PLATFORM PROFESSIONAL

Technique 11: Speak to the Audience by Speaking Like the Audience

The idea is to speak in simple declarative sentences.

A simple, declarative sentence is just what it sounds to be—a direct, uncomplicated combination of nouns and verbs to make one idea instantly understandable.

The rule you must follow is this: one idea per sentence.

"People in the audience can't go back to read and reread what I say," reports Beth Marden-Kane, 33, who runs a small-business consulting service in Dallas. "So I just follow the KISS formula—keep it simple, stupid."

In addition to using simple, specific, and concrete words, and short sentences, try to use the active voice wherever possible. What's the difference between the active and passive voices?

Active is when, "You promoted the idea."

Passive is when, "The idea was promoted by you."

Active verbs suggest energy. They are the lift beneath your speaking wings. They give your ideas motion and energy.

Technique 12: Illustrate Rather than Explain

When you explain anything more than is absolutely necessary, your speech comes across as a sermon or lecture. I cannot think of a faster way to run off an audience. Sure, there are points that need to be covered.

"I could've gone over a laundry list of details about the last selling idea I presented but it would've taken hours and left everybody numb," reports Andy Cross, 33, regional manager for one of the door-to-door cosmetics companies, based in Newark, Delaware. "Instead, I told a little case history about one of our most successful reps. She uses one of those computer thinkpads to build her product database and customer activity file. Afterwards, three other reps came up to ask about her system—so I know the message really got through."

Andy's right. The simplest, fastest, and by far the most practical way to get anybody to understand anything is to think up a little story.

Technique 13: Use Body Language to Say What Words Can't

A university study reveals that what the audience sees has more impact than what they hear.

Professors say the words account for about 10 percent of what an audience believes, tone of voice about 40 percent, visual messages the remaining half.

Here's my take on the research: Whatever the oral message of your speech, the ones that are unspoken are at least as important.

I am talking about the messages that tell the audience you are credible, honest, forthright, forthcoming—all the good things you'd like them to think about you.

These come out in your dress, your physical attitude, the gestures you make. Obviously what you wear depends on who you are speaking before, and the setting. A good rule of thumb is to wear what your immediate superior might choose to wear if he or she were in your position.

Generally, if you speak at an off-site management conference, casual clothes are just fine. More formal situations usually demand conventional business dress. For men this usually means a fairly subdued business suit, contrasting shirt, solid or simple-patterned tie.

Women are best dressed in a dark blazer with contrasting skirt, low heels, tailored blouse, and very simple jewelry.

In addition to dressing in a way that meets the expectations of the audience and its setting, you've got to give off an aura of pride.

Don't forget: You are a living visual aid for yourself. Make sure your body language says you've got worthwhile things to say.

Walk to the podium with confidence. Stand tall. Do not lean on the podium. Keep your hands out of your pockets. Your movements and gestures must be few, slow, and deliberate. Act like you belong in front of the crowd.

To make eye contact as you speak, pick three faces in the crowd: one on either side of the room, the third at the back of the hall. As you speak, slowly pan from one to the other to the other.

"I get a chance to see a lot of speakers and I can tell you just the kind of speech they'll make by watching them walk to the mike," reports New York meeting consultant Horace Judson, 49. "If they don't stand tall, no matter how many words they throw at the audience they're not going to say anything worthwhile. It's just the opposite with the ones who look confident: I expect them to be worth listening to."

Technique 14: Visual Aids Are Highway Billboards

Properly used, visual aids jumpstart understanding.

And while they have no place in purely emotional kinds of talks where you want to sustain a mood without interruption, they certainly help explain complicated ideas—especially where numbers are involved.

"Visual aids are like highway billboards," reports Chicago art director Marty Stevens, 50, who designs multi-media presentations for the auto shows around the country. "If you can't understand them perfectly at 55 miles an hour, they're not doing you any good."

Marty's point is a biggie. There are several more worth making about visuals to support your words.

▶ One idea per visual

▶ Illustrate major points, not details

▶ Use as few words as possible

▶ The headline must explain the visual

▶ Without fail, read each headline word for word

We've covered a lot of important ground in this chapter on public speaking. Before we move on, it is probably a good idea for you to go over a quick summary of my fourteen techniques to see if there are any you might have missed:

▶ Get tense

▶ Steadily buildup confidence

▶ Prepare to win

▶ Rehearse, don't memorize

▶ Put last things first

▶ Meet time constraints

▶ Flesh out your ideas

▶ Open with a grabber

▶ Make it worthwhile for them to listen

▶ Close with a recap

▶ Speak to the audience by speaking like the audience

▶ Use body language to say what words can't

▶ Visual aids are your highway billboards

Platform professionals—men and women who earn their living behind a podium or in front of a camera—tell me that the art of speaking in public is to appear artless. The more natural your speech comes across, the more likely you are to win the confidence of the audience.

What is true of communicating with hundreds of people at once is equally true in one-on-one situations—especially when the other party's of the opposite sex.

If the concepts of public speaking and breaking the ice with the opposite sex appear strange bedfellows, I suggest you turn the page as quick as you can.

We're going to be talking about everything from taking that first step and summoning up the courage to ask for a date to winning the heart of the one you are after.

Read on . . . I promise you'll see exactly how to get the one you love to love you back.

Fourteen Workable Ways to Break the Ice with the Opposite Sex . . . Even if you Are Very Shy, on the Quiet Side, or Simply Not the Social Success You'd Like to Be

"Herb Cooper was my guest at a gathering of The Grape Nuts—30 congenial people with a common interest in wine. We meet three times a year to talk and taste."

Half an hour into the evening, Herb, 44, who works in finance for the March of Dimes, was standing next to Rita Walton, 39. She's the wine buyer for a national restaurant chain.

Aimlessly, Herb lifted bottles, read labels, put them down.

Rita looked on with amusement. She said nothing.

Finally, he turned to her with a boyish smile.

"My name's IIerb. My wine IQ is only a little lower than my shoe size. You look too comfortable to be a wine-dummy. Tell me, which way is up?"

"Well, hello, Herb," she replied warmly. "I'm Rita. You are welcome to taste with me."

Later, as Herb and I were leaving, he thanked Rita.

"I don't know what I would have done without you," he said.

"My pleasure," Rita beamed.

A week later, Herb telephoned me.

"Suppose two people were going to have dinner," he said. "And suppose she is going to cook crabs and he offers to bring the wine. And suppose that she knows a lot about wine. What wine should he bring?"

From time-to-time over the next few months I heard from both Rita and Herb.

She spoke of his dedication to a philanthropic cause; he, on the other hand, respected her wide-ranging knowledge of food, wine, and the cultural scene.

Between the lines, I sensed romance taking hold.

So it was no surprise when, a year or so later, they announced their intention to marry.

HOW TO GET THE ONE YOU WANT TO WANT YOU BACK

Happily, Rita's and Herb's courtship is living proof that for the few willing to make the effort, you can break the ice to win the true friendship and love you want.

But sadly, too many efforts end in loneliness and frustration.

For these men and women, be they straight or gay, the world remains filled with strangers.

Facing the bleak and disappointing prospect of a loveless destiny, many decide nothing can be done to break through the glass barrier that separates them from that very special someone they can admire now only from afar.

If you count yourself among the isolated majority, the good news in the pages of this chapter is sure to be the answer to your prayers . . . even if you are very shy, on the quiet side, or simply not the social success you'd like to be.

You see, I firmly believe that breaking the ice with a complete stranger doesn't happen by accident, mere chance, or blind luck.

In fact, it is as predictable as sunrise.

BREAK THE ICE BY SATISFYING NEEDS

Think about what went on between Herb and Rita.

Herb quickened Rita's pulse by saying what he said the way he said it.

What goes for Herb and Rita goes for the world:

The things we choose to say and the ways we choose to say them determine our ability to make the kind of friendship that marks the start of every enduring relationship that ever was or will be.

And here is why:

We all have a deep psychological need to be cared for in a special way that is somehow different from the next person's.

Breaking the ice, like so much else about human communication, is a matter of satisfying a particular person's specific need.

Take Rita, for instance. She wanted to be appreciated for a bunch of reasons—among them, her wine expertise.

Herb obliged. Bingo! They broke the ice. Like Herb, when you communicate your understanding of the other person's needs—through the words you say, the tone in which you say them, your gestures and eye contact—you ignite desire.

Choose words that fill the needs of the one you want and this much I guarantee:

The one you want will want you back.

HOW TO SUMMON UP THE COURAGE TO TAKE THE FIRST STEP

I don't know exactly what's going on in your life at the moment, but the fact that you are reading this chapter suggests there might be a special someone out there whose friendship and love you can now only dream about.

What I intend this chapter to do is show you that that special person may not be as far out of reach as you think.

Follow the principles of romantic behavior I lay out in my fourteen workable ways to break the ice with the opposite sex and you cannot possibly fail to win the loving friendship you desire and deserve.

THE FUNDAMENTAL PRINCIPLES OF ROMANTIC BEHAVIOR

▶ Though everybody's tendency is to avoid initiating contact with a stranger, once such overtures are made to us our natural urge is to respond.

▶ We like to like people who like us first.

▶ Rejection can always be overcome with patience.

▶ Happiness is contagious.

▶ The human need for appreciation is far stronger than any human's ability to resist it.

▶ The opinions of others have more effect on what we think of ourselves than self-affirmation.

It's all here: Everything from summoning up the courage to take that first step to the body language that says you care in ways that words alone can't convey. Read on to discover:

▶ How to build self-confidence

▶ How to speak with enthusiasm

▶ How to listen like a lover

▶ When to flatter

And that's not all.

In this chapter, I'll more than amplify and expand these ideas. I'll show you how to take the lead in romantic conversation, how to gain trust, how to make yourself irresistibly likeable, how to keep the object of your desire interested, and, finally, how to demonstrate commitment.

It all adds up to

- -

Love—the Biggest Benefit Life Offers—Yours When You Master the Secrets of Romantic Behavior

Never again will you be forced to settle for anything or any one less than the object of your dreams, and the fire your conversation ignites in their heart will burn for you and you alone. By understanding and using the secrets of romantic behavior to fill the needs of others, you are certain to win the heart of the one you want.

"It was his smile, his big brown eyes, his cute tush, the way he laughed. I met Allan at a research presentation and I knew right away he was the one I wanted," reports Tish Powers, 28, a Los Angeles line producer for the CBS network. "I tried to make my interest obvious but he was too shy to pick up on it. At that point I knew I had to make the first move but I was afraid to look foolish. One day we bumped into each other in the cafeteria. I'd read one of his reports and had a couple of questions. We talked about them over lunch. When he called later with some more data, I felt he was responding to me in his own way, and it was now or never! I suggested that since we were both on the list for an off-site seminar later that week, it made environmental sense to go together in one car. It's taken time to get Allan to lower his defenses but it is worth the effort. We've been dating for nearly six months."

Allan's need was to be recognized in a way he could accept and safely act on.

By filling that need, Tish broke the ice, encouraged him to come out of his shell, and created the conditions that made his more serious interest possible.

Too often we sit back and wait for others to make the first move, show us how much they care before we are willing to care back. But if Tish simply waited for that to happen, she might never have connected with Allan, the one she wanted.

And here's the funny part: despite what she thought, there was almost no risk in taking the first step. After all, it's a fundamental principle of romantic behavior:

We like to like the people who like us first.

DO YOU KNOW HOW TO TALK YOUR WAY TO LOVE?

To determine where you stand when it comes to breaking the ice with the object of your desire, it is definitely in your interest to take a look at the following exercise.

Below you will find ten brief statements. After reading each, you will be asked to make a choice. Just check the response that, in your judgment, is the better approach.

1. Someone you are attracted to makes eye contact with you. Your heart pounds, your spirit soars. What's the first thing you do?

   ❏ A. Play hard to get?

   ❏ B. Start a conversation immediately?

   ❏ C. Take a deep breath to relax?

2. Some people think the best way to get a reaction from someone you are interested in is to act first. Others say it is better to hold back. Where do you stand?

   ❏ A. Better to act first

   ❏ B. Better to wait and see

3. The best way to handle coolness or even a rejection is to:

   ❏ A. Exit the situation with as much grace as you are able to muster under the circumstances.

   ❏ B. Continue to meet the other person's needs even if they are rejecting yours.

4. The wonderful thing about a relationship is the joy it creates. Experiencing it is a pleasure, but developing it takes work. Do you believe that basically unhappy people can work to create happy relationships?

   ❏ A. Yes

   ❏ B. No

5. Some of the most important moments of a relationship surround the first words out of your mouth. Is it better to:

   ❏ A. Speak with positive enthusiasm?

   ❏ B. Speak with absolute honesty?

6. The first difference of opinion between two people in a potentially romantic situation usually comes up early in the conversation. Do you think it is better to confront such differences early so as to head off a long-term problem, or would you go along with what they want for the time being on the grounds that it is too soon to make any decision?

   ❏ A. Confront early.

   ❏ B. Go along for a while.

7. The very best way to form a romantic alliance is to

   ❏ A. Stand up for your independence.

❏ B. Go along to get along

8. The difference between listening, and listening like a lover, is the difference between hearing and caring to hear.

❏ A. Agree

❏ B. Disagree

9. Nothing kills the magic of romance faster than criticism. Which of the following are examples of veiled criticism?

❏ A. Advice

❏ B. Asking a person to justify what he or she says

❏ C. Both

10. The secret of strengthening a budding relationship is first to recognize the deeper worth of a person and, second, to express how much you benefit from these qualities.

❏ A. Agree

❏ B. Disagree

Now that you have completed the exercise, simply compare your answers with this list:

Answers: 1. C, 2. A, 3. B, 4. B, 5. A, 6. B, 7. A, 8. A, 9. C, 10. A

A score of five or fewer correct answers suggests an urgent need to improve your ability to break the ice with a stranger of the opposite sex. Please read this chapter with great care. Do not try to put every one of its precepts to an immediate test. Instead, try to practice the one you are most comfortable with. When you've mastered that, move on to the next.

A score of six or more correct answers suggests you are already benefitting from your conversational skills but not to the full extent required in an ice breaking situation. The areas where you are likely to benefit the most are the ones in which you made the wrong answers. Pay special attention to these as you read on to take what is good and make it even better.

FOURTEEN WORKABLE WAYS TO BREAK THE ICE WITH THE OPPOSITE SEX . . . EVEN IF YOU ARE VERY SHY, ON THE QUIET SIDE, OR SIMPLY NOT THE SOCIAL SUCCESS YOU'D LIKE TO BE

Technique 1: Relax

Ever notice that when you are around someone you'd like to get closer to, you suck in your gut or fuss with your hair, your posture braces, your eyes shine, and your heart thumps?

Ever wonder what makes it so?

I'll tell you in a word: adrenaline.

Your body's getting ready for the mating game.

The birds, the bees, the Cohens, the Kelleys—every living thing on this earth gets nervous around the object of its desire. It's perfectly natural, usually helpful, and no cause for concern—I'd be more worried about not feeling nervous.

So hey, let's face it: nervousness isn't the real issue.

No, the real problem is even worse: It's the nervousness about being nervous in the first place.

That's what does us in. It sets off a chain reaction. So we spend all our effort on trying to hide it. Which leaves the real job—ice breaking—undone. Which only makes us even more nervous.

I think you get the point I am driving at: Somehow, you've got to actively take steps to break the vicious cycle.

The best and by far the most practical way to do it is this: Relax. Accept your nervousness and the possibility you will be rejected. Then get on with ice breaking. Sure, I understand—you don't want rejection. But, so what if it happens? It hurts? Well, yes it does, but it's not the sort of hurt anybody dies from. After all, nobody bats a thousand.

The cure is to pick yourself up, dust yourself off, and get on with your life.

Here's better news. Rejection also has a useful side to it. If you are at all normal, you'll come out of it knowing more than you knew going in. That means next time you'll have a better idea of what works for you and what does not.

Let me nail down the point with some words from Thomas Edison, the world's most famous inventor.

He conducted 50,000 experiments before he created the electric light bulb. Some people thought he wasn't learning much. That made Edison mad. "How dare they," he wrote. "I have learned 50,000 things that do not work. Can they say as much?"

So, relax and do what Edison did:

Make failure your friend instead of your enemy and you cannot lose.

Technique 2: Act Instead of React

When it comes to breaking the ice, it hardly ever pays to sit on the sidelines and wait for something to happen so that you can react to it.

People die of waiting. I tell you this because of a paradox I've observed in romantic behavior, and I am sure you have, too. Though everybody's tendency is to avoid initiating contact with a stranger, once such overtures are made to us our natural urge is to respond.

"One of our most active seniors is a man of 85 whose got a reputation for chasing women," reports retirement community social worker Bev Naismith, 36, out of Pensacola, Florida. "They no more put their bags down and he's talking with them and they are both laughing. I hope I can be as active at that age."

No matter what your age, you can't beat Bev's logic: The best way to get a reaction is to act first.

So, if you truly wish to succeed with the object of your desire, you must seize the initiative, act to get a positive response.

Do nothing more than that and your breakthrough will have begun.

Technique 3: Stay Vulnerable No Matter What

"To tell you the truth I never admired Richard Nixon's campaign politics but I thought his ability to win the heart of Patricia Ryan, the woman he eventually married, was one of the best examples of hanging in there I ever heard of," reports San Diego marriage counselor Bernardo Warres, 36. "Nothing stopped him, he never got mad, never tried to get even. Rejection after rejection, he just kept on keeping on—being positive when she was negative. Eventually his vulnerability won her over."

Bernardo's observation confirms my belief in the principle that rejection can always be overcome with patience. Look, when you are trying to break the ice, the hardest thing to take is indifference and rejection.

The common impulse is to withdraw or somehow punish the other person with an attitude that says, "If you don't want me, I don't want you . . . so there!"

Either way tells the other person you don't have what it takes to be a true friend—the only real basis for romantic involvement.

Your defensiveness only further justifies their reason for being standoffish in the first place.

Far better for you to do what Nixon did—hang in by continuing to meet the other person's needs even if they are rejecting yours. Yes, you risk looking foolish. But in the end, the payoff more than justifies the potential pain:

Eventually, by continuing to meet their needs for acceptance, attention, and understanding, their attitude towards you will change and they will probably come around.

There is no shame in showing patience. The more you show, the stronger your relationship will eventually grow.

Technique 4: Let Your Happiness Show

Happiness is contagious. You catch it from the people you want to get close to. And vice versa.

"Every time we met she was so happy and excited, I found myself getting happier and happier," reports newlywed Amos Barrish, 29, a Boston software technician. "I figured it had to be love."

By allowing your happiness to infect others, you create two happy people where once, perhaps, there was only one. This idea of two happy people is terrifically important. And the reason is this: Unhappy people create unhappy relationships. It takes two happy people to achieve a happy one.

The logic is inevitable: The more happiness you bring to the party, the happier the party is likely to prove in the long run. So it's a good idea to show some early excitement. You don't need any abracadabra words to get across an I'm-happy-to-see-you attitude.

Say it with a smile or the way you listen, with the clothes you wear or the way your voice sounds. Be glad to be around the person and your pleasure is bound to light up their life.

Technique 5: Make the Downbeat Upbeat

Whatever you choose to say to open the encounter make it positive and enthusiastic.

"I guess the best opening line I ever went for was when he walked past me, came back, and asked me the name of the fragrance I was wearing. He thought it was just so wonderful. Who could resist?"

reports Nicole Longwood, 39, who works for the California Tourist Commission, in Sacramento. "That was 10 years ago and we're still married and counting."

If you are out to get someone to spend some time with you, you must have an upbeat attitude. This does not mean you must rid yourself of all your problems before you speak.

What it means is nobody's interested hearing about them, at least not right away. In those first few minutes of the encounter, perhaps the most important moments your relationship may ever know, the important feelings to get across are

▷ Enthusiasm for life even with all of its absurdities

▷ A willingness to laugh at yourself

▷ An attitude of fairness that never seeks to make more of you by making less of somebody else

These are winning character traits people simply cannot long resist. Nobody is born with them. But it is possible to learn them, make them part of your inner life. You don't need a lot of fancy rules to follow.

Just make the personal determination that from now on, you are going to see both the dark and the light sides of life, but you are only going to talk about the brighter.

You'll be amazed at how fast people come to think of you as a positive person worth getting to know better.

Technique 6: Let the Other Person Do Most of the Talking

One of the most pressing needs you'll find in people is the need to talk about themselves and their interests. The more they do it, the better they feel.

Trouble is, they rarely get the chance to do it freely. Which is where you enter the picture. Simply by encouraging the object of your attention to keep on talking about himself or herself, you satisfy one of their highest-priority needs.

How do you offer encouragement? With quiet listening and questions that draw people out—questions that can't be answered with a yes or a no, or a simple fact.

For instance,

"Where do you want to be two years from now?"

"What don't you like about opera?"

"Where do you go when you're not working?"

"I wondered how you felt about X."

With these examples and others you think up on your own, I think you get the point I am making about drawing people out.

Now, let's spend just a minute or so on the other encouraging factor—listening like a lover.

Basically, listening like a lover—which I will discuss with you in detail a little further ahead in this chapter—is listening with honest interest that makes itself felt to the other person in the quiet way you lean toward them, the alertness in your eyes as they speak. It's a matter of not just hearing what the other person says, its a matter of caring to hear what the other person says because you are genuinely interested in finding out what affects their lives and happiness.

Technique 7: Flattery Will Get You Almost Everywhere

To hear most people, flattery is a dirty word. But of course, most people are wrong, dead wrong. Flattery is really a good way to show your sincere appreciation of the style, personality, and easily-seen charms that make the object of your desire the object of your desire.

People hesitate to use it for fear their praise will be dismissed as insincere. But that's not the sort of flattery I am suggesting you use.

The fact is, even if they don't show it, people are deeply affected by *sincere* flattery.

This is true because the human need for honest appreciation is far stronger than the human ability to resist it.

"We met at a candlelight wedding party, and in the warm glow she looked wonderful. I told her that the way her eyes and hair caught the flickering light made her quite the handsomest woman I ever met, but she brushed the comment aside," reports Lew Ervine, 34, a New York lawyer. "Three months later she asked if I really meant what I had said."

Flattery is like good brandy: A little bit whets the senses.

An overdose numbs them.

Follow Lew's lead: Don't give in to the desire to pour it on by the bucketful just because the other person doesn't seem to be responding right away.

Trust what you have said to build and strengthen your friendly relationship. Eventually, the one you want will respond. Just give it time and your sincere flattery will get the object of your desire to see you as someone whose company they enjoy.

Technique 8: Go with the Flow

Every good love story begins with a combination of joys and disappointments. Give and take—it's the natural ebb and flow of a relationship.

Suppose you have an expectation about something and the one you want sees it differently. Under these circumstances, now is not the time to press hard for your point of view.

Remember, everybody's got the right to a personal perspective, which of course means they have the right even to be wrong.

"It's like driver's ed when they teach you about a skid," reports Nan Kerrlander, 27, who works in Sears' Chicago head office. "The trick is not to go against it. You go with it so your relationship doesn't slide off into a ditch."

Nan is saying that, if the person doesn't want to accept what you want, and you value the relationship's potential, going along with what they want doesn't mean you give up your wishes. Quite the contrary.

What it means is that by going with the flow, you are giving yourself and the other person time to gently guide things to a track you can both accept.

No matter what, don't let minor differences lead you to turn off your charm. In fact, use them to turn it on even more, to smile bigger, to be even kinder.

Everybody admires that kind of grace under fire. Hardly anybody resists it for long. So go with the flow and you will eventually get what you want.

There's just one thing you've got to be careful of, and that is not to be a pushover.

Technique 9: Stand Up for Your Independence

"Show me a stock clerk with a goal in life and I will show you a person capable of making history," said merchant J.C. Penny. "Show me someone capable of making history but without a goal and I will show you a stock clerk."

It is very important for you to be able to communicate the essence of J. C. Penny's message to the object of your desire. Whatever the particulars you focus on, the sense of the message should be this: You have personal goals you intend to achieve no matter which way the friendship goes.

"It's much easier to get involved with a man who knows he is going places no matter what I do than it is with a guy who is basing everything on me," reports Yolande Chin, 23, a fashion assistant for a Miami swimsuit manufacturer. "If I go along, my heart is always going to have to beat for two. It's more responsibility than I can handle."

It seems to me the technique of standing up for your independence offers you two pretty good benefits.

First, it represents a commitment to create your own climate of opportunity by growing to the outer limits of your talent and ability. And second, it invites and encourages the one you want to see, accept, and be empowered by your vision.

Stand up for your independence. It's the only way to make a strong alliance.

Technique 10: Don't Kiss Up

Life has a way of teaching us to get along by going along.

Which is fine, maybe, in business. But, it is definitely bad karma when it comes to breaking the ice with someone who catches your fancy.

Here's the thing: If you try to please too hard by making other people's opinions more important than your own, you not only diss yourself, you invite the object of your desire to think you lack backbone, too.

"No matter what you feel inside, it is very important to come across as an independent person who couldn't care less what they think of you," reports Deanna Brisco-Singleterry, 47, who writes a syndicated advice column for singles. "It's that air of indifference that gets 'em every time."

Don't kiss up no matter how much you might want to or how politically sound a move it may appear to be.

Only by your willingness to show your independence as a person can you encourage romance to flourish.

Technique 11: Don't Take the Relationship's Temperature

Let me make this short and sweet: Asking someone how they feel about you—directly or by fishing around—corrodes trust, rots understanding, and eats away at happiness.

It hints emotional uncertainty on your part. After all, goes the line of reasoning, if you were more secure in yourself you would know without having to ask exactly where you stand.

Now I am not saying you should not feel a little uncertain from time-to-time. That much seems only human. I am saying *all* you should do is feel it. The moment you give it voice, the appearance of an emotional shortcoming makes you a much less attractive partner in the eyes of people with whom you seek to break the ice.

Remember, what you don't say can't be held against you.

Technique 12: Listen Like a Lover

There's a big hole in your education and it concerns listening.

For instance, my guess is that you have been taught to think that listening is a passive act—just let the words in and understanding is automatically yours.

I'd say you have another think coming. Listening is anything but passive. In fact, good listening takes more active effort than you might imagine. But learning to actively listen is learning to listen like a lover.

It starts, as I pointed out a few paragraphs back, not with just hearing what the other person says but *caring to hear what the other person says because you are genuinely interested in finding out what affects their lives and happiness.*

SEVEN WAYS TO LISTEN LIKE A LOVER

Don't interrupt. Let the other person speak as long as they want. The more they talk the more understood they will feel. Given the luxury of ample time, most people come to realize that with you, they don't have to speak in 10-second sound bites. They become less guarded and more open the longer they remain in your company and talking. Encouraging them with respectful silence gives you an opportunity to learn about their needs so that you can satisfy them with the things you may later choose to talk about.

Communicate without words. Get across, in body language, the intensity of your interest in what the object of your desire is saying. If you are standing, put your arms at your sides, palms facing them, lean slightly towards the other person. If you are seated, rest your hands comfortably in your lap, plant both feet on the floor pointed directly at them, and lean forward slightly. These moves encourage the speaker to really open up by suggesting just how intensely receptive you are.

Signal understanding in small ways. Nod your head to signal understanding, pinch the bridge of your nose to show deep involvement, smile to encourage the other person to go on.

Maintain eye contact. You should be looking at the person roughly 60 to 70 percent of the time. Avoid harsh eyeball-to-eyeball confrontation by focusing on a spot just north of the bridge of the other person's nose. When eyes meet, they bridge the biggest gap of all—the one between two minds.

Feedback to build and drive momentum. When the other person pauses to get your input, say what it is you heard. Mind you, I didn't tell you to say what you think you heard or you wanted to hear. I said, "say what it is you heard." Do it in your own words. For instance, someone is telling you their boss doesn't believe in getting down with the troops, and you say, "Yeah, like managers know it all and people like us have to do it all." No lengthy speeches, no comments, just say out loud your understanding of what is being said.

Practice acceptance. Acceptance means allowing the other person's point of view to be, without approval, comment, or criticism. Acceptance is purely neutral. Its intent is to create an atmosphere of fairness that both justifies and rewards them for opening their souls to you.

Make time your ally. Don't push, guide, or shape what the other person is saying in any way. Allow them to reveal whatever it is they want you to know in their own sweet time. Just hang in from moment to moment, understanding each thing that comes along as well as you can. With enough patience, a pattern will reveal itself and you'll have a better sense of the direction the conversation is taking.

Listen like a lover and you will say, without words, an awful lot about the way you care.

Technique 13: Criticism Kills Desire

Every budding relationship needs some magic to transform interest to desire.

Nothing kills the magic faster than criticism in any form. Failing to remember a commitment is a form of criticism. Prefacing a sentence with words to the effect of, I'm only saying this for your own good, is a form of criticism. Subtle or out of the closet, criticism comes in every form imaginable and some too fierce to mention.

Look, if you want to make it with the object of your desire, you've just got to accept the fact that for you, job one is good listening, not good instructing in the lessons of life according to you.

You say you've got opinions about what they should be doing, how to make this and that better?

Good!

Just keep them to yourself.

Don't give advice.

Don't ask them to justify what they say.

Don't criticize by claiming not to.

Criticism is poison in the well.

Everything the water touches dies a little.

Avoid being at all critical.

Technique 14: Give Them What They Cannot Give Themselves

"I can pat myself on the back all day long," reports Sue Erzein, 31, a Tucson school teacher. "It doesn't make me nearly as self-confident as a single pat of recognition from a friend I am interested in being with."

The point Sue makes confirms a basic psychological truth: The opinions of others have more effect on what we think of ourselves than self-affirmation. Said another way, recognition of our positive virtues needs to be confirmed from outside ourselves to mean anything at all.

That was the basic point I was making several pages back, when I talked about using flattery to make yourself more attractive to the object of your desire. But even when it is sincere, flattery only skims the surface. It is based on what you pick up very early in the game. Alone, it won't satisfy the deeper emotional needs of the one you want to be with.

So now, I'd like to take the discussion a little further to give you the secret of developing the thoughts that recognize the deeper worth of the person you want to be with, the thoughts that encourage a friendship to develop more fully.

In a word, the secret is time.

Getting to know the person over time will reveal that person's best qualities.

Once you begin to see these, the name of the game is to find a way to tell the object of your desire *how much you benefit from their best qualities.*

"We planned on going to an outdoor concert at the Blossom Festival, but never talked about dinner. When we met, Rafe was carrying a picnic basket, and it made me see what a caring person he is," reports Nicole Oberlin, 29, who runs a small business in Cleveland. "The food was wonderful, the music lovely, and when it was over I told him how important it was to me to feel cared for. I think it drew us closer to the kind of relationship we both want to develop."

When, with the passage of time, you are able to give the object of your desire the admiration and feeling of worth they cannot give themselves, you will truly have broken the ice and made a friend.

If you will practice the fundamental principles of romantic behavior developed in my fourteen workable ways to break the ice with the opposite sex, your life is certain to be far richer.

Let me recap these for you briefly before we conclude this very important chapter:

▶ Relax

▶ Act instead of react

▶ Stay vulnerable no matter what

▶ Let your happiness show

▶ Make the downbeat upbeat

▶ Let the other person do most of the talking

▶ Sincere flattery will get you almost everywhere

▶ Go with the flow

▶ Stand up for your independence

▶ Don't kiss up

▶ Don't take the relationship's temperature

▶ Listen like a lover

▶ Criticism kills desire

▶ Give them what they cannot give themselves

Isn't it curious that, despite all kinds of advances in technology, the only way to break the ice with someone is still the old fashioned way—through talk.

No other human skill comes close to conversation in importance—and that is true whether the subject is love or leadership or anything in between.

Everyday contacts with family, friends, business associates, relatives, and strangers place us in situations where what we say and how we say it mean the difference between acceptance and rejection, cooperation, and conflict.

If you are pressed to solve a specific conversational problem immediately, by all means turn the page. Whether it is a matter of winning the attention of your boss to the fact that you deserve a raise, or zeroing in on the cause of conflict with a neighbor, or anything in between, you'll find specific, concrete, and practical help to turn your problems into opportunities.

APPENDIX

Ninety-Three Instant Solutions to Talk Your Way to Whatever You Want, Everywhere You Go

If your problem or issue is . . .	Please refer to Chapter(s)
Abuse, verbal	7
Acceptance	1,7
Accountability	5
Advice, giving/getting	1,8
Aggression	1
Alienation	7
Anger	7,9
Anxicty	7
Appreciation	4,5,6
Argument	7,8
Assertiveness	6
Backfires	1
Belittling	1
Benefit	2,6,11,12,13
Blaming	1,4
Body language	2,3,5,7,8,9,12,13

If your problem or issue is . . .	Please refer to Chapter(s)
Calming others	7
Changing minds	6
Children, handling, pesky	6
Closings	11,12
Commands, instructions, orders	5
Communication barriers	5
Complaints	7
Complimenting others	1
Conflict	7,8
Confusion	7
Control	5
Conversational leverage	2,4
Coverups	7
Criticism	9,13
Defensiveness	1
Distrust	1,7
Emotions	1,2,5,6,7,8,10
Empathy	8
Empowerment	4,8
Encouraging others	4
Expectations, unwarranted	1
Exploring issues	4,7,8
Fears	7
Feelings	7
Flattery	13
Friends, making new ones	6
Frustration	7
Gathering information	4
Gender blindness	1
Getting the one you want to want you back	13

If your problem or issue is . . .	Please refer to Chapter(s)
Gossip	2
Gripes, handling	4
Habits, force of	1
Hidden interests/unmet desires	2
Hot buttons	2,4,5,6
Impatience	7
Inattention	3
Inner confidence	10
Interruptions, handling	4,10
Isolation	7
Job interviews	3,6,8,10
Joy	7
Labelling	1
Leadership	5,7,8,9,10
Listening	1,2,3,4,6,7,8,13
Loyalty, building	2
Mistrust	7
Moodiness	4,7
Motivating others	6
Name calling	7
Needs	2,6,12,13
Negotiations/compromise	8
Nervousness	7,12,13
Opposition	6
Persuading others	6,8
Praise	9
Promotions	11
Questions	2,4,6,8,9
Raises, how and when to ask	2,3,8,10
Rejection, handling	13
Resentment	9

If your problem or issue is . . .	Please refer to Chapter(s)
Respect	8
Self-confidence, ways to build	3
Self-esteem, lack of	5
Self-interest	1,2,8
Selling	6
Shyness	13
Sincerity	1
Speaking publicly	12
Team play	6
Teasing	7
Temper tantrums	9
Tension	7
Time sickness	1
Understanding what other people want	2,4,7,8
Vocabulary	1,10,11
Writing better	10,11

INDEX